the Recording Guitarist

A Guide for Home and Studio

By Jon Chappell

© Andrew MacNaughtan

ALEX LIFESON, of Rush, displays his studio

ISBN 0-7935-8704-2

HAL•LEONARD®
CORPORATION

7777 W. BLUEMOUND RD. P.O. BOX 13819 MILWAUKEE, WI 53213

Visit Hal Leonard Online at
www.halleonard.com

the Recording Guitarist

A Guide for Home and Studio

To Mary, always

Acknowledgments

I would like to express my appreciation to the Hal Leonard Corporation for the opportunity to write this book, and especially to the Reference Book staff who provided inspiration, enthusiasm and wisdom throughout the project. Special thanks to designer Alex Lindquist, illustrator Kevin Stoohs and photographer Rick Gould for their superb contributions and talents. Thanks also to my various guitar and recording colleagues who have helped out in the making of this book or who have influenced me as a writer, guitarist and recordist. Among them are: Sean Ballou, Buck Brundage, Steve De Furia, Doyle Dykes, Allan Holdsworth, Craig Jackson, Pat Kirtley, Eddie Kramer, Mike Levine, Alex Lifeson, Bernard Matthews, Emile Menasché, Gil Parris, Greg Perry, Steve Pouliot, Paul Rivera, Marshall Toppo, Carl Verheyen, Alex Wright.

THE ecording Guitarist

A Guide for Home and Studio

PART TWO: APPLICATIONS FOR THE RECORDING GUITARIST

ntroduction

Recording guitar and playing live guitar are about as different as night and day. Each requires different skills, different equipment, and a different philosophical approach, or "head," if you will. I've known plenty of guitarists who can do one brilliantly but the other not to save their life. In fact, most guitarists, I've found, are naturally suited to one and must work like hell at developing the other. For example, you might be a great improviser, and your best musical moments occur in the heat of passion—the drums pounding, the stage lights blazing, the crowd screaming. Then, in the cold reality of the studio, nothing seems to work. You can barely play the right notes, let alone capture the fire and spontaneity of last night's live performance. If that describes you, you're not alone. The majority of guitarists are more comfortable in jams than under the microscope of studio scrutiny.

If you've never really recorded before, but have tried to leave an impromptu outgoing message on your answering machine, only to find yourself transformed into a tongue-tied imbecile, you have a glimpse of what it's like to record professionally and under real pressure for the first time. Something happens when you hit that little switch and the red light is on. Nothing flows freely. What was once delivered naturally, without thinking and with no pre-meditation, becomes leaden, self-conscious, and error-ridden. You have entered the Recording Zone, a seemingly hostile, unforgiving place that presents an endless series of snares, booby traps and trip wires, all designed to prevent you from capturing anything usable much less musical onto tape or disk; that is, until you learn its ways and the completely different rules of physics by which this world operates.

Once you recognize that you are in fact in a foreign land, you begin to understand that to succeed here, you must essentially learn a new language and new customs. Once you do, though, all your musical instincts come back to you. Technology is not intimidating and the performance pressure of playing to a click track seems as natural as performing for an attentive audience. Recording can be just as rewarding as playing live if you know how to do it right. The first step to successful recording is to acknowledge that it is different from playing live.

We will explore the world of guitar recording from beginning to end, which means starting with the guitarist himself, continuing through the instrument, into the signal chain, out the other side and landing finally onto tape or disk. There are many diversions and side roads to take, but the focus will be on capturing the best sound possible within a given setup. That setup could be as simple as an acoustic guitar in front of a mic going directly to stereo DAT, where you're just trying to keep the finger noise to a minimum. Or it could be an elaborate ensemble situation where an electric guitar is going through a rack and into a mixer, and then competing with other instruments for a place in the mix. Each setup presents its own set of problems and opportunities, but all involve the recording process.

We will not distinguish between what is a performance-related issue or what is a technologically related one, as often the two are blurred. For example, most people who have played in live situations all their lives who then sit down to record find that they play too hard. Although backing off on the attack might seem solely related to performance, it also involves other issues, like mic placement, compression, EQ and even the choice of instrument. Successful recording guitarists don't distinguish between performing and technology, they simply make all the right choices. But getting to that point takes experience, judgment and a whole lot of listening to yourself and others.

IT STARTS AT THE BEGINNING AND WORKS FORWARD

The more experienced at recording you become, the more you realize how important the beginning of your signal chain is. The signal chain is nothing more than the road map of your guitar sound from start to finish. The start is the instrument itself, and many people ignore or skirt past this crucial, initial step. If you don't take care of business with your instrument, it's usually too late by the time you're tweaking the reverb decay to fix the tone. Take the time in the beginning and you'll find that your sound is not only easier to manipulate and make good-sounding, setup time is quicker as well. Working with a good tone provides more usable options than working with a bad tone. You might even have to go back to the step that's even before the instrument—you the performer. If you can't quite play in time, or pull off passages that are just beyond your technical capabilities, no gear or technology in the world will save you. A '59 Les Paul through a Plexi Marshall sound can still sound hideous, if not in the right hands. Never rush through this first step.

You must also consider that what is bad and good are not inherent in the sound itself, but a matter of context. Not only must your instrument be in good working order, you the musician must make the right choices as well. Sometimes that involves the selection of the instrument itself. Don't always reach for your Les Paul if you think an SG or a Telecaster might provide the best solutions. And if you're playing a distorted lead sound, experiment with the neck pickup as well as the bridge pickup before locking in to one particular sound over another.

The same is true for amplifiers. Get the sound on the amp using its own controls before you use external effects to compensate for them. For example, you may have EQ in several different places in your signal chain: on the guitar, in an outboard EQ unit, on the amp, and on the mixer channel your amp mic is connected to. How should you proceed to make EQ adjustments? Start with the guitar's tone controls, move to the amp's and spend the bulk of your time between these two places. If you still experience problems, try solving them with only enough outboard assistance to correct the deficiencies, not to get a core, usable sound.

This does not mean that finding your sound has to be a dull, bloodless exercise. By all means, turn on the reverb, switch the pickup selector around, and play different styles. Just be sure to focus on the sound itself and not aspects of the sound—like effects or gimmicks. If you don't know what a good sound is, listen to your favorite records, and try to get close to that. Being a good musician means having the ears to get the sound you want, not just the coordination to play all the right notes.

PART ONE:
THE SIGNAL CHAIN

CHAPTER ONE

Guitars for Recording

GUITARS

There are literally thousands of guitar models and vintages to choose from to develop your own individual voice. No one can say "X is a better recording guitar than Y" any more than he can say that one guitar is better than another for writing songs. But you can define certain basic categories that will help you cover 90 percent of all recording and musical situations, and organize your approach to assembling a recording arsenal of guitars. You'll always be adding, changing, and modifying the guitars in your collection, but there is general agreement on which guitars you should acquire first, and that any reasonable producer could expect you to have up and running with little or no notice. That's the approach we'll take here: that every guitar mentioned in this section is a reasonably expected primary instrument or "double" (non-guitar or guitar related fretted instrument, like Dobro or banjo).

The most basic division in guitars is whether they are acoustic or electric. The term "acoustic guitar" means a guitar that produces its sound through the unaided vibration of the wooden sound chamber (body). An electric guitar produces sound not directly by resonating wood, but by creating an electronic signal through the pickups that is amplified and output through a speaker. An acoustic guitar produces its audible sound through the guitar itself; the electric guitar through a speaker.

Nowadays an acoustic guitar can be fitted with a pickup system, so that it can be handled in much the same way as an electric one; that is, as an electronic signal from a pickup. And electric guitars don't need speakers if they're plugged directly into the mixer or into an amp simulator. But there still exists the tonal differences between an electronically amplified acoustic and a miked acoustic that create the near-unanimous agreement that a well-miked acoustic is superior to an electronically rendered one. The same is true for an amped guitar versus a direct-recorded one. If you can't use an actual speaker, you can use electronics to simulate one.

With that in mind, we'll first consider acoustic guitars for their ability to generate unamplified sound, and discuss the different electronic capabilities (piezo vs. magnetic pickups, built-in mic and pickup combinations) later in the book.

ACOUSTIC GUITARS

The best way to determine how an acoustic guitar will sound on a recording is to listen to it with your ear. This sounds like overly simplified advice, but remember you're

Fig. 1.1

A *variety of*
acoustic guitars

listening to the guitar now from the vantage point of how it will record. This is quite different than judging a guitar from how it will sound live. For example, the guitar must be completely buzz and rattle free, something your ear might let you forgive or block out while you listen to the more musical aspects of its live sound. But once on tape, little buzzes and rattles that are forgiven in a live performance somehow become prominent, self-conscious and unbearable on a recording. As for the sound itself, the recording process tends to "compress" the natural sound of an acoustic, because it must capture the sound from only one or two angles (depending on the number and types of mics used), rather than the way a listener experiences the sound live—surrounding him from all sides and from all parts of the instrument, especially (and ideally) if the listener is in close proximity. Some savvy auditioners even have another person play the instrument while they stand several inches to several feet back listening with one ear plugged (the one away from the guitar). This lets them hear the instrument as a microphone would.

Typical "translation errors" between the live sound and the recorded sound involve focus: the sound changes from warm to muddy, or resonant to boxy. Musicians will often refer to an acoustic guitar by its recording qualities: This is a good recording guitar, they will say, which can mean several things, but usually that it's not overly boomy (boom—or low-frequency emphasis—is great onstage but problematic in the studio), and that it's well balanced (even tonal response across the entire frequency spectrum through the guitar's entire range). A "good recording guitar" doesn't need to be loud, either, and often is not a good stage guitar precisely because it's not very loud. As a guitar becomes inherently more capable of projection, the "boom factor" increases. A more even response across the frequency spectrum (where the lows don't boom and the highs don't cut through) is often more versatile in the studio, though the sound might not be as initially impressive in a live context.

FLAT-TOP STEEL-STRING GUITARS

The steel string acoustic holds a variety of connotations. Martin dreadnoughts, Gibson Jumbos, National Steels, Ovation Elites, and Taylor Grand Concerts, and models by Larrivée, Santa Cruz, Lowden and Collings are all examples of acoustic guitars with steel strings. (See Fig. 1.1 for a variety of acoustic models.) As a recording guitarist, you may need to own only one nylon-string, but you'll eventually encounter situations that call for several of the above mentioned steel-string guitars, plus an acoustic 12-string and guitars optimized for slide and Nashville (also called high-string) tuning where the lower four strings are substituted with lighter gauges and tuned an octave higher. The term "flat-top" is sort of an old-fashioned name that differentiates acoustic "folk" guitars from acoustic "jazz" guitars, which have carved, or arched, tops (often with f-holes). When someone says "flat-top," they're referring to the world that involves 90 percent of all acoustic guitars made—non-arched, non-jazz models (see Fig. 1.2).

To generalize greatly, but nevertheless relay beliefs held by many recording guitarists, Martin dreadnoughts and their ilk are good for warm, full-bodied parts, especially fingerpicking or chording in open-position. Gibson Jumbos are good for strummed rhythm parts, and are one of the most versatile models for all-purpose acoustic session work. In general, smaller-bodied acoustics have better balance and are preferred for intricate work, like up-the-neck fingerpicking parts. Big-bodied models are better for rhythm. The most important aspect in choosing an acoustic guitar, though, is its basic sound and how well it contributes to the mix. And as a final disclaimer, the above generalizations are just that—generalizations. Fingerpick a Gibson Jumbo and slam-strum a small-bodied Martin 000-28 if that's what sounds good for the cue. Since the sound you'll create is ultimately up to your ears, you should keep searching for the guitar that's right for you.

If you're specializing in acoustic music, you'll want to have fresh strings before every session. This guarantees two things. First, the guitar will sound its absolute best and play with the most accurate intonation; second, it ensures a tonal match for subsequent overdubs, passes, or edits. This can't be done if different strings are not in the same period of their life cycle. One sound will always be a little brighter or ringier or duller than another if the string sets are of different ages. But you'll always have a match if the strings are brand new every time you sit down to record.

Fig. 1.2

Steel-String Guitar

Steel strings are usually strummed with flatpicks or fingerpicked with bare right-hand fingers. Most people do not don fingerpicks for recording, though many players do use a plastic or nylon thumbpick, especially country blues players. The thumbpick yields a cleaner, more direct attack, because the angle that the thumb strikes the string is somewhat oblique as compared to the way the fingers hit the strings (which is at a more perpendicular angle). Fingerpicks are used for banjo, Dobro, lap steel and pedal steel, so players who have facility on these other instruments will sometimes use picks on acoustic parts, but it's generally not done.

Flatpicks are used for any acoustic rhythm parts, and the preferred gauge is medium or heavy. Generally, the better player you are the heavier gauge pick you prefer. Since a heavy-gauge pick offers the most resistance, less string energy is transferred to it, so the best tone and responsiveness is yielded with heavy-gauge picks. Many people like the slight clicky, percussive sound that the pick attack gives, and will try to incorporate that into the sound. Obviously, for lead playing, the best results are obtained with a pick as well. Playing the guitar forcefully gets the top vibrating so that the sound-to-pick noise ratio is highest and the guitar sounds best when the whole instrument is excited. The trick is to find the place between strong playing that yields good tone but not to "overdrive" the instrument enough to create buzzing, rattling, or a splatty, compressed sound.

Fig. 1.3

Cutaway Steel-String Guitar

THE CUTAWAY CONTROVERSY

Special mention must be made of the growing use of the acoustic cutaway. A cutaway is a scoop out of the upper treble bout, allowing better access to upper frets (see Fig. 1.3). This can be especially valuable in the studio where the increased range offsets any possible tonal detriment created by the non-traditional body design. Although the traditionally shaped dreadnoughts, jumbos, and concert-sized guitars will always have a place in the hearts of collectors and traditionalists, the irksome fact remains that whenever you pick up one of these models, you can't play them past the 12th fret. Since a cutaway tends to attenuate the bass frequencies more than any others in the spectrum—and since it is those frequencies that are the most problematic when recording because of the boom factor—most recording guitarists have come to appreciate the cutaway versions of classic guitar models as a viable instrument. Then there is the advantage of the increased playable range.

The guitar is already a low-range instrument. Even though it's notated in the treble clef (where a written fourth-space E is played with the open first string), it actually sounds one octave lower. When you see a written third-space C and you play it correctly on the first fret, second string, it's actually *sounding* middle C (first ledger line below the staff). If someone writes out a part for you and doesn't realize the guitar is a transposing instrument, you'll have to play it an octave higher. That's where the guitar's limited range can cause problems. A cutaway can save the day if you suddenly have to play your part an octave higher, and a non-cutaway acoustic would make this cumbersome or even impossible. Consider that a cutaway allows for up-the-neck playing with a capo on, say, the seventh fret. (More on capoes below.)

Fig. 1.4

Nylon-String Guitar

NYLON-STRING GUITARS

A nylon-string guitar refers not merely to a description of the string material, but to a type of guitar whose design and construction is entirely different from a steel-string's (see Fig. 1.4). Nylon-string guitars are synonymous with classical guitars (except for some nylon-string fitted acoustic-electrics, like the Gibson Chet Atkins CE model), and typically feature a slotted headstock, wide neck, and a conventionally shaped body. Even though the materials are similar to steel-string flat-tops (mahogany neck, rosewood back and sides, spruce or cedar top), the internal structure of nylon-string guitars are not, so the method of tone production involves more than just the strings.

Another significant difference between a nylon- and steel-string is that the nylon-string guitar's neck joins the body at the 12th fret, not the 14th, as a steel-string's does. This is a limitation you don't want to discover halfway through an important take when you have surreptitiously switched guitars to impress the producer, and suddenly find you can't play the running eighth-note passage at bar 17, because it extends to the 15th fret—something that was accessible on your Martin but is now out of reach on your Ramirez.

One solution to the neck limitation is to use a cutaway nylon-string. Many classical guitarists consider a cutaway sacrilege, but it can make your nylon-string more viable in situations where playing above the 12th fret would preclude the use of a nylon-string altogether. Especially if you're playing with a pick, consider a cutaway, as the tonal variation is not as noticeable in single-note playing and the increased range is a more than equitable trade-off.

Nylon-strings can be played with either a pick or the right-hand fingers, but the traditional sound is with the individual fingers, with a little bit of fingernail on the attack. This requires that you let your right-hand nails grow longer than the left-hand ones, which can be disconcerting at first. But the biggest problem in keeping long nails is the care and maintenance they require. Nails can and do chip, rip and tear, especially before an important session when any normal activity—like opening a car door, zipping your coat or picking up your amp—is now fraught with peril. There's not a classical guitarist in the world who doesn't have a litany of contingency plans for *what-to-do-when-I-break-a-nail*. Nevertheless, a well-groomed nail produces the ideal sound on a nylon-string guitar, and is well worth the emery boards, emergency prosthetics and fussing it takes to keep your nails in shape.

A nylon-string can sound good with a pick as well, though a standard flatpick sometimes results in a "clicky" sound that produces a prominent "transient" (pitchless attack noise). This may be desirable for its percussiveness, but if it's too much, many guitarists try a felt or leather-coated pick to reduce the initial pick noise. This more resembles the nail-and-flesh sound of the right hand fingers, but gives a confidence level to guitarists more accustomed to playing guitar with a pick than their fingers.

A well-written nylon-string guitar part shouldn't exceed the guitar's natural range, which is about the 15th fret on the high E string (a written G, four ledger lines above the treble staff), and should avoid passagework (many consecutive fast notes) above the 12th fret. But with a cutaway, higher notes are possible, and while not necessarily an orthodox sound, is well worth considering for the expanded note range.

Many modern nylon-string guitars feature not only a cutaway to allow for better upper-fret access, but internal electronics for the direct recorded sound. Just as electronically amplifying an acoustic-electric has become a standard approach for a live sound in the steel-string guitar world, so has plugging in a nylon-string. But in current recording practices, plugging in a nylon-string is still rarer than plugging in a steel-string.

For expressive, melodic passages, nylon-string guitars respond quite well to the *rest stroke*, where a right-hand finger strikes a string and lands, or "rests," on the adjacent string below. This powerful motion extracts maximum tone from the note, partly due to the fact that the finger is drawn perpendicularly across the string. The two limitations are that you can't use this technique for extremely fast passages, and that you render the adjacent string momentarily unavailable while it serves as an anchor or stop for your finger.

The *free stroke* is the other type of finger motion, which is the most natural and intuitive fingerstyle method. The right hand is placed over the strings at roughly a

60-degree angle with a stationary but not stiff wrist. The strings are plucked with the fingers in a hinged motion. The term "free" refers to the fingers' position after striking the string—dangling in the air in a neutral, "free" position, poised to strike again. Arpeggios are the most common application of the free stroke.

Whichever way you play the nylon-string guitar—using unadorned right-hand fingers or a flatpick—recording a nylon-string usually involves getting a pretty sound with subtle and expressive characteristics. One of the most difficult things in the world is getting a good tone on a nylon-string, but recording it is fairly straightforward and follows the same guidelines as recording an acoustic steel-string guitar. One major difference though is that nylon-string playing is sometimes played at much lower volume levels, which means that breathing noises, rustling of clothing and even moving the guitar in the air will cause problems. To practice your "recording chops" on a nylon-string, get used to sitting very still and breathing in a controlled and even manner.

ARCH-TOP STEEL-STRING GUITARS

These are synonymously known as "jazz" guitars, although that name was applied later to distinguish these instruments from "flat-top" steel-string varieties. If you hold an arch-top guitar with its face up and back parallel to the floor and raise it up to eye level, you can see that the top is arched, or curved, so that it swells upward in the middle, reaching its highest point under the bridge, and slopes down at the neck joint and tailpiece. The bridge usually floats (is not attached) on the top surface, held in place by the tension of the strings bearing down from above. Often, the top has f-holes (so named because they resemble a lower-case *f*). This is not where the sound emanates from, though. The sound comes from the top, just like an acoustic flat-top, though the response is totally different due to its shape, bracing structure, and bridge system.

D'Angelico and D'Aquisto are two of the most famous makers of arch-tops, and Gibson produced them too. Robert Benedetto is one example of an active maker of high-quality arch-tops (see Fig. 1.5). Although most arch-tops around today are electrified, the acoustic quality of an arch-top is a distinctive sound in swing music, and is especially apropos in a trio setting of acoustic bass, fiddle or clarinet, and guitar. The sound is not quite as full-bodied and resonant as a steel-string, but there's a snap and a brassiness to an arch-top that makes it ideally suited to four-to-the-bar swing rhythm parts.

Anyway, comparisons of an arch-top to a flat-top are moot if you consider that an arch-top evokes a strong association with a certain period of music—small combos of the middle 20th century. Nothing sounds like an arch-top except an arch-top, so if you're recording a scene where *verisimilitude* is important, nothing else will do. Verisimilitude is where the producer wants you to mimic the sound of the café jazz sound in a 1930s Paris restaurant. Non-verisimilitude is having Bryan Adams sing a power ballad with synths and gated snare drums during a medieval love scene in Kevin Costner's film *Robin Hood*.

Fig. 1.5

Benedetto Arch-Top Guitar

ELECTRIC GUITARS

When Charlie Christian attached a wire-wrapped magnet under the strings of his guitar in the early part of the 20th century, he not only made things louder, he changed the entire character of the guitar. An electric guitar, that is, a guitar with a pickup, produces a sound that is completely different than an acoustic guitar with a mic hovering just above the strings. When they first came into common usage, the initial benefit was that a pickup-configured guitar was louder than an un-miked, unamplified guitar, and less problematic with respect to bleed and feedback when compared to a miked guitar (see Fig. 1.6).

The real importance of the pickup, though, was that it was tonally different than a miked guitar, which was really the critical distinction. Even without the mondo distortion and fuzz effects we're used to today, a clean electric guitar has more sustain and brilliance than its miked acoustic counterpart. Response is also different, meaning certain frequencies behave differently depending on the loudness of the signal. For example, a soft-picked acoustic guitar dies away much more rapidly than a similarly attacked electric.

Hollowbody, semi-hollowbody, and solidbody represent the first level of separation among the various types of electric guitars. These divisions have more to do with body density than pickup configurations or onboard electronics. The denser the body cavity, the less the energy is lost or dissipated from the vibrating string to the resonating wood, and hence the longer the string rings or sustains. It should be noted that these are the inherent properties of the guitar itself. All bets are off if you plug these guitars through compressors, distortion pedals, and overdriven amps.

HOLLOWBODY GUITARS

A hollowbody guitar has the least natural sustain potential of all electric guitar types. It is so named because it's essentially an acoustic guitar (which is also hollow) with a pickup either floating on the guitar's top (as in the Gibson Johnny Smith model) or sunken into carved-out cavities or holes (like Gibson's ES-175 and L-5 models). But whether floating or built-in, hollowbodies retain a distinctive woodiness to their sound, despite the fact that virtually all of their sound information comes to your ears electronically—through the pickups.

Traditional jazz electric guitar players like Joe Pass, Tal Farlow, Barney Kessel, and Herb Ellis, use hollowbody jazz guitars (see Fig. 1.7) as do modern players like Pat Metheny and George Benson. The characteristic sound is mellow, full-bodied, with a slightly "dull" (though not in a negative sense) or creamy high-end response. Even with electronic advancements in EQ and other tone-shaping circuitry, it's almost impossible to capture the "woody" character of a hollowbody guitar with any other type of electric guitar, and therefore a recording guitarist can't consider his arsenal complete until he has acquired a hollowbody guitar. Hollowbody guitars are the best of the three electric guitar types for playing fingerstyle, as Chet Atkins and Joe Pass have shown us.

Fig. 1.6

Gibson Les Paul

Fig. 1.7

Ibanez
Hollowbody Guitar

Fig. 1.8

Epiphone Semi-Hollowbody Guitar

Fig. 1.9

A popular solidbody: the Fender Stratocaster

SEMI-HOLLOWBODY GUITARS

This guitar was wildly popular in the '70s due to the cool jazz-rock stylings of Larry Carlton and Lee Ritenour, but the semi-hollowbody guitar has been a favorite guitar of blues players since long before that, as well as with modern guitarists like Eric Johnson who, though most closely associated with a solidbody Strat, creates memorable and unique colors with his Gibson "dot-neck" ES-335.

A semi-hollowbody guitar has a thinner body than a hollowbody, and therefore less resonance capabilities in its sound chamber (see Fig. 1.8). It also has a solid block of wood of varying mass (depending on the model) running up the center of the guitar, which decreases further its "hollow-ness," and adds to its sustain capabilities. The retention of the f-holes are largely cosmetic, and may even be a liability, as they increase the possibility for feedback at high volumes (which is not usually a problem in a recording situation). Some newer semi-hollowbody guitar models are now coming out with no openings in the top (B.B. King's signature guitar, the Gibson Lucille, is one such example).

SOLIDBODY GUITARS

The solidbody guitar makes up the majority of all electric guitars in existence, and includes all the household model names, like Stratocaster (see Fig. 1.9), Les Paul, Telecaster, Flying V, Explorer, SG, Jaguar, plus all the companies whose names are synonymous with solidbody manufacturing: Jackson, Steinberger, Ibanez, Dean, Paul Reed Smith, etc. You can go your entire recording career playing nothing but solidbodies, so varied are the choices within this domain. Because the influence of the body's resonating abilities is at a minimum in a solidbody, the sonic characteristics are more the result of other factors, such as the neck's scale length (which affects the string tension), the pickups, and the electronics.

This does not mean that differently shaped solidbodies will sound the same with identical pickups. Solidbodies are unique in the way they handle sound from shape to shape, material to material. But pickups factor greatly into the sound of a solidbody. Les Pauls (see Fig. 1.6) have double-coil, or "humbucker" (Gibson's own name for this model, though the term is used generically), and Strats use single-coils. Why people don't replace a Les Paul's humbuckers with single-coils is largely a matter of tradition, but many "hybrid" guitar builders adopt an approach of mixing classic solidbody body styles with different pickup types.

As a recording guitarist, you should have several solidbodies, representing the different "schools," so that producers can request a guitar by name. Typical producer requests sound something like this: "I want a Les Paul bridge pickup sound here," or "Give me an out-of-phase, *waka-waka* Strat sound," or "Let's try a neck-position Tele rhythm sound." All of these are bona fide requests, and are meaningful to students of classic and archetypal electric guitar sounds.

You don't necessarily have to own these specific models, but you should understand the principles that create the types of sounds represented by these classic axes. That includes understanding the differences among:

- **Pickup types**: single-coil, humbucker, PAF, P-90, lipstick tube, etc.

- **Pickup configurations:** three vs. two, relative placement and angle along the string length

- **Pickup wiring schemes**: whether the pickups are in or out of phase with each other, what the resistor values are in the pots, whether they have coil taps, whether there is additional circuitry—such as a preamp or presence boost—present, whether it's three-way vs. five-way vs. eight-way switching

- **Pickup controls:** master volume vs. individual pickup, master tone vs. individual tone, etc.

While guitarists can get away with owning one of each type of amp (one Vox, one Marshall, one Fender), they'll often have several of the same model guitars (e.g., a vintage Strat, a Stevie Ray Strat, a Hot Rails Strat) to satisfy different musical requirements.

BEYOND THE GUITAR

SLIDE GUITAR

Every guitarist who records, either at home or as a sideman, should have at least a rudimentary, working knowledge of slide guitar. That means that you can play in tune with decent, rattle-free technique, and have under your belt a couple of licks in a couple of styles that you can use as a springboard for creating parts. Different tunings favor certain idiomatic licks, so it's a good idea to work out parts in open D (D A D F# A D), open G (D G D G B D), their relatively tuned counterparts, open E (E B E G# B E) and open A (E A E A C# E), and standard tuning. You don't need to play like Duane, but knowing when to add a slide part could be just the icing on the cake a certain part needs. (See *Chapter 9: Tricks and Tips* for some creative uses for slide.)

Fig. 1.10

Sonny Landreth playing slide guitar on an electric solidbody

Most recording guitarists will have a separate guitar set up for slide work, because the higher the action, the better the tone (see Fig. 1.10). A guitar with intolerably high action for normal playing is a good candidate for slide parts, because it allows you to really bear down on the slide (thus getting a better tone) without the fear of buzzing or fretting out. Intonation is not a problem either, as you use a combination of visually sighting the slide over the fret wire and your ear to play in tune. Since intonation and precision fretting are factors that are not as critical for slide guitars, many players feel you can get away with less expensive guitars for this purpose. A slide guitar (for most mortals) is not as good as their principal instrument. Also slide sounds better if the instrument itself is a little funky.

Guitar Synths & Other Gizmos

Many people feel the jury is still out on guitar synths for occupying a legitimate place in a playing arsenal, and some even question whether they belong more to the synth family than the guitar family. But as a recording artist, owning and mastering a guitar synth can give you an edge in the studio and just might make you a hero one day. You could think of a guitar synth as a double, along with the other non-guitar instruments in your arsenal. A guitar synth uses the notes you play to "trigger" a synth module (either internal or external) that plays whatever sound you have dialed up: a sampled flute, a sine wave, a snare drum sound, or a ray gun effect. It's not so much about guitar as it is being able to produce and utilize effectively creative and unusual sounds using your skills as a fretboard player. Many guitar synths allow you to mix the sound of the real guitar in with the pure synth sound, creating a layer. It may not be what the producer expected of you when he called for a guitar player, but in the right context, a guitar synth can produce an entirely new color. For home recordists especially, a guitar synth can help flesh out orchestration ideas without having to dust off their keyboard chops or employ a MIDI sequencer.

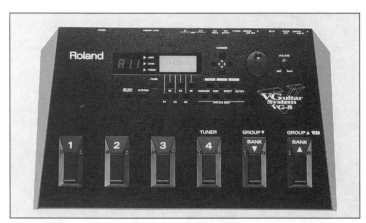

Fig. 1.11
Roland VG–8

The Roland VG-8 (see Fig. 1.11) is not a synth, but is treated like one by many guitarists as a viable alternative to a straight guitar. The VG-8 (the "VG" for "virtual guitar") uses physical modeling as the basis of its sound generation, but it's not triggering external sound sources as a synth does. It uses the vibration of the string, complete with all the nuance your hands imbue it with. Therefore, there's no "tracking" issue (where the synth has to first "read" the pitch and then produce a tone, creating a lag between when the note is played and when the unit triggers a sound), as there was with earlier guitar synths, and sounds seem much more organically produced.

But modeling affords some astounding tonal variations, including the ability to move pickups around on the neck (virtually, of course), emulate various pickup, mic, and amp responses, and provide re-tuning capabilities (instant open-D, instant 3rd-fret capo, etc.). A VG-8's emulation capabilities are not quite as good as the genuine article (its acoustic 12-string is no match for a real one in a critical listening environment), but when used judiciously or mixed a certain way, it can prove indispensable. The VG-8 also features some very un-guitaristic sounds, which can also add to your sonic palette.

Other Instruments for Doubling

If you specialize in certain acoustic blues and folk styles, you may want to have a National steel guitar, a 12-string acoustic, a high-string guitar, and even a 12-string slide for doubling tracks. As far as doubles go, it used to be that players would buy Dobros, lap steels, mandolins, banjos (tenor and five-string), etc., and tune them like the top strings of a guitar (changing string gauges when necessary), but that practice is fading out in favor of playing idiomatically in the proper tunings. There is simply no way to get a convincing Scruggs-style part on a five-string banjo if you don't tune the drone string (the one played with the thumb) to a high G and base your patterns on forward rolls.

Bouzoukis, balalaikas, kotos, and ouds are ethnic instruments that can still be acceptably tuned to suit a particular situation, and most people just borrow or rent one of these before a session (and familiarize themselves with it) if a producer calls for one. Again, if you're considering any one of these doubles, make sure it's buzz and rattle free, intonates properly, and holds its tuning. Many an exotic "wall hanger" can be found in antique stores, but there's no guarantee that their playability condition is up to the rigors and critical demands of a recording environment.

PARAPHERNALIA POTPOURRI

Accessories: tuners, capoes, slides, E-bows, peg winders, wrenches.

There is a scene in James Cameron's undersea action-thriller film *The Abyss* where the two heroes are trapped in a crippled and leaking two-man submarine. They realize that if they don't plug the leak, they'll drown in minutes. But the leak is behind an electrical box bolted to the sub's wall. Access to the leak is blocked. Efforts to bare-handedly rip the box from its mount prove futile. They can't loosen the bolts with their fingers, and they didn't bring their tool box in their haste to chase the bad guy (who's responsible for their leaky predicament). As the frigid water rises to neck level, one of them cries in frustration, "I don't believe it! We're actually going to die because we didn't bring a crescent wrench."

How many of you have had that same sinking (sorry) feeling at a gig because of the lack of some stupidly simple item—like an E string or a fresh battery or an amp fuse? Well, on a gig you can actually get away with some catastrophes (e.g., finishing a set with a missing string). On a recording session, where everything is under a microscope, it's virtually impossible (though there are some legendary stories). Even the best-equipped guitarist can't ensure totally against disaster, but there are some essential tools that should always reside in your bag or on a nearby shelf to troubleshoot common mishaps. When assembling the guitar portion of your rig, don't forget all the little stuff that accompanies them. They might just mean the difference between sinking and swimming.

Tuners: To sit in a long uninterrupted recording session, you'll have to tune occasionally, sometimes surreptitiously, so as not to disturb other activities (playback, rehearsal of upcoming cues, producer giving notes to the ensemble, etc.). There are many time-sensitive sessions where you can't even make noise, much less find a break in the action to tune, so you need to have an electronic tuner placed inline with your guitar, effects and amp, so that you can check your tuning periodically. Tuning visually, when you get the hang of it, can actually be faster than tuning by ear, and is definitely more reliable when ear fatigue sets in.

An electronic tuner can also aid you in alternate tunings within the same piece of music, or within a quick segue that would normally prohibit a retune. You could, for example, play one cue in standard tuning, rest for eight bars, come back in drop D tuning, rest again, and again re-enter in standard tuning for the next cue. Many multi-effects processors even mute the output when you enter their onboard tuning mode, which is a great convenience, especially in the sometimes tense goings-on of the recording studio.

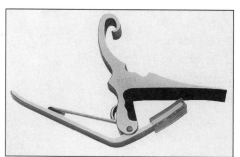

Fig. 1.12

Capo

Capoes: Capoes (see Fig. 1.12) are devices that clamp around the strings and underside of your neck, pulling the strings to the fretboard at a given fret—like a permanent 1st-finger barre. This allows you to transpose the guitar chords from the actual "concert" (true or absolute) key you're actually in. For example, if you want to play D chord you can either play it as an open-position D, or capo the 2nd fret and play a C chord, which will sound as D. This might seem arbitrary until you consider what happens if the chord is A♭ major. Here, you can either barre the 4th fret as an F-type chord, or you can capo the first fret and play an open-position G chord. If it's supposed to sound like a ringy, open-string, fingerpicked part, it's better to pop on the capo and play it in "G" than to grip an A♭ barre chord. Capoes can save your life when people decide to switch keys up or down a half step, which often happens when recording with vocalists.

By playing a part in "C" that's really in D (to take our previous example) you also end up playing C licks instead of D licks. Each open-position key on the guitar has idiomatic properties to it. For example, some people find it easier to play acoustic blues in E than in G. So if they encounter a song in F or G that's supposed to have a swampy, Delta feel to it, they'll probably slap on a capo at the first or third frets, respectively, and play out of an E position.

But capoes can work for adding "color" parts too. Say you've just recorded a song on acoustic guitar using A, D, and E7 chords, all in open position. The producer likes the full-bodied sound of the part, but thinks the overall mix lacks some sparkle and high-end activity in the accompaniment. This is a perfect opportunity to put on the capo at the 9th fret and play the open chord-forms C, F, and G7, which will come out sounding as A, D, and E7—the original chords in the rhythm part. The difference is, these capoed chords are played way up the neck with higher notes. What's more, the capo gives them an open-string quality. If you're the one who laid down the original part, you can usually play the new exactly in rhythm, which can sound more like a "doubled" guitar than two different guitars playing at once. Suddenly your double-tracked guitar sounds more like a 12-string, but with an expanded range. As an aside, this situation would work well for a Nashville-tuned guitar, which would yield a similar effect.

Slides: There are a variety of objects that can be fashioned into a slide, from the medicine-bottle type (Coricidin was a commercially obtainable cough medication whose bottle was just right for an average human left hand to perform slide guitar with) to a length of brass pipe to a wine-bottle neck to an actual nickel-chrome machined slide for a pedal or lap steel. Which one is right for you is largely a matter of individual taste and comfort (as is the decision to play the guitar itself, on your lap or upright in normal guitar-playing position), but a well-versed recording guitarist should have some slide facility in several styles. Facility means not only having a clean, noise-free and in-tune technique, but also being able to play idiomatically, i.e., knowing some licks. Slide players play both in open tunings (G and D, and their relative transpositions A and E, being the most popular) as well as standard tuning.

E-Bow: An E-bow is a nifty little device that fits in your right hand and uses a battery-powered magnet to excite the string directly under it. What you can do then is play the guitar as you do normally in the left hand, substituting the E-bow placement for right-hand picking. This produces attack-less notes, emulating the sound of a bowed string instrument, like the violin, viola, or cello. Because the E-bow has to magnetically oscillate (vibrate) the string into producing a pitch, the response is not as immediate as if you'd picked it, so it's generally better on slower, more lyrical melodic passages. It doesn't take that much technique to master one, and it can contribute a completely different flavor to a guitar part, especially as an overdub.

Wrenches, Peg Winders, and Other Tools: I once interviewed Eric Johnson to publish an article on his guitar technique. As we chatted casually, he picked up his Strat and began to play, stopping almost instantly because it had developed a slight 1st-fret buzz on the 3rd string. In a matter of mere seconds, he reached into his case, pulled out a truss-rod wrench, administered a couple of cranks, and eliminated the buzz—without ever breaking his conversational stride.

This shows what an intimate knowledge of your instrument can bring. You can not only play it, but you can make adjustments and minor repairs to it too—often on the fly. These repairs can be as simple as fixing fret buzzes and intonation problems, which can happen as a result of an environmental change, or some other misalignment occurrence to your guitar. To do this, you must know the mechanical elements of your guitar and be facile in dealing with them.

If you have a floating bridge system with a locking nut, make sure the corresponding wrenches are within reach should a string break. A small Phillips-head screwdriver is usually what's required to raise and lower pickups, if they ever get too far or close to the strings. Pliers and wire cutters can accomplish in seconds what might take an unaided human hand minutes to complete. A peg winder will bring a string up to pitch from total slack much quicker than winding the machine head by hand. Peg winders also have a built-in notch in the tuning-head sleeve that allows you to pop stubborn acoustic-guitar bridge pins. A socket wrench will allow you to tighten or even remove the output-jack nut, should you ever develop a problem down there.

Depending on the guitar and rig you have, you should develop a miniature tool-kit that includes extra fuses, alligator clips (for making temporary electrical connections), spare batteries, and even extra tubes for your amp, so that you can problem solve virtually any situation within your technical abilities.

SOME OTHER SEEMINGLY OBVIOUS ITEMS

Extra Strings: Seems obvious, right? But there is a way to be smart about something as simple as extra strings. For example, don't just pack one extra set. Keep three Gs, Bs and high Es, because these break more than the lower, wound strings. It's not uncommon to break the same string twice in one session, especially if you're doing multiple takes on some outrageous bent-note passage.

Batteries: Take an inventory of what kind and how many you use in your setup and have a complete replacement set. Upon insertion of any new battery, I stick white masking tape on it and write the date. Come to think of it, pack the tape and the marker in your bag, too. Tape can be used to reduce rattle on a trapeze tailpiece or Dobro cone.

Cables and Adapters: The cable part is easy: Have at least one long and two short in reserve. Don't wait for total failure before substituting cord, either. Intermittent crackles can kill a take just as dead as a totally non-working cable, so at the first hint of trouble, swap for a new one, and work on the problem after the session. Adapters are items many guitarists don't pack, but they can be the "crescent wrench" that saves the day. In a pro studio, you probably don't have to worry about scaring up, say a direct box, but in a demo studio, if you bring your own, you'll be self-sufficient should you decide to go direct and there's not a spare D.I. around.

Needle-Nose Pliers, Reversible Screwdriver, Pocket Knife, Alligator Clips, Electrical Tape, Soldering Iron, Length of Wire, Penlight: This is your guerrilla-electronics repair kit. You can fix everything from a crackling cable to a broken volume pedal pot with one of the above devices. Music electronics is a surprisingly simple, intuitive affair if you can locate the source of the problem; sometimes a cursory look will reveal the defect—a broken solder joint, a loose wire, a dirty contact. Alligator clips will hold two contacts together, but if you have the time drop a glob of solder onto the connections.

Cable Tester and Volt-Ohm Meter: Each of these items costs about $12 and $20 respectively, and earn their keep the first time they diagnose a bad or reverse-wired cable. Learn how to use the volt-ohm meter with respect to your equipment, i.e., know what power supplies you have and what the appropriate settings are on the meter. You can impress your friends with your "gearhead geek" aptitude.

Fuses: Any new environment—even a studio—can have unpredictable wiring schemes that could cause havoc with your gear, and especially to your amp. Your amp's first line of defense is its fuse. If the house current is weird, the fuse will blow. Having replacements is your responsibility, just like having extra strings. If you blow subsequent fuses, alert the engineer and asked that your amp be moved to a different circuit.

Duct Tape: This is the musician's baking soda—an all-purpose utility product that cures a multitude of maladies. You can use it to fix everything from a rattling tailpiece to a broken mic clip. Even the roll itself is handy: you can use it to tilt your combo amp up for better monitoring.

Pencil and Paper: I can't tell you the times I've scrambled to find these two mundane items. You can take notes, dash out substitute chord changes, and even pass notes to the other session musicians where conversation is discouraged or impractical. Write your cheat notes on a separate piece of paper, not on the chart, so that you can take your scrawlings with you, and no one will ever see "Hit the E chord when the big fat tuba player gets ready for his entrance."

Penlight: It doesn't have to be dark to use a flashlight. Shadows and small sizes pose as much a problem for diagnosing an electrical problem as the complete absence of light. If you're trying to locate a bad solder joint inside a volume pedal, you may not see a glob of solder that's causing it because of a shadow. You can hold a penlight between your teeth as you reach into the back of your amp to fix a broken speaker lead.

GUITARS FOR RECORDING: A REAL-LIFE SCENARIO

Fig. 1.13 Strats and Teles

Veteran studio player Carl Verheyen has developed his arsenal of guitars over many years of playing in the studio. While he owns about 40 guitars, he doesn't take nearly that many to a session. "I have about 24 guitars delivered, and that prepares me for anything that might be thrown at me," Carl says. "I have 12 guitars in one trunk and 12 in another—an acoustic trunk and an electric trunk. Those get delivered just about everywhere I go. Even if they say, 'Oh, just bring your Strat,' I always carry a few extras just in case."

Carl keeps everything in a warehouse maintained by his cartage company. "For me, the nice thing is, the warehouse is about seven minutes from my house, so if someone calls and asks for just a 12-string overdub, I can just drop by the warehouse on my way to the session. That's not too much trouble. If I need them serviced, I'll call the warehouse and tell them pull trunk #2 and take out my thinline Tele, or whatever, and that I'm on my way over to pick it up."

Carl gives this advice for assembling a recording arsenal of guitars: "Composers and producers are hipper than ever, and know the difference between a Strat and a Les Paul. You might be playing a line on a Tele and they'll walk right up to

Fig. 1.14 Semis and Les Pauls

you out of the blue and say, 'Hey, could I hear that on a Les Paul?' You're just expected in the studio world to have all these various instruments covered.

"You can specialize, of course," says Carl. "As far as my individual style is concerned, I'm pretty much a Strat man. I've got about seven Stratocasters and they all sound different. Three of them are old, four are new, and those I take on the road and change the pickups. But my ground-zero guitar is an old Strat, a '65 or '61. So I got real good on my instrument, which in my case was a Strat, before moving on."

Once Carl had the Strat thing down (see Fig. 1.13), he moved on to other "bread and butter" models. "If you start with a Strat, you realize, well, Fender also had the Telecaster, which is a classic instrument, and doesn't sound anything like a Strat," as Carl points out. "You can't get that sound out of a Strat, so you need one of those. Then you need that Gibson sound, that humbucker sound. So I have an ES-335 and a couple of Les Pauls (see Fig. 1.14). The 335 is a great half-jazz type of axe. Not the most rocking guitar, but it does that down-the-middle thing pretty well. I used it for years on the TV show 'Cheers.'

"But of course that doesn't sound anything like a Les Paul," continues Carl. "I use those for power chords and for really thick-sounding songs. I bought a 1969 Les Paul that had the mini humbuckers in them and took them out and put PAFs in it. So I have the poor man's '58 or '59. I also have a 1954 Les Paul with the soap bar pickups, the P-90s, which I find to be a wonderful blues guitar. It's got a single-coil sound, but much thicker than a Strat. It's one of the most usable guitars for playing solo because it just cuts through everything. I've got a '69 thinline Telecaster, a hollowbody one. And that sounds great with just a little bit of distortion playing the chords. It's a great rhythm guitar. One of my tricks is to combine that with a 1965 Rickenbacker 12-string played clean. Those two things just jangle like crazy. It's good for a Tom Petty or Byrds retro thing. Even a grungy sound.

"I also have a 1959 Gretsch 6120, the Chet Atkins model with a Bigsby. That's a completely unique sound, and it sounds great through a Vox amp distorting just a little bit. In addition to the Chet Atkins/Duane Eddy thing, which it does real well, I've found all sorts of crazy, silly applications for that. But I'll also use it to play jazz. It sounds great when you mic the f-holes and use the amp signal in combination."

Besides the Strat, Tele, Gibson, Rick and Gretsch sounds, there are other instruments that come up for more exotic sounds. "I have a 1957 Supro Dualtone that I've set up for slide," notes Carl. "It's a huge, fat-sounding guitar with pickups that are about three inches wide, but they're single-coil. That's been very valuable. I also have a couple of hot rod Strats, set up with Floyd Roses. They're sort of stunt guitars, for that radical

Fig. 1.15

Carl's acoustic armada

sound. I've also got a Strat with lipstick tube pickups for that Jaguar, Jazzmaster, Nirvana sound. My Parker Fly is becoming quite useful because of the piezo. I go from the piezo into a D.I. into the board and route the magnetics into an amp for a dirty sound."

"For acoustics, I have several Gibson Jumbos, and those are my favorite all-purpose, acoustic rhythm guitars. I also carry a Martin dreadnought, a 12-string, a Nashville-tuned acoustic and a nylon-string to every session. All of those are in my acoustic road case" (see Fig. 1.15).

The example set by Carl is that it's not only important to have a variety of sounds, but to know how those sounds can be used. This involves having a historical knowledge of the way the guitar sounds and being able to produce musically useful sounds yourself. You have to know *when* to play a certain guitar as well how to play it.

CHAPTER TWO

Amplifiers for Recording

GUITAR AMPS

The guitar amplifier carries with it connotations almost more mystical than the guitar itself, because it's all about an evasive, intangible factor: tone. There's no real evaluating the color, look, or feel of an amp—it's just an electronic box. All your judgments about an amp's capabilities must come only from the sound it produces. But an amp doesn't merely make the sound of the electric guitar louder; it adds its own character to the total tonal makeup, interacting with not only the guitar, but also the player. To understand what a guitar amp does in the first place, let's begin by considering it compared to another type of amp: the kind used to power the speakers of your stereo system.

CLASSIC HI-FI APPROACH VS. GUITAR AMP

A so-called hi-fi (high fidelity), or power amp, such as you'd find in your home stereo system or driving a recording studio's monitors, behaves just like an amp "should." It reacts quickly and truly to the incoming signal (your guitar sound, let's say) and reproduces that signal faithfully in its output stage—only a whole lot louder. Loud enough to drive a pair of speakers. The best amplifiers are the ones that are the most sensitive to the preamp's signal and can reproduce those fluctuations accurately, quickly and evenly across the frequency spectrum and at all power levels.

But an electric guitar sounds terrible through a conventional power amp. Its requirements from an amp are totally different than a conventional signal's. Amp designer Paul Rivera explains: "The problem is basically in the preamp EQ and the speakers. Every EQ has a hinge point between the bass and treble. On a hi-fi system it's placed a lot higher than on a guitar amp. Full-range signals sound better to human ears with a higher hinge point than do guitar signals. That's why electric guitars don't sound good through stereo systems. Acoustic guitars, by contrast, sound good through stereos and lousy through combo amps."

Then there's the issue of distortion. A guitar amp behaves like a theoretical high-quality amp only up to a certain point and then it starts to distort. Distortion in any electrical signal is usually a bad thing, except in the case of electric guitars, where certain kinds of distortion are not only tolerable, they're preferred to the undistorted signal. This is what tube amps do that make them unique, and it's why they're considered by most people to be the best type of guitar amp. They distort. They color. They do not deliver a true representation of the electric guitar's sound as it comes through the cord. They can't react quickly to successive current spikes, like when you play a series of hard downstrokes. The first one is a little louder than the rest. But whatever it does, it's beautiful and finding an amp with that perfect distorted tone is the holy grail of amp builders and guitarists.

The other aspect to a guitar amp's sound that Rivera alluded to is not strictly in the amp stage, but goes hand in hand with the system—the speaker. Again, a speaker optimized for a guitar amp is not like the speaker you'd use in a stereo or studio monitoring system. For one thing, stereo speakers are usually two-way systems. They have a tweeter for handling high frequencies and a woofer for the low (three-way speakers have a tweeter and two woofers for high, midrange and low frequencies). "A guitar amp with a tweeter sounds terrible, unless it's designed for acoustic-electric guitars," assures Rivera. "Not only do they have no place sonically in a guitar amp, but they're easy to blow. If you need a setup with both an acoustic and electric guitar, use separate cabinets."

Guitar speakers are one-way systems, even in a two-speaker cabinet running in stereo. One midrange speaker is used for both high and low frequencies. Guitar speakers have a more limited frequency range than these other two types, especially in their ability to reproduce the high end. Consequently, a guitar speaker is more a midrange device, rolling off the high end of any signal that gets put through it.

Again, you don't need to know exactly how all this works, except to say that your ears will be the judge once you hear it. Try plugging your guitar into your stereo sometime to hear how harsh the high end is and how over-pronounced the low end is. (One thing speaker simulators do is mimic the EQ response a midrange-oriented, guitar-amp speaker produces.)

Similarly, your CD player sounds pretty lame if you patch it through your guitar amp. Power amps and guitar amps are designed to do two totally different jobs. But there are occasions where you will use a power amp for your guitar signal, and if you know the differences between power amps and guitar amps and what each one was designed for, it will help you from becoming confused.

PARTS AND STAGES OF THE AMPLIFIER: PREAMP, POWER AMP, CHANNEL CONFIGURATION, FRONT PANEL

When you enter the recording environment, it's important to understand what happens to your signal at each amp stage along the way. Gain stages are the separate changes an electrical signal goes through to prepare it for the next step in the circuit. You can't hook a 4x12 speaker cabinet directly to a headphone output jack and you can't plug your guitar directly into a power amp input jack, because these devices aren't properly matched with respect to gain. The gain has to proceed through certain steps to be compatible for the next stage. Let's explore those stages.

Preamp: A preamp is designed to accept a low-level signal, like that produced from guitar pickups or a microphone. Since the preamp has to be ultra-sensitive to weak signals, the output it produces is commensurately weak. "Weak" here is not a bad thing; it's what allows for subtle variations in the fluctuating current that we perceive as sensitivity.

A good example to illustrate this principle is the microphone. A microphone has to have an extremely delicate mechanism (the diaphragm) to be able to move exactly in concert with the differing air pressure that the human voice or other acoustic instrument produces. As the diaphragm moves in minuscule motions, a proportionately minuscule current is produced. That current, though weak, reflects with remarkable accuracy the character of the original signal. This explains why microphones have such a low-level output, and why microphone preamps (called "mic pre's" for short) are so important in recording. Still, the signal doesn't do anybody much good at this low level, especially if it has to drive an array of large loudspeakers and be heard by thousands of people.

Power Amps: Enter the power amplifier. Here, the circuitry does not have to be as sensitive to air pressure (as a mic and pickup do) and minute electrical fluctuations (as does the input on a preamp), because it's not starting from zero; it has a preamp signal to deal with. The power amp is sort of a booster rocket for audio. A "good" power amp will take a preamp signal and increase its level without changing the basic shape of the signal. Generally, you don't want the amp changing or coloring the sound of the preamp, you just want it to drive the speakers.

That's the theory, anyway, but you don't have to be playing guitar long to realize that what is theoretically accurate is not what's necessarily musical. There's no greater living example of this than the guitar tube amp. Here, the older and more inefficient vacuum-tube technology produces (it is generally agreed) more musical results than modern solid-state components.

Tube, Solid-State, and Hybrid Amps: Certainly there is a lot of hype about just how good tubes are and how bad solid-state technology is, but the fact remains that old Plexi Marshalls, Fender Princetons, and Vox AC30s have a sound that is much sought after, and these are tube amps. Any modern guitarist should know how to derive a good sound out of any amp, and how to capitalize on its particular strengths, but tube amps will always occupy a special place in the guitar aficionado's heart.

Different types of amps include:

- *All-solid-state:* Both the preamp and power amp sections use solid-state technology

- *All-tube amps:* These use tubes for the preamp section (the 12AX7 is a popular preamp tube) and tubes for the power amp section (the 6L6 and EL34 being two well-known types)

- *Hybrid amps:* These try to achieve the best of both worlds by providing a tube preamp, where most of the tone shaping occurs, and a solid-state power amp, where manufacturers can keep the price down and where the effect on tone is not as critical

Separating Pre and Power: The power amp section may not contribute as much to the sound as the preamp, but it does have an effect on overall tonal quality, especially on a tube power amp, which tends to react more dynamically. The harmonic structure of the notes changes depending on the current in the tubes. Tweaked preamps tend to sound the same at low and high volumes, which is a giveaway that someone is deriving all their sound from an overdriven preamp and using either a solid-state power amp, or a tube amp that's not driven very hot.

Because of this separation of preamp and power amp, many guitarists will use one or the other but not both. It's possible to go into the preamp of a combo amp, come out of the effects loop or preamp out, and go off to another device for the power amp stage. Older amps have no place for you to tap in, but newer amps feature several places, notably the Preamp Out jack, or the Effects Send jack. This adds a whole host of options when trying to combine preamps, power amps, and speaker cabinets.

Channel Configuration: If you're going to use just the amp to derive your clean and distorted sound, you'll need to know what happens when you switch channels. Is the second channel (the lead one, usually with more front-panel controls) using any of the first channel's circuitry? In some amps it does and in others there is completely isolated, dedicated circuitry (including, sometimes, separate reverb controls) for this purpose.

Also, many amps now come with three channels, which makes a whole lot of sense. Most electric guitarists really need three basic sounds: a clean sound for fingerpicking and clean chords for ballads; a crunch rhythm sound that is nice and fat but still retains definition among the individual strings so that chord tones can be discerned; and a lead sound that sounds great for single-line work but would otherwise be too distorted for rhythm work. Especially if you're anti-stompbox, preferring no artificial means to derive a tone, consider a three-way amp.

It may seem obvious to point out that guitarists need to know their front panels but it's important to realize that not all front panels treat signals the same way, despite similar labelings. For example, a Marshall's EQ stage occurs before the preamp, while a Fender's is post-preamp. This has an effect when you go to dial in more treble. Also, if your amp has a sweepable, or semi-parametric, midrange control instead of a passive one, you should know how that operates. A contour control is sometimes included, and rather than blindly turning it, know that it changes the response curve of your tone. When do you use the Presence control over the Treble? What's the difference between pushing the Bright switch in and rolling off the treble versus the other way around? You might have to look at the owner's manual to see what exactly the Bright switch is doing (though many manuals won't print exactly what, but you can find out). You should always make adjustments by ear if possible, but if you don't know how your controls are "voiced," you may make a situation worse rather than better if you're asked to make an adjustment—especially under pressure. Don't rely on just one or two settings. Work to be as versatile on your amp as you are with pickup selections, distortion settings, and effects programming.

OTHER FEATURES: PRE OUT, POWER IN, EFFECTS LOOP, CLASS/POWER SWITCHING, SPEAKER OUT, SLAVE OUT

All of the following features (except for class/power switching) are found on the amp's back panel in the form of in and out jacks, or sockets, that you plug a 1/4" cable into. It's important to remember that even though the jacks for all these various features are the same, the electronic functions are very different, so make sure you know exactly what you want to do before you start plugging in cables.

Pre Out: This taps the signal after it's been through the preamp and EQ stage, but before it goes to the power amp. There's no way to quantify what exact percentage the preamp contributes to the signal's character, but it's certainly a large majority. So tapping the signal of an amp at this stage captures the essence of the sound and gives it to you in a versatile form, electronically speaking. You can route the signal to another power amp with a lower output wattage, for example, and drive that amp harder for a more distorted sound at a lower overall level. You can pass the signal through effects, such as reverb or delay, before going back into the power amp (although an effects loop will accomplish the same thing). If you want to process your signal in stereo, this is an excellent way, as you can run an un-effected preamped signal through one power amp and a processed one through the effects loop of, say, a multi-effects processor (you want to avoid the multi-effect's preamp stage if it has one, as you're already "preamped" through your favorite amp) and into another power amp.

Power Amp In: Patching a signal directly into the power amp jack avoids the preamp stage and effects loop (if included). This is handy if you've set up miking on a combo, but want to use a different preamp. You might, for example, use an external preamp for a super fuzzed-out tone, and come back into the amp at the power amp to utilize the power amp stage and speaker cabinet. If you have a particular preamp that you like—from an ADA to a Mesa V-Twin—this is the way to get that sound coupled with the dynamic response of a power amp and speaker cabinet—plus, you don't have to move the mic.

Effects Loop: The effects loop is a neat and tidy solution to tapping your signal between the preamp stage and the power amp. Most modern high-end amps have an effects loop built in to their back panel, and they come in two varieties, serial and parallel (see Fig. 2.1). A series effects loop passes the entire signal through the loop, affecting 100 percent of the signal. It essentially shunts the whole signal off to be processed and brings it back. A parallel effects loop taps only part of the signal (typically 50 percent, but sometimes the ratio is adjustable), leaving a portion to pass through unaffected. Whether you go the parallel or series route depends largely on how much you like to tweak your sound (or on the type of amp you buy). If you're more "mixer" oriented and like to blend your signal and adjust the balance with care, you might prefer the parallel approach. If you're more oriented to the "inline" school, where your signal runs all in a row, the series scheme will be a lot simpler to operate and give you signal responses more typical in a stompbox configuration.

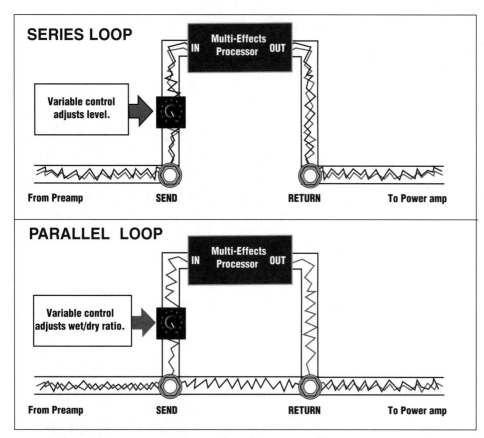

Fig. 2.1

Signal path of series and parallel loops

Loop preferences aside, if you have to come to the party with your own effects (and not rely on the engineer to apply them at the mixdown), it's best to plug them into your effects loop, especially if they are the rack-mount variety and are used to receiving line-level signals. Guitarists for years have been putting stompbox versions of reverb, delay, choruses, and flangers before the preamp, but the ideal way to get a pure raw sound to the preamp is to have no effects inline. Once the straight guitar signal passes through the preamp, then quality (i.e., rack-mount) effects can be added via the loop. Your amp's effects loop runs at either -10 dB or +4 dB, so determine which level applies to you, as it will help you prepare the proper level for your effects to receive the signal. A +4 signal is hotter and better suited to higher-end units, but it can overdrive stompboxes, which tend to react better to -10 signals and below (guitar output levels).

Class/Power Switching: Class/Power Switching is useful in recording situations for the same reason it's employed in live ones: it allows you to get your amp working hard (and sounding good in the process!) without having to be unduly loud. In a power soak or reduced wattage mode, the components react electrically the same at a lower power setting as they do in a higher one. It's just that the overdriving of the circuits happens at a much lower current, which results in less overall loudness. Bleed is a problem in all but the best high-end studios, and especially if you're recording the guitar amp along with other acoustic (miked) instruments. If you're overdubbing in the control room and your amp is down the hall, you probably don't need to use the power switching feature.

Speaker Out: The primary function of this jack is fairly obvious. This is where you connect the speaker(s) to the power amp out to receive that signal plus all the stuff that comes before it (preamp, EQ, stuff from the effects loop). As long as you observe the ohm-rating requirements, you can attach a variety of speakers and speaker arrays (multiple speakers wired together, usually in the same cabinet). You might prefer a higher-wattage EV for clean sounds and a lower-wattage Celestion for your distortion settings, and you would make these substitutions at the speaker out jack—again, assuming you observe the speaker load requirements. Don't use speakers with lower ohm ratings than indicated on the back panel, as you could do damage to your amp.

This is where you would attach a "load box," that converts a speaker signal to a line level. Caution: it's best not to attach anything to the speaker output except the speaker unless you really know what you're doing. If you take away the amp's natural load—the speaker—and attach some doohickey that doesn't load the amp properly, you can cook your amp (i.e., do irreparable damage) real quick.

Slave Out: This is similar to the speaker out in that it offers a tap opportunity after the power amp stage, but it's usually hotter as it's tapped from the power output transformer. If your amp has one of these jacks, it's better to use this as your signal to drive another power amp—after you've treated the signal correctly.

With skilled guidance from a qualified amp tech, you can get the most convincing signal from the speaker out or the slave out jack, because there's interaction with the power transformer as well as the preamp.

Fig. 2.2

A Vox AC30 combo amp

CONFIGURATIONS: COMBO, HEAD & CAB, PRE/POWER AMP + CAB

If you love amps, old and new, British and American, you may not think much about their configuration. A Fender Vibro-Luxe is a combo and it is sacrilege to imagine it in some other anatomically parsed form. Similarly, the only way to conceive a Marshall series 800 amp is as a head with one or two 4x12 cabs sitting underneath. But these two amps represent more than just a different aesthetic in amplifying a guitar signal. They represent a different approach to configuration, and configuration has particular meaning to recording guitarists. The Vox AC30 (see Fig. 2.2) is a combo—the amplifier section and speaker cabinet combined. A Marshall 800 series is a head and must be used with a cabinet. A head-and-stack configuration allows you to use one 4x12 cabinet for a small club and two 4x12 cabinets stacked on top of each other (thus the term "Marshall stack") for larger clubs and arenas (see Fig. 2.3).

Separate heads allow you to mix and match cabinets (as described above in the one- vs. two-cab scenario), or to keep one cabinet and mix and match heads. For example, you may want to set up one cabinet and mic for a recording session, and then try running different amps through it. This saves striking the cabinet and setting up a new one between each cue. Session ace Carl Verheyen takes six heads, give or take, on typical big sessions. He taps each one at either the speaker out or slave out jack, runs it through a line-level converter and then through an FET power amp to a cabinet. This allows him to switch quickly from head to head while retaining a consistency between the effects rack and power amp stage.

Fig. 2.3

A Marshall head and stack

What gives you the most flexibility in a short time is the rack approach (see Fig. 2.4). It may give you the least psychological feeling of purity, but with some thought it can

Fig. 2.4

A rack-mounted system

provide you with the most versatile and flexible setup, especially if you must produce a variety of sounds in a short period of time. The rack approach dictates that you have separate components for each step in the chain. That means a separate preamp, effects system, and power amp. For example, you might plug into a Marshall JMP-1 preamp, go into a Lexicon PCM 80 multi-effects processor and then into a Crown power amp. If you decide at some point during the session you want to change, you can swap an ADA preamp for the Marshall, and come up with an entirely different sound. The same is true for the effects rack. You can just as easily fly in an Eventide H3000 with all your favorite chorus and pitch-shifting programs.

In the 1970s, rack-mounted gear was all the rage. It was common for session guitarists to bring case after case of outboard gear, and to have complicated switching systems to access it all. The trend has turned away from that super-processed, more-gear-is-better sound to a purer, stripped-down approach. But what has still remained is the practice of rack-mounting certain pieces of gear, especially preamps, and power amps—the essential components of even the most Spartan approach to guitar. Most true tone aficionados will use a head, such as the Soldano SLO 100, and depending on the recording situation, will employ rack gear, creating a sort of hybrid of the head-and-cab and rack approaches. But for recording in a variety of situations, especially ones with a degree of unpredictability to them, the rack way is the neatest solution.

Speakers and Cabinets: Open and Closed Back, Replacements

Open/Closed Back: If you're miking the speaker, you'll need to be aware of the two basic types of cabinets: open-back and closed-back. If you'll notice, most combo amps feature open-back cabinets, and most head and cab configurations sport closed-back cabinets. Open backs allow the sound (mostly bass frequencies) to escape through the back of the amp, which results in a more "open" sound, preferred by blues players. The bass frequencies are less directional than treble ones, so they tend to fill the surrounding space by emanating from the back as well as the front. This means you can place a mic above or even behind an amp with successful results. A closed-back cabinet, by contrast, pushes all those bass frequencies back through the speaker and out the front, creating a punchier sound. All things being equal, a closed-back sound is thumpier in the low end and more compressed sounding. If you use a two-amp setup, as Allan Holdsworth and Eric Johnson do, you'll probably want to play chords on the open-back amp and lead or low-note, metal-type riffing on the closed-back amp.

Replacements: Speakers, like the amps themselves, have definite characteristics guitarists have come to associate with a certain sound. Just as you wouldn't install a Tele bridge pickup in a Les Paul, so you wouldn't put a 30-watt Celestion in a Vibro-Luxe. But sometimes you can improve an existing cabinet or create a new cabinet with replacement speakers, closely related to, but not exact copies of, existing ones. Obviously, if you blow a speaker, you'll have no choice, so know what speakers you're working with and what you can replace them with should the situation arise.

AMPS FOR RECORDING: A ROUNDUP

"Producers know when to ask for a Les Paul over a Strat, and the same is true for amps," says Carl Verheyen, our guide through the studio guitarist's supermarket. "I find it easiest to think of amps in two categories: clean amps and dirty amps. Lots of new amps come and go, and there's always a new flavor of the month, but the staple amps for me that last through the years are Fenders and Voxes for clean sounds. When I sit at home and practice I have two old blackface Princetons. It uses 6V6s, and I've set them up with matched tubes, which makes them work well together in stereo. For a bigger sound I've got two '63 Vox AC30s. I've got two newer models, which are quite good, especially if you get them with the old blue Bulldog speakers. I use an old Jim Kelly amp, which Allan Holdsworth turned me on to.

Fig. 2.5

A selection of Carl's recording amps (with pedalboard in foreground)

"For a dirty sound, I've got a '66 JTM-45 Plexi, with a white Plexi back. I have a '68 Plexi, a 50-watt, and a '69 100-watt. It really gets up and honks. I have some newer amps: a THD, Electroplex Rocket 90, an Egnater four-channel head that's really versatile. I use a couple of '60s Marshall basket-weave cabs with 25-watt Greenbacks. Allan Holdsworth told me years ago to never play out the same speakers for your clean and dirty sounds. He always makes it different. And he was right." (Fig. 2.5 shows some of the amps Carl regularly uses on sessions.)

On speakers, Carl advises to stick closely to original manufacturer specs for replacements. "I use Jensen and Vox Bulldog speakers for my clean sound, and the 25-watt Celestion 'Greenbacks' for my dirty sound," he reports. "The lower-wattage Celestions give me that nice, slight break-up at a reasonable volume. If I'm going for a clean sound, I might run 75-watt speakers from the same head."

Though it's a bit of a generalization, recording musicians tend to use Fenders as a reference for clean sounds, and Marshalls as the springboard for distorted sounds. Obviously there are scores of other manufacturers making a living by producing quality amps for recording guitarists, but the fact remains that just as you can't have a discussion about microphones without mentioning Neumann, you can't talk about amp tone without touching on the Fender and Marshall aesthetic. You must have experience with both schools, not only with respect to your ears, but also how to tweak and manipulate them during a session.

CHAPTER THREE

Recording Guitars: The Setup

ELECTRIC GUITAR RECORDING

Recording the guitar is never done in isolation. There is always a context in which the guitar will appear. Is it electric or acoustic? Hard rock or folk? Historically stylistic or wholly original? These are all musical issues you must consider. Then there are the realistic or logistic considerations. Will you be printing effects or adding them in the mixdown? Will you be playing through an amp and will it be miked or will you be going direct? If you're playing through an amp, can you play it as loud as you need to or will you have to keep the volume at a reasonable level? These are all issues that affect your setup and approach to the session.

DIVERSIFY YOUR SOUNDS

Your favorite amp might be a non-master volume 100-watt Marshall cranked to 10, but if you're to be sharing the studio with a string section, you'll have to keep your sound way below that, even with heavy baffling. Thus, you'll probably have to employ a distortion box, power soak, or another method to achieve the same distortion quality at a lower volume. Be aware that your amp will now respond differently and so might your playing, if it's not what you're used to hearing.

Just as you wouldn't play at the same volume level and intensity for an entire performance, so should you avoid the same pickup setting. A mistake many beginning guitarists make is that they play on only one pickup setting. Worse, they develop a sound for only that one setting—usually the bridge pickup if you're a rock player, the neck if you lean toward jazz. To be musically interesting and compelling, you must have good sounds for most if not all the pickup settings on your guitar, whether it's a two-humbucker, three-single-coil, or hybrid configuration.

While most guitarists will have their secret weapon be one setting—let's say it's the bridge pickup with your favorite distortion pedal tweaked for that pickup—you must, if only for the sake of variety, have alternate pickup configurations and sounds that complement that setting. This might involve multiple distortion pedals in the same chain, but never used together. It's a matter of logistics as well as sonic ideals. You can't be constantly twisting the knobs on your Turbo Distortion pedal to fit both the neck and bridge pickups, but you should be switching between those pickups fairly often in a typical pop song that has varying levels of dynamics and drama. If you need to have distortion on each of those pickups, you may have to have two identical pedals, or two distortion pedals (or a single pedal with dual-mode distortion), each optimized for a certain sound.

Having a multi-effects processor, or at least a programmable preamp, can solve the headache and redundancy of stompbox logistics. Then you need to plan your program switching by means of a foot pedal which acts solely as a switcher, and have that action coordinated with your pickup switching. However you solve the problem, though, you should cultivate a wide sonic palette of sounds—clean, crunch, and distorted—for a variety of pickup settings.

SINGLE-COIL VS. HUMBUCKER PICKUPS

Guitarists using single-coil pickups need to be aware of noise and brittleness, the two primary pitfalls of single-coil technology. If any single pickup is making too much noise (using two pickups together doesn't result in as much noise), there are several things you can do (though not necessarily on the spot): You can adjust your "attitude" (position) toward the amp, turning to and away to find the lowest noise position; you can replace your stock single-coils with a "stacked" version, which will cut the noise, but keep the original routing of your guitar body intact; you can switch to active pickups, such as those made by EMG; or you can employ a gate, which will keep the guitar from buzzing, except when you're playing.

Finally, volume-attenuation machinations—like rolling off the volume pot with your right-hand pinky or working your volume pedal—is a way to reduce the pickup noise when you're not playing, which keeps the irritation level in producers low. A gate will do this for you automatically, freeing up your hands and feet, but you have to experiment with the threshold and release times to ensure a natural performance. If your amp is loud and your pickups are vintage, get used to noise; it's an inextricable part of the rock and roll sound.

Brittleness can obviously be handled by EQ, but a better way is to use a tube preamp or even slight compression to take the edge off, but not enough to rob the natural highs. EQ acts indiscriminately over all frequencies and doesn't behave dynamically as a tube compressor does. Fortunately, brittleness is usually only a problem when the bridge-only pickup position is used and in relatively undistorted situations. Other single-coil combinations don't suffer from the brittleness problem.

Humbucker pickups, like those found on well-known Gibson models, don't suffer from noise or as much brittleness as single-coils (in fact the impetus for their invention was noise elimination), but can sound mushy, especially in the middle range (this is their most common weakness). Usually EQ solves this, and graphic equalizers have been used to good effect to brighten up an otherwise dull-sounding humbucker performance. Under heavy distortion, it's the top end that usually needs a little help, so you can apply some judicious EQ here as well.

Humbuckers are less bright than single-coils because the very act of "bucking hum" cuts some of the high frequency response. But the bridge position in a humbucker guitar tends to be more usable than the bridge position of a single-coil guitar, all things being equal. That's why the most common *hybrid* (mixing single- and double-coil) pickup configuration is single-single-double (neck to bridge), with the optional coil tap (a switch that splits a humbucker into a single-coil) on the bridge-position humbucker. Compression and distortion throw all of these general guidelines out the window, as most of the tone then comes from the boxes and not the inherent response of the pickups. But in getting a core tone, start with the pickups through the amp, and then dress up the basic tone with effects.

MIKING VS. DIRECT

Regardless of how you get your pickup tone, your approach must be influenced by the method of recording. If you mic your amp, you'll create the sound completely differently than if you're recording directly into the board. Direct recording was at one time something only done in emergencies, but that attitude is rapidly fading. Though it's generally considered inferior to miking an amp, direct recording can in some situations be the preferred method for capturing guitar sounds, for a variety of reasons. These days, direct recording isn't limited to plugging into a box which goes into the board. As we'll see, there are many ways to record without miking a speaker, many of them involving the preamp and power amp of your favorite vintage amplifier.

AMP SETUP AND PLACEMENT IN THE STUDIO

If you're going on a session, whether it's a song demo, record date, or jingle, establish beforehand what the amp situation will be. The first step is to make sure you and the producer agree on what kind of amp it is that you'll be playing through. He may say, "Oh, you know, basic rock stuff," but that doesn't tell you whether you're going to be playing through a Marshall or a Fender. And people can get very upset if they're expecting one and you bring the other.

Also, who will supply the amp? Most big studios are outfitted with an arsenal of guitar amps, but you really should bring your own, unless specifically instructed not to, or the situation demands using a house amp. Sometimes engineers and producers will prefer to work with the house amps, and in that case, make sure you and an engineer have a detailed discussion as to what's available and what modifications, if any, have been made. Amps of the same make and model can sound very different, especially in older amps, so be prepared to do some tweaking.

ROOM ACOUSTICS

When you record your electric guitar, the room may or may not play a part in it. If you're on a jingle or movie session, the chances are nil that the room will play any role. You'll be in the studio playing with all the other instruments, like strings and horns, because it's cheapest to have all the musicians together for one studio call. As the guitarist, you'll be off in one section, usually against a wall, with a gobo or baffle that severely restricts the sound from traveling out into the studio. For those cases you don't have to worry about anything except getting a good amp sound, preferably at a low level. This means you should be accustomed to getting good sounds—distorted as well as clean—at low levels.

But if you're on a record date, or recording your own demo, you'll likely have access to a large room that has some character, and you'd be wise to capture it via the microphones. The advantage of using the room is that it's a natural setting and you can use your ears. What sounds good to you, the guitarist standing six feet back from your cooking Marshall, will sound good to the mic as well.

Studios are not just big rooms, or people would just go down to the local elementary school's gymnasium to get ambient sound. Studios are acoustically engineered with care and analysis in their construction to avoid flutter echoes, standing waves, resonant frequencies, and other nasty artifacts that plague non-acoustically designed rooms. Learn to appreciate those times when it's just you and your amp in the live room of a commercial studio. It'll get you through those times when you're at home stuffing your amp in a closet or bathroom and surrounding it with a mattress.

GETTING THE RIGHT SOUND THROUGH THE MONITORS (HEADPHONES, SPEAKERS)

When you record at home and act as your own engineer, you have a lot more opportunities to hear what's really going to tape—and it may or may not be what you hear in the room. The act of listening to what's going to tape is called "tape monitoring." Standing in the room and listening to your amp as you play through it is not tape monitoring. Even listening to the sound through headphones is not tape monitoring. Technically, that's called "source monitoring." What you want to listen to is what the tape actually recorded—sometimes available only on playback on certain machines.

So getting a good monitor sound is a three-step process. You must produce a good source sound using your ear and a natural environment, and then switch to tape monitoring to see that nothing is lost in the translation. (By the way, whether or not you're actually using tape is immaterial; you may be monitoring off a hard disk or MiniDisc.) Allan Holdsworth points out that when you mix, you have to be careful to monitor what the two-track machine is hearing rather than what the multi-track is playing. In this case your multi-track—even though it's a tape machine—is the source, and the two-track stereo-mixdown machine is your "tape" monitor. "Sometimes I've monitored off the multi-track when mixing, only to be horrified when listening back to the two-track mixdown," he warns.

It's extremely important not to rush the first step of source monitoring, first in the room, then in your monitors. Get the sound early in the session while you're fresh, while you have the most time, and while other people (if any are present) still have patience. Then stick a mic in front of the speaker, or take the amp's Slave Out to the board, or perform whatever process that gets the amped sound to the recording machine. After you've done that, put on the headphones and see if what you're hearing is what you thought you had in the room. If not, go back to square one and tweak. Check your levels to make sure it's not some gain-stage problem going to the board.

What you're doing is adjusting the sound so that your headphones or monitor speakers deliver what you ultimately want to hear on the recording itself. If you're amping the guitar, you'll obviously need to isolate the live sound from the monitor sound, whether that's in a set of headphones or over near-field monitors. That means you can't stand two feet from your amp with headphones on to get an accurate reading. It may feel better to you because the amp is thumping you in the chest and you feel the interaction of the air pressure on your strings, but it won't sound the same on playback.

Near-field monitors (see Fig. 3.1) work by delivering sound to your ears between the range of when you can't perceive the tweeter and woofer as two sources and when reflected sound dominates the direct signal. In other words, if you put your ear directly in front of the tweeter and then moved it to the woofer you'd hear the different sources. Moving a little bit away, you'd still be able to hear the speakers' directionality. But after a few feet, you can't perceive the bass and treble as coming from two different sources. As you move slowly back, though, the character of the room starts to contribute to the sound so that eventually the ambient sound has more influence over what you're hearing than the direct sound. (Some manufacturers prefer the term "direct-field" over "near-field" to describe monitor speakers designed to work this way.)

Fig. 3.1
Near-field monitors
by Mackie Designs

Headphones are great for isolation and allow you to hear stereo separation, but they lack a true bass-frequency response as well as the natural way people listen to music, which is through air. If you must mix via headphones, be careful not to put too much bass in, as a good bass sound in the headphones will sound unduly prominent over speakers. If you must spend the bulk of your time monitoring over headphones, leave time to check your mixes over near-field monitors.

AMBIENCE: NATURAL VS. ELECTRONIC

If you're going to mic your guitar, whether acoustic or electric, you have a choice of including the room sound or not. If time and environment allow, most engineers prefer to capture some of the room along with the straight guitar, as it's the way we hear instruments naturally. Miking the room ensures we get on tape what our ears have already naturally dialed in as a good sound. The room usually complements the sound, and that's why studios are designed with great attention toward acoustics. That's also why if you're in a good room, an engineer will usually set up an omnidirectional (picking up sounds from all sides) mic, because that is the way we hear—omnidirectionally. Even if the reverberant sound is minimal, there is still the fact that air is between the vibrating speaker and the mic diaphragm, and this is a form of ambience as well.

If you don't have a good room to record in, or if the good room is taken up by a string section, and the guitar is banished to a corner where baffles, or gobos, stand sentry to prevent any sound from escaping (or ambience coming in), you have to add ambience electronically. This is a little more difficult because you must artificially re-create the good sound you just produced standing a patch-cord's length away from the speaker. But reality dictates the increasing use of electronically produced ambience, most often supplied by that indispensable outboard effect, the digital reverb.

But whether you're recording the room sound, or close-miking the guitar and adding ambience via the reverb unit, it's important to place your sound in some environmental context. Although we'd like to always record an amp or acoustic guitar in a nice live room without external processing, it's just not feasible or even necessary all the time. So using a reverb is pretty much a fact of life, even to get a basic room sound. Also, a reverb gives you the choice of many environments, whereas a room gives you only one, unless you have a mansion's worth of variously shaped rooms all devoted to getting good live sounds for guitars.

Chances are if you're not a top-call journeyman session player performing in a variety of acoustically stellar live rooms, you'll usually record using one room sound, or with a reverb, or a combination of room and reverb. To get the greatest versatility from a room, it should be neutralized somewhat, to get rid of annoying idiosyncrasies. These include *standing waves* (certain frequencies given undue prominence resulting from the room's dimensions), *flutter echoes* (the splatter sound that occurs in live rooms near the wall and ceiling union), and other nasty artifacts. Since there is no ideal of what a live room should sound like, people agree to have fairly dead-sounding rooms as a point of departure, leaving the ambience to electronics, which can be duplicated exactly, because the machine can be brought to any session, or the same program can be used in identical machines at separate locations. You just bring your ambience with you on a memory card or floppy disk—or written down on paper.

DIRECT RECORDING WITH PICKUPS

This section deals with capturing guitar sounds without a mic. Though it's generally agreed that recording "direct"—that is, plugged straight into the mixing board or recording device—lacks realism, there are compelling reasons to go without mics. Most are for convenience, but some (like the technique of "re-amping," discussed later) are actually rooted in sonic principles.

USES FOR DIRECT RECORDING

Though the most natural way to record electric and acoustic guitars is with a mic, we'll begin with direct recording, because it's easier, more commonplace (especially in lower-end and mid-level situations) and more foolproof, due to advances in direct-recording technology. After we get some direct sounds to the board, utilizing good acoustic-emulation guidelines, we'll back-step into using mics and see how mics take care of acoustically what we had previously dialed in electronically.

TWO-WAY NOISE ELIMINATION

There are several advantages to recording direct, almost all of which have to do with ergonomics and convenience. When you record direct (as opposed to using an open mic), you don't have to worry about environmental noise. You could record with the TV on, big trucks driving by, the telephone ringing, and your guitar sound will still be isolated. Recording direct means no outside noise can get in.

By the same token, no noise from you gets out. If you plug into a direct-recording processor, go into the board, and monitor on headphones, it's virtually silent on an electric guitar, and no louder than you would be normally on an acoustic guitar. This means you can record anywhere anytime, without disturbing housemates and neighbors. This has tremendous advantages if you're traveling or have an unpredictable schedule.

CONTROLLING VARIABLES

Less obvious but just as handy are some sonic factors. Because recording direct is an all-electronic endeavor, you're guaranteed the same sound every time you sit down to play. This means that after you find your tonal sweet spot, you can leave your controls set in that position and achieve the same tone and orientation every time (this is especially handy for punching). As anyone who has ever dealt with miking can tell you, it's extremely difficult to get the same miked sound from day to day. You'll see people mark out not only mic positions with masking tape, but chair, body and leg positions as well. Even the room's humidity and how long a mic's been on (especially if it's tube-driven) can alter your tone.

Because speaker simulators and acoustic-environment simulators have gotten so good, many guitarists examine a recording situation to see if the difference between an actual miked guitar or amp and a simulated one will even be noticed. If, for example, the guitar is to be mixed way down or processed heavily, the subtle differences between a good emulator and a well-miked setup will be lost on the listener. This is similar to having a Ferrari and a Yugo in rush-hour traffic. The performance difference between the two is lost on the 15-mph, stop-and-go environment.

SIGNAL QUALITY

Then there is the issue of pure quality. Though no one necessarily prefers a straight pickup-recorded acoustic to a straight miked one per se, when combining pickup and mic sounds, the pickup will deliver a stronger, less "airy" signal, especially in the bass. This is why some players, like Al Di Meola, create a composite sound using pickups and mics. It could be argued then that if you're looking for a direct-to-board sound, direct recording, by definition, is the best tonal choice, and not just a compromise for convenience.

The advantages for recording direct are that it is highly convenient, "good enough" for many situations, and provides an incredible variety of convincing sounds that would otherwise require extensive setup time. Let's look at a couple of ways to record directly into the board.

HIGH-TO-LOW IMPEDANCE VIA DIRECT BOX

Although you can stick your guitar cord into the mixing board, tweaking the Trim control and fader to get a sound, it won't be very good. That's because the impedance and levels a board expects to receive are different than those output by a guitar. The quickest and most inexpensive solution is a direct box. A direct box is a passive (no external power required) device that converts a guitar's high impedance pickup output to a low-impedance signal. This allows you to plug straight into the mixer's mic input channel for the best results. Many other boxes will do the same thing—that is, take a guitar signal and convert it to a signal a mixer more appreciates—but to get the raw, unadulterated sound of your pickups onto tape with no coloration or processing, a direct box is the way to go. (One advantage of recording clean this way is that you can take your signal and "re-amp" it at a later time. See *Chapter 9: Tricks and Tips*.)

SPEAKER SIMULATORS

Speaker simulators, or emulators, are enjoying increasing popularity these days, because they are getting better and better at what they purport to do, and so make life so much easier, especially for the home recordist. Because the only natural way to hear an electric guitar is through a speaker, the speaker coloration of a signal is considered a primary element in the sound of an electric guitar. When you take away the speaker and try to create the same thing electronically, you have to ask what the speaker's contribution was and how are you now going to simulate that.

There are four basic issues:

Frequency Response: Because a guitar-amp speaker is not a full-range system (as a two- or three-way studio-monitor system is), it can't produce high frequencies very well, and so "rolls off" after about 8 kHz (the same is true, though to a lesser extent, in the low end). So the first thing we do is knock off some high end.

Compression: Because a speaker is mechanical (a metal voice coil, a paper cone), it's not nearly as responsive to or as malleable as the incoming electrical signal which it seeks to reproduce. A speaker driven hard cannot reflect in its travel the same impulses going into the coil, and so a form of compression occurs.

Distortion: A speaker's paper cone is hardly a sensitive electronic meter, and the wave forms of incoming complex signals can't possibly all be reflected in one speaker (in multi-speaker systems, a cross-over circuit divides up high and low frequencies and sends them to different speakers) and wave forms compete for the same turf, each asking that section of medium to reflect its characteristics. What happens is a form of distortion where both wave forms are compromised, resulting in a cross modulation.

Ambience: The final step in a speaker's coloration has to do not so much with the speaker itself but the environment. In order for us to hear a speaker, it has to be miked, which means there is the conversion of the electro-mechanical action of the speaker into pressurized air (sound waves), the travel of those waves through an environment (even if it's only a couple of inches), and then its conversion back again into electrical energy via a microphone. It may seem like an extra step electronically, but that's what helps give a guitar signal its psycho-acoustic realism.

You don't need a dedicated speaker simulator to satisfy the above requirements. Through some dedicated external processing gear, you can come pretty close. With a graphic equalizer, you can roll off the high frequencies of your signal, experimenting with the hinge point (the point above which all frequencies are affected). A little compression from an external compressor can provide the smoothing effect a speaker has, and an exciter or sonic enhancer can provide the intermodulation that occurs. The last step is to provide the ambient character of a miked speaker and this is easily accomplished with a small room setting on a digital reverb. Look at Fig. 3.2 to see the "a la carte" method for producing a speaker simulator for direct recording.

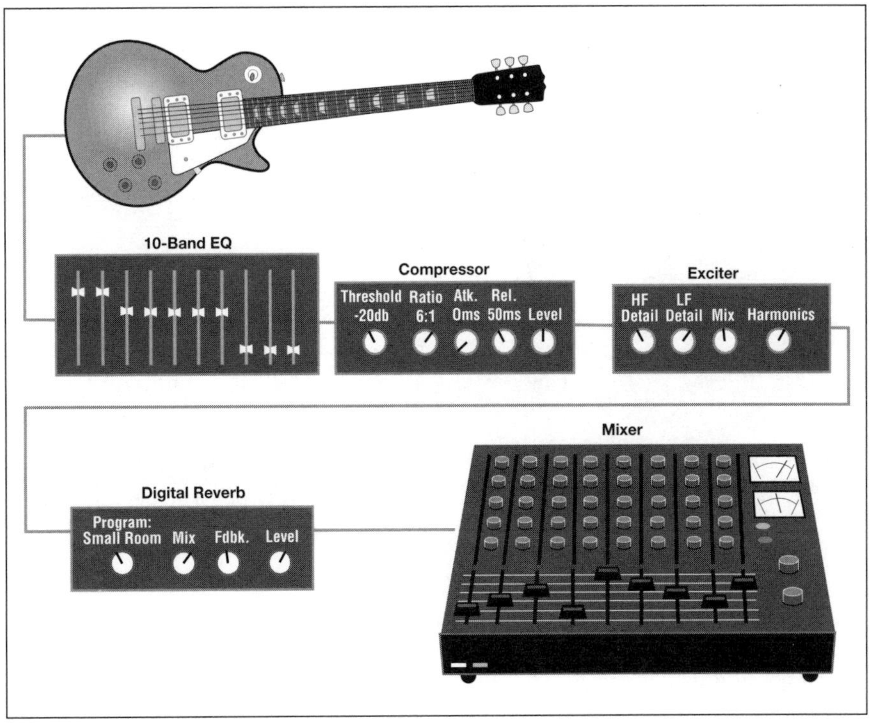

Fig. 3.2

A do-it-yourself speaker simulator

In dedicated speaker simulation devices, the manufacturers have designed special algorithms based on the dynamic interaction of all the above factors in real time. Using laboratory instruments to study speakers as they actually behave under certain conditions, speaker-simulator makers construct convincing models that typically behave better than our homemade version, but by tweaking your settings, you can come up with very usable results.

MICS AND GUITARS

Miking guitars is surprisingly simple, but not simple enough that there's not infinite variation within a fairly defined set of guidelines. The mic basically stands in for your ear, so use your ear to find the optimal listening position and sweet spot, then place the mic there, listen, adjust the mic position slightly, listen again, and repeat ad infinitum until you've got it. Just because you find the perfect mic position one day does not mean you can duplicate it the next. No one knows why this is so, but everyone acknowledges that you must start from zero every time you set up a mic, because no two situations—musically or acoustically—are alike. You can certainly resort to short-cuts by avoiding setups that won't work, but what does work must be newly discovered each time.

UNDERSTANDING MICROPHONES

There are hundreds of mics available, all with a vast history of uses, associated mythology, and ardent champions who argue for one brand over another, or one model that to them represents the sonic ideal. For the serious recordist, mics should be treated almost like another musical instrument, so sensitive and varied are their different qualities. But you can delimit your search enough to the "instruments" that are particularly suited to recording guitars.

Fig. 3.3

A Sennheiser 421 dynamic mic

DYNAMIC VS. CONDENSER

The two most popular types of mics these days are dynamic and condenser. Although there are other types, notably the ribbon, tube, and PZM (pressure zone microphone that affixes to a solid surface, such as a reflecting wall), 99 percent of all mic applications for guitars involve either a dynamic or a condenser mic. The world of microphones for recording guitars is almost as rich and diverse as that of guitars themselves, and it takes a lifetime of experience to appreciate the qualities and nuances of them all. But for now, let's concentrate on some of the standard-bearers, both for acoustic and electric recording.

A dynamic is the most widely used and economical type of mic, found on performing stages everywhere. The Shure SM-57 and SM-58 are two popular dynamic microphones, used for vocals and instrument miking. The Sennheiser 421 is a higher-quality dynamic mic that is also very popular in recording applications. Dynamic mics (see Fig. 3.3) are rugged, can handle a high SPL (sound pressure level) and are generally flattering to a human voice. Flattering means that there's a certain character or color that the mic adds, rather than being "flat" (adding no frequency "bumps" and so delivering an accurate or graphically flat response curve) or "transparent," two other words that describe mic qualities. Because humans expend large amounts of air with their soundwaves, they exhibit high SPLs, as do kick drums and the speakers of cranked-up guitar amplifiers. Because people speak or sing into mics intuitively, they get most of their experience with microphones this way, and so are used to the characteristics of dynamic mics. Dynamic mics sound good on guitars and guitar amps as well.

Although there are no strict rules, dynamic mics are usually used on amps in close-mic situations. Again, a dynamic mic is comfortable with high SPLs and yields great results when placed 1–3 inches from a speaker at a volume too loud for a human ear to endure comfortably. Since they tend to reject frequencies at the top end, they're very forgiving on subtle rattles and other artifacts that more sensitive mics would pick up.

Condenser mics (see Fig. 3.4) use a different method for producing signals than dynamics, requiring a constant electrical charge in the pickup element. For this it must draw power from an external source, such as a battery, the phantom power supply in your mixer, or an outboard mic preamp with built-in phantom-power circuitry. Condenser mics need voltage to operate; if you plug in your mic and forget to turn on the phantom power switch (or if you plug into a board with no phantom power supply at all) no sound will result. (But if you plug a dynamic mic—which requires no external powering—into a phantom-powered jack, you won't do any damage to the mic; it simply ignores the voltage.)

Condenser mics are generally of higher quality than dynamics, and are more sensitive. This is usually a good thing in microphones (despite the quality of dynamics to reject rattles, mentioned above), as they yield better results in aspects such as high frequency detail and transient response. Transients are the initial attack noises of a note, which on the guitar are percussive in nature, meaning they yield no pitch information. Although transients are quite short, often they are the loudest part of the signal. Since the transient has to overcome the inertia of the mic's element (that is, it has to stimulate a metal plate into vibrating), the more-sensitive condenser mic will respond quicker and truer, reproducing with better integrity the attack sound. You will hear words like "transparency" and "clarity" used to describe the qualities of condenser mics.

The diaphragm is the surface that the source sound collides with to get the element moving that creates the current. A small diaphragm has less mass and therefore takes less energy to move. This is why you'll often see the long, thin cylindrically shaped mics on acoustic guitars (including the AKG 451 or C-1000, the Audio-Technica 4041, and the Shure SM-81). These diaphragms are very responsive to the small, high-energy frequencies produced by the plucked string. For the same reason, small diaphragm condensers work well as overhead cymbal mics. What small diaphragm mics are not good for is capturing warmth, receiving high SPLs and responding to complex or pronounced low-end frequencies. For sounds with those qualities, you'd enlist a large-diaphragm condenser.

Fig. 3.4

A Neumann U87 condenser mic

CLASSIC MODELS AND USES

The family of large-diaphragm condensers include the best and most well-known mics in the world, including the Neumann U87. No mic aficionado considers his mic locker complete until he has at least one of these, and preferably a closely matched pair for stereo recording. Other well-known mics in this category include the AKG 414 and the Audio-Technica 4050. Large diaphragm mics are extremely versatile, finding good use in recording acoustic guitars from any position, and amps, both in close and ambient positions. Because they are condenser mics, they're very good at high-end detail and transparency, and their large diaphragms make them good full-frequency choices as well.

If you're a home studio owner with a good mixer and an MDM (modular digital multi-track, like the Alesis ADAT or TASCAM DA-88), you should be thinking about dropping between $700 and $1,000 for a good, multipurpose large-diaphragm condenser mic. Many mics in this range will feature selectable pickup patterns, which also come in handy. The two most common pickup patterns guitarists will encounter are cardioid and omnidirectional (or "omni" for short). There are others, but these are the two most widely used for guitar applications.

PICKUP PATTERNS

Fig. 3.5a

Cardioid pattern

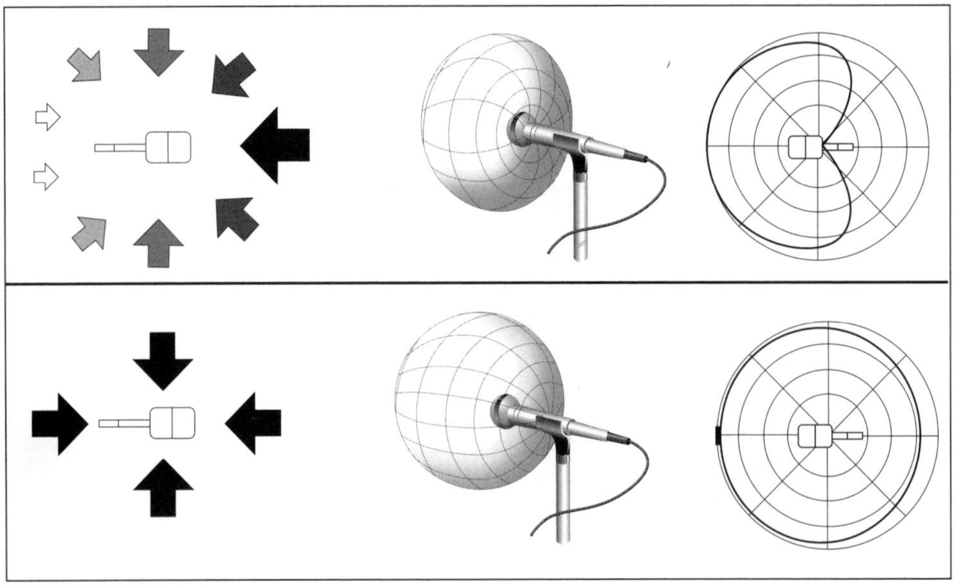

Cardioid: A cardioid pattern (see Fig. 3.5a) is heart-shaped, which means the pickup has the greatest "field of vision" in front of the diaphragm, with response tapering off as you get off axis from the mic until there is almost complete rejection of sound as you go around toward the rear. Because they pick up well in the front, less well from the sides and poorly from the rear, cardioid mics are known as "directional" mics, and are good for the stage because they block out side noises (like other instruments) well and rear noises (like monitors) very well. There are variations on the basic cardioid pattern, including super-cardioid (a wider pattern favoring greater off-axis response) and hyper-cardioid (which has a

Fig. 3.5b

Omni pattern

narrower response yielding almost no off-axis response), but all cardioid mics have a characteristic known as the "proximity" effect, which means bass response increases drastically the closer you get to the mic. Comedians produce low, thundering voices by putting a cardioid mic right next to their lips. If you're miking a boomy acoustic, the proximity effect can work against you, but having it on a thin-sounding arch-top can work for you.

Omni: An omni pickup pattern (see Fig. 3.5b) receives sound equally well from all directions. It has no proximity effect and doesn't favor a sound approaching it on axis versus one coming at it off axis. For guitarists, omni mics make great room mics because they listen to everything around them not just the source at which they're aimed. For acoustic recording that requires a warmer, natural sound, omnis can't be beat, because they capture the entire air around the guitar, rather than focusing a narrow headlight beam at a certain region of the guitar. But because they pick up sound from all around, they are much more sensitive to room noise and performer noise (breathing, rustling, even gurgling stomachs). If you have a really great-sounding room, an omni mic is the best way to capture its quality.

ACOUSTIC GUITAR RECORDING
MIKING TECHNIQUES

Acoustic guitars that sound good to the ear will generally record well, regardless of the type of mic or where it's placed. Great results can be obtained from either dynamics or condensers, used singly, in a blend, or in stereo. This is not necessarily true of electric guitars, where the best mic does not always produce the best sound in any configuration. But in acoustic guitars, generally what you hear is what you get. If you use a better mic, you'll get a better sound simply because the mic is providing a more accurate picture of what's really there. And while it's true that the characteristics of some mics are preferable to others for capturing the acoustic guitar, the better the guitar sound, the less those factors need play into the equation.

You can get good results with either condensers or dynamics, but condensers are preferred for their generally better ability at picking up transients, or the high-frequency artifacts (noise) of the plucked string. A quality dynamic mic works very well, though, like a Sennheiser 421, pointed at the bridge, 18–24 inches away and pointed slightly off axis—as if the "beam" emanating from the top of the pickup were pointed at the 12th fret, and not perpendicular with the guitar's top. Good miking technique is nothing more than a lot of trial and error with placement, and then exercising good judgment when you listen to your placements over the monitors.

You'll often hear people talk about an acoustic guitar's "sweet spot," and all that is is a particular, narrowly defined point in space where the guitar sounds best. This can be found by plugging up one ear and using the other as the mic, pointing it at the guitar and moving around the general area. In this way, you are behaving like a directional mic. Go from fretboard to bridge, the upper bout to the lower, and vary your distance and angle to the guitar. Your ear doesn't have the exact "pickup pattern" a mic does, but this can sure give you a head start as to which region gives you more the tone you're looking for.

ROOM ACOUSTICS

Though an acoustic guitar and an electric couldn't be more different in terms of quality, you still listen for the same quality in a room sound: an ambience that makes the guitar sound good. You don't necessarily need to know the acoustical theory to know when the room is working for you or against you. If things are sounding good in the room, use a mic to capture that quality. If there are harsh echoes and things rattling, take steps to cut the room out of the picture.

ACOUSTIC PICKUPS

Many acoustic guitars, both steel-string and nylon, come with built-in electronics that allow you to plug a normal electric guitar cord into the endpin jack and plug the other end into a guitar amplifier, mixing board, or effects processor. If there are onboard electronics (which include a preamp and EQ), they're usually found inside the guitar body, with tone and volume controls on the top side of the upper bout.

Pickups are used more and more in live situations, even by the best acoustic guitarists, because of their convenience and manageability. In a recording situation, where logistics are not as much a factor, some engineers and guitarists like the tonal quality of a pickup and blend that in with the pure mic sound. One reason is that pickups can deliver a more focused bass response than a microphone, and often people will blend in the pickup sound of an acoustic guitar to boost its low-end while using the mic to capture the mid and upper frequencies which it delivers so well. And of course you can use just the straight pickup sound (no mic) of the acoustic guitar. It's still unmistakably an acoustic guitar, but very different sounding than the guitar recorded with just a mic. This sound is described as somewhat "compressed," "focused," or "cutting" and is good for lead lines that must cut through a busy or noisy mix. There are two types of pickups for acoustic guitars, referred to as magnetic and piezo.

Magnetic: The magnetic pickup is most like an electric guitar pickup in function (though it's optimized for the acoustic guitar) in that it uses a coil of wrapped wires surrounding magnets to capture the vibrating steel strings above it. Since this pickup type is based on magnetic energy, it won't work on nylon strings. It typically sits in the acoustic's soundhole.

Piezo: Piezo technology uses a thin membrane that's placed between the saddle (the bone- or ivory-like strip that sits in a slot in the bridge) and the bottom of the bridge. It works not magnetically, but by varying pressure caused by the vibrating string bearing down on it from above. Contact pickups that adhere to the soundboard are also piezo-based, and some systems have multiple contacts at different points on the soundboard, which are then blended together. Because of recent advancements in piezo (pronounced pee-AY-tzo) technology, the membranes have gotten more sensitive and responsive, and are generally preferred over magnetic pickups for a truer acoustic sound. There are notable holdouts for magnetic pickups, though, including Leo Kottke. And of course, you can always choose one or the other based solely on a sound you're looking for or a certain situation.

COMBINING PICKUPS WITH MICS

A potentially negative phenomenon to watch for in pickup-equipped acoustic guitar playing is finger noise. This is the unavoidable *skritch* the left-hand fingers make when fretting, releasing, and moving along the strings. While this is a natural and listener-tolerated result of playing the guitar, recording guitarists usually try extra hard to keep finger noise to a minimum. A pickup tends to give undue prominence to finger noise, because it picks the sound up directly, from the string itself, rather than from a distance, as a mic does. Since the mic is some distance away, the musical information (vibrating string) is usually much louder than the string noise, and the string noise is placed in the background. But the pickup tends to give the string noise a bit more "presence," as if it's closer to your ear than normal.

One trick that works particularly well in a rock context is plugging an acoustic through a combo amp's speaker to get an even more compressed, focused sound, and then miking the speaker. You shouldn't plug straight into the amp's input, though. A better way is to go into a dedicated mic preamp or even the preamp of your mixer's channel input. This provides a better match for the two impedances—the output impedance of the piezo and the input impedance of the mic pre. Then, via an aux send, take the acoustic guitar's signal out of the mixer and run it into the effects return jack of a combo amp, bypassing the preamp stage (because your signal is already preamped). You then have a properly preamped piezo signal run through a nice tube power amp and a midrange-oriented speaker. See Fig. 3.6 for an illustration of this scheme.

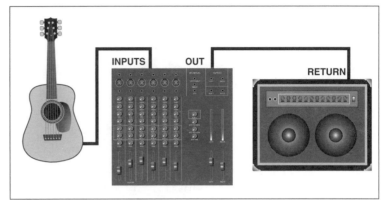

Fig. 3.6

Acoustic through combo amp

This happens to work well if you're already in the studio playing an electric through a combo amp and the producer asks you to switch to a direct acoustic sound (and he doesn't want a miked guitar, as isolating it and setting up a mic isn't practical). As Fig. 3.7 shows, you can have both instruments plugged in simultaneously, and without re-patching, switch between the two guitars. Just remember to pull down the fader on the acoustic when you switch to the electric, so that no noise enters via the amp's effects return jack. This non-conflict of jacks between the electric and acoustic works even if you're not recording via a speaker, but using the slave or speaker out of the amp and continuing on to a load box and beyond.

MIKING GUITAR AMPS

Though direct recording gear is a godsend, many misguided guitarists make their lives more complicated by using thousand-dollar effects processors, rack-mounted amp-simulators, and parametric EQ wizardry to try to emulate a simple, amped guitar sound. After all that, it still sounds pinched and largely unconvincing. The irony is that expensive signal processors have to jump through hoops just to come close to capturing the sound of a mid-

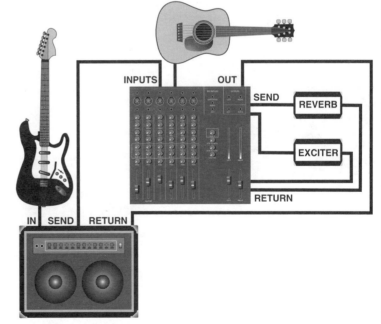

Fig. 3.7

Switching between electric and acoustic guitars

priced combo and an inexpensive microphone. And they usually fail, because they're trying to do electronically what is basically an acoustic phenomenon. The fact remains that nothing beats a miked guitar amp for sound. If your setup and environment allows, this is the best-sounding and simplest way to go.

If you've wondered why you can't hook your pedalboard up to your Portastudio and get a good sound, it may reassure you to know that it doesn't get much better when you use higher-priced multi-effects processors and digital recorders. But with even a modest amp and inexpensive dynamic mic, you can get realistic and exciting guitar sounds. And best of all there's no magic, only a couple of well-established guidelines. The key is to let the sound come out of the speaker, naturally, fully, and preferably at a high volume, and to use the right type of mic.

CLOSE MIKING: 1 OR 2 MICS, IN A BLEND OR STEREO

If you have only one mic, you should close-mic your speaker and apply ambience electronically. Run the mic into the mixer's channel input so that you have one channel with the straight, un-effected sound. Then take an aux send from that channel, go through the reverb and back into the board, via the aux return, or, for more control, back into another input channel (this will give you EQ and panning control). Pan them both center and create a blend.

If you have two identical mics, you can set up a stereo sound by placing the mics in an X pattern (where one mic crosses the other in an "X" and you aim the center of the X perpendicular to the amp's face), so that one mic picks up one side and one mic picks up the other, similar to the way a human hears a speaker. Pan the mics hard right and left and maintain an even balance between the two channels. Arranging two mics this way is also known as a "coincident pair."

The mic of choice for years for close-miking guitar amp speakers was (and still is, though others work just as well) the Shure SM-57. This is an inexpensive dynamic (as opposed to condenser) microphone that has a good-sized diaphragm and can withstand high sound pressure levels. In other words, this mic is happiest being slammed by a loudspeaker at close range pumping out low and midrange frequencies. Placing the mic about one to two inches away from the grille cloth yields optimum results, and positioning it slightly off center (looking at the edge of the bull's eye, not straight on) results in a fatter sound (see Fig. 3.8).

No one really knows why setting the mic off-axis from the cone works the way it does, but engineer Bernard Matthews expresses the view of many by summing it up this way: "The best placement of the mic is a few inches away from the cloth and one to three inches from the center of the dome at an angle, so that the diaphragm is not parallel to the cone. This prevents certain frequencies from jumping out, similar to the standing-wave principle in a room with parallel walls. You don't want the width of the diaphragm—which is pretty wide, as it's a dynamic—to resonate unnaturally with any particular frequency."

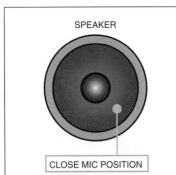

Fig. 3.8

Mic on speaker

N.S. "Buck" Brundage, has contributed his technology and production talents to such artists as Al Di Meola, Fate's Warning, Steve Morse, and keyboardist/producer Jan Hammer (Mahavishnu, *Miami Vice*). He describes his procedure for miking amps in the studio: "After setting up the amp to sound good to my ears, I put on head-phones to hear what the mic is picking up. Sometimes I'll replace the guitar with a noise generator and have the engineer send white noise to my headphones via a monitor send so I can move the microphone until I find the 'sweet spot' on that particular speaker. If you use a boom stand, you can easily adjust the vertical and horizontal axis of the mic. I prefer starting the miking process with a Shure SM-57, to get my ears acclimated. I may change mics later on, but I'll usually begin with the 57. I often like to use two mics, an SM-57 and a Sennheiser 421, because each will pick up some quality the other misses." Generally, Brundage advises, a 57 (and mics like it) will provide definition and the 421 (and its ilk) will deliver body. Put them each on their own channel and see if they sound good as a blend (layered together for a total sound) or in a small stereo spread (with slightly different pan positions when mixing down to stereo).

The distances and angles of the mic placement are all variable, as is the choice of mic itself, but miking the speaker using the above guidelines will yield the best results, because the sound of an electric guitar exists through a speaker. You have the best chance of getting on tape exactly what it sounds like to the ear if you use a mic.

Nowadays there are dozens of mics on the market that conform to the high-SPL, large-diaphragm spec, and some are even optimized for miking guitar cabinets (the SM-57 was originally designed as a vocal mic). But the de facto standard for close miking a guitar amp speaker is the SM-57, so look for mics that have the same general characteristics and frequency response.

A ROOM WITH A V-U: CLOSE AND DISTANT MIKING

Once you've secured an amp and a mic, the next thing you need is a place to put it. We've already explored close miking, where the mic picks up only the speaker and none of the room (reflected) sound. But if our goal is to capture the sound as we hear it naturally, we have to also record what the amp sounds like a few feet back, both from the speaker and from the room.

If you have the budget, you can put a high-quality condenser mic, like a Neumann U87 or AKG 414, about waist high, on axis, several feet back from the amp. This will help capture ambient or room sounds (see Fig. 3.9).

With two identical mics, you can set up a stereo sound by placing the mics in an X pattern, so that one mic picks up one side and one mic picks up the other, similar to the way a human hears a speaker. Pan the mics hard right and left and maintain an even balance between the two channels.

Fig. 3.9
Two-mic setup

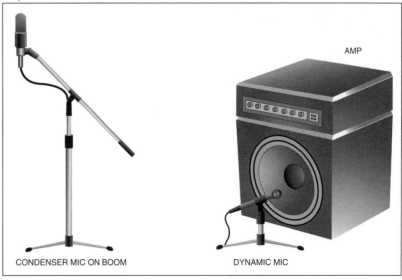

CONDENSER MIC ON BOOM   DYNAMIC MIC

AMP

Matthews describes how he mics a room sound using condensers: "When I use a large diaphragm, I back off to let the sound develop, depending on how live the room is. I use an omni about six feet from the speaker in an overdub room. I like using condensers in omni, because a cardioid is only cardioid above 3k. The pickup pattern becomes more circular the lower in frequency you go. If you have a cardioid, you get the full reflection of low frequencies, but only partial reflection as the frequency gets higher, and then you actually get rejection of certain frequencies. Omni removes that kind of coloration. And after all, your ears hear in stereoscopic omni."

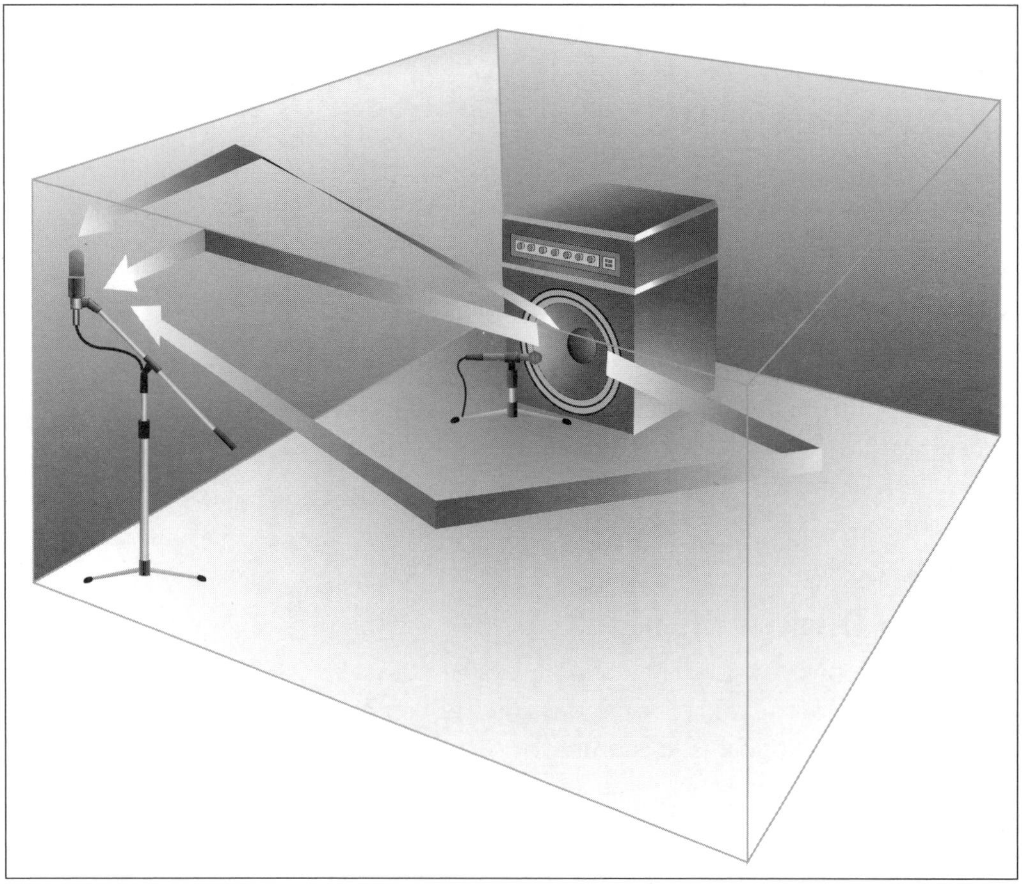

More budget-friendly dynamic mics can also work well for room miking, especially ones like the Sennheiser 421. In general, less expensive mics work great on guitar speakers for two reasons: one, they don't pick up every little high-end detail, like rattle and noise, and two, they won't be so easily overpowered like more expensive ones that have sensitive diaphragms.

Fig. 3.10

Two mics showing reflected sound

THE PHASE FACTOR

Whenever you have more than one mic picking up the same source, you have to beware of phase problems (different parts of the same soundwave hitting two mics simultaneously). "Multiple mics can create phase coherency problems," cautions Matthews. "The proof of this is how easy it is to create a chorus effect with just mic placement. To avoid this I'll put, say, a 57 faced into the grille, and a room mic in the air away from the direct throw of the speaker. That eliminates timing problems of sound hitting one mic first then the other (see Fig. 3.10). Many amp simulators suffer from phase coherency problems."

If you're miking a 4x12 cabinet instead of a combo, your options are even more varied. "When you have four speakers to choose from, you can put one mic on one speaker in the cab, and the second mic on another," says Brundage. "This increases your tonal possibilities."

PHONING IT IN FROM THE CONTROL ROOM

Working with a head and cabinet allows you to set up your room sound in the studio, then take the head with you into the control room for further tweaking. This way an assistant makes the mic adjustments while you sit in the control room, listening to the results over the studio monitors.

Matthews elaborates: "As an engineer, I like to have the guitar player in the control room and the cabinet in the studio. It's face to face, and you can communicate. I take a line from the speaker out in the amp head and go to a tie line, female to female. Some studios have a mouse hole, and I'll pass the cord through and then stuff it up with foam. Speaker lines can go pretty far, 50 feet or so, before signal loss." (See Fig. 3.11.)

Fig. 3.11

Amp in control room, speaker in studio

Of course on a combo you can't separate the amp from the speaker. You shouldn't try to run a 50 foot guitar cord from the control room to the studio. "I'd rather have a 50-foot speaker cable than a 50-foot guitar cable," says Matthews. "I use Monster speaker cable because it's very thick—eight-gauge copper wire run in parallel. A guitar cord is unshielded. Impedance is significantly lower in a speaker cable, which is why it can run a long ways. That's why there are speakers on the ceiling and amps on the stage."

A neat way around the limitation of recording from the control room with a combo in the studio is to use two direct boxes. Direct boxes are inexpensive, no-frills, passive (non-powered) gizmos that convert high impedance signals (your guitar output) to low impedance signals (such as that found in a mic), or vice versa. Plug your guitar cable into a direct box in the studio and take the XLR (low-Z) out with as long a mic cable as you need to reach the amp (e.g., 50 feet). When you reach the amp, deploy another direct box that will do the same thing in reverse—go in with the XLR and out via the 1/4" jack. You can use the same type of box, since the box is passive and has no inherent signal-flow direction (see Fig. 3.12).

Once you've achieved your sound, any minor tweaks can be accomplished at the board using the individual channel EQ. It's at that point that you can add or monitor effects such as chorus, delay and reverb. Effects can be monitored but preferably not printed.

Before we begin discussing final EQ and effects applications, consider some real-world applications for getting a good miked-speaker sound in a less than state-of-the-art environment.

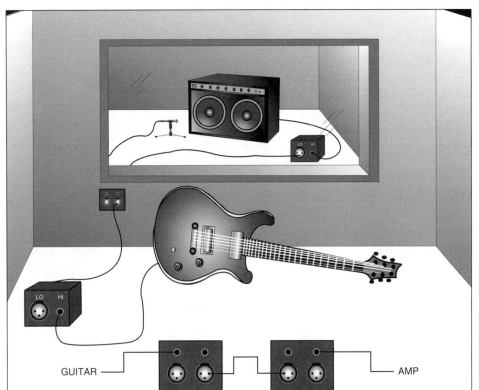

Fig. 3.12

Covering long distances with two direct boxes

MONSTER IN A BOX

Most of you do not have ready access to a studio with an acoustically tuned live room and an isolated control booth every time you want to record a guitar sound. This means that you will probably be in your house or apartment when recording your amp. If this is so, you immediately face two problems: 1) the loudness to your ears, and 2) the loudness to the ears of other humans in the vicinity. Loudness to your ears is a problem because many amps don't sound good unless they're cranked and cooking. But if you're not a good distance away, you won't be able to hear anything in isolation; the room sound of the amp will creep through your headphones, rattle your fillings, and generally put you in an acoustic fog while you're trying to work. Almost as important is the consideration of those around you. Guitar amps turned up enough to sound decent to you become a nuisance to those trying to read or watch a ball game.

There are two ways to solve this. Since the primary sound comes from your close mic, you're getting virtually no ambient, or reflected sound. Plus, we're going to add that with effects later (that's easier to simulate than a good mic sound). So the first method to consider is enclosing everything (your amp and mic) in a huge wooden cabinet made out of plywood and lined with shag carpeting or an old mattress. It won't be soundproof, but it will cut the decibels dramatically and attenuate annoying frequencies (mostly the highs). Cardboard will not work, by the way. To gain any foothold in the soundproofing arena you must employ mass. Cinder blocks are great but too heavy and hard to put together (unless you're a mason); particle board is best (it's what most speaker cabinets are made of), but it's too expensive; plywood is just the right balance of economics and sound-squashing effectiveness. Make a big box and create a door that closes flush with the box's sides and can be secured with clamps or hooks and eyes. Leave a hole for the heat to escape and rig up a fan inside at the back if you're going to be at it awhile (see Fig. 3.13).

The second method is to put the amp in a different room, like a basement, closet or a bathroom, and run a long cord to where you're recording. This is actually the preferred method for guerrilla home recordists, because you can choose the room (bathroom for live sound, closet for dead) and get better isolation than with the enclosed-box method. If you have the luxury of taking up two rooms to do your recording, consider this method and employ direct boxes.

Remember, a mic cord is low impedance, so running a 40- to 60-foot length of it won't degrade your sound significantly (especially when you're dealing with mid-range heavy guitar frequencies). Another point to people living in apartments: Take your amp off the floor, as the low frequencies will pass right through if the amp is in direct contact with the floor. Remember the adage "One man's ceiling is another man's floor."

GO TO YOUR (VIRTUAL) ROOM

If you can't afford the extra mic, don't have the environment for room-miking (e.g., the amp's in a closet), or are relegated to going direct via a speaker simulator, you can use a reverb or multi-effects unit with a good room-simulation setting to act as a second mic. Room simulators are programs that are not used as a reverb effects per se, but as an ambient enhancement. You can use one of these programs to fill in for a condenser mic in a midway position (3–10 feet from the amp).

If you've ever used a drum machine and listened carefully to the individual sounds, you may have noticed that the samples (drum sounds) are not completely dead sounding. They have a little bit of "air." You then usually add a longer reverb (e.g., large room, hall) to your final mix. But the room sound is still heard as part of the original sample. That same approach should be used in setting up a basic guitar sound. Before adding cathedral-like reverb washes and 330-millisecond delay repeats, spend some time setting up a room sound with short reverbs and different EQ schemes.

You can even run the room reverb sound inline—as this is a constant effect—and add EQ to the reverb itself (but not to the straight signal) to simulate the size, shape and character of the room.

If you're using one signal to create both the close miked sound and the room miked one, split it so that one runs off to another mixer channel. This most closely reflects how you'd be running two mics—each in its own channel, and blended accordingly. Split the signal by taking the guitar's input channel and feeding a second mixer channel via the direct out jack. Go through a reverb and/or delay and set it for 100% effect. (Do not use the second channel's effects send to derive the reverb/delay, as this results in a mix of effect and straight signals.) The first channel, the input, is set up for the room sound only, and the second is the longer reverb/delay–only sound. Note that since only the reverb/delay is heard in the second channel, EQ'ing acts only on the effected signal (see Fig. 3.14).

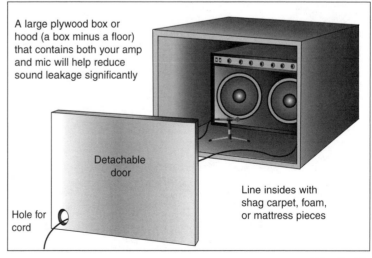

A large plywood box or hood (a box minus a floor) that contains both your amp and mic will help reduce sound leakage significantly

Detachable door

Hole for cord

Line insides with shag carpet, foam, or mattress pieces

Fig. 3.13

A homemade iso-cab

If you can devote only one channel to the miked guitar sound, you can still get the two perspectives by running the more intense ambient effects (long reverbs, delays) through an effects send rather than inline. This allows you to mix the straight sound with the effected one from the board, which is much easier than trying to achieve the balance with the effect inline.

In either case, keep the room sound on constantly and employ a concert hall reverb program or digital delay when the situation warrants it. Obviously, flanging, chorusing, and other miscellaneous effects (tremolo, etc.) are employed according to the musical context. But the above approach will leave you with a staple sound that is pretty much "set and forget."

Buck Brundage cautions not to scrimp on the two front-end steps of close miking and room simulation. "Spend as much time as possible moving the mic around to find the sweet spot. This is absolutely critical. Then, if you have a room simulator in your effects processor, tweak that until it sounds right. There are many units that will do this, but I use ART's DRX 2100 SE, which uses a system called AES—acoustic environment simulation. Here, I can control room size, frequency response, mic position, and objects in the room—such as wood plus rug, pews with people, etc."

Fig. 3.14

Splitting a sound to additional channels and running through an inline effect

Room simulation can be done with a direct signal as well as a close-miked one. But however you get your basic sound, the EQ and "effects" (long reverb, delay, panning, chorus, etc.) should be added last. Taking care in these early steps will pay off in great sound and tonal education.

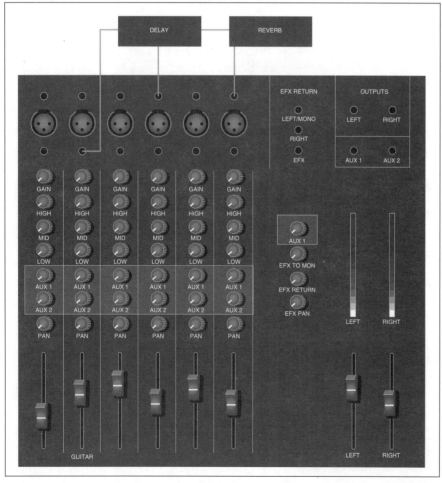

EQ: A DASH OF LOW ... A PINCH OF HIGH ...

Practically every gizmo in a studio has tone controls or EQ, so where should you begin to make tonal adjustments, should you need to? This section outlines the best approach for EQ'ing your overall sound.

AT THE AMP OR THE BOARD?

Once you've got your amp and mic set up, you're ready to add EQ and effects. Follow the advice given above and work to get practically all the tone from the amp itself. The only external EQ you might want to add from the board is at the very top and bottom ends. I like to get the amp sound just right and then add board top end for a little sparkle. I find that if I go to the amp's front panel to add top end, I change the whole dynamic of the tone controls' interaction with each other. But adding the sound from the board just takes the existing tone and highlights the top end. Also, board EQ's are much more precise and controllable than a guitar amp's, so the process is a little more scientific. Generally, a push in the 2–4 kHz range works wonders, and I sometimes add just a tad of 10 kHz for a little sizzle (see Fig. 3.15).

The same "spectrum highlighting" assistance applies to the low end, though you won't need as much help there. A guitar amp's frequencies (and the guitar's range itself) are skewed to the lower end of the musical range, so what you hear is usually what you get. Still, a little boost in the 100–200 Hz range will add bottom without creating mud. Be more sparing here with the dB push than you would with the top end.

Most of your board work will be in the top end. That's where you lose top-end definition as you start adding other instruments to the mix (keyboards, cymbals, horns, strings, etc.). Then the guitar—which sounds perfect in isolation—can lose a little luster.

MICS AND EQ

Virtually all the sound should come from the mics. If you have to make excessive EQ corrections, the miking is probably at fault. "If you have to push or pull any part of the EQ past 6 dB, you should re-position the mics, or even switch mics," says Brundage. "Get it with the amp and the mics before going to the board. The danger with board EQ is that you risk adding or subtracting something that's not even there. If, for example, you try to boost the highs and there are no highs in that range, you'll just add noise."

Matthews offers this additional advice: "Bring the mics through a good mic pre. Then you can work on your recording sound as well as your guitar sound. The number one thing is starting with the right mic in good condition, with no EQ, no compression. If I hear something that's not right, I alter the guitar sound or move a mic before touching the board. The biggest mistake people make is adding drastic EQ or compression—because that's what distortion is."

USING THE CONTROL ROOM TO CREATE FEEDBACK AND SUSTAIN

After enduring all the leg work of positioning your mics and tweaking your EQs, reverbs, and delays, you're probably ready for a treat. Here's a great trick that will simulate what happens when you stand in front of your cranked amp rather than two rooms down the hall "behind the glass." Of course, we're talking about feedback. Buck taught me this trick, and I use it shamelessly. All you need to do it is an available aux out of your preamp or mixer. What we'll do is set up a separate line out with your guitar signal that will be used solely to generate controlled, user-specified feedback. Here's how we do it.

Run an aux send from your mixer (all mixers have at least two of these per channel, so select the one not being used for reverb or other global effects) into

Fig. 3.15

Using Board EQ: Guitars can benefit from a hint of top end, a slight presence boost (2–4k), and a smidgen of low-end bump

a smaller amp that you keep in the control room with you. It's best to use a small 12" combo with a decent clean sound. The idea is to sit in the control room and use the small amp to generate feedback at desired spots during your solos. Feedback works when certain frequencies from the speaker oscillate the strings into producing more sound which in turn creates more frequencies, ad infinitum, and thus the phenomenon known as *feedback*. We'll be using the control-room amp to act as our "string exciter."

Remember, we're not actually going to be recording this amp, we're just using it to move the guitar strings. We're looking only for some octave feedback and perhaps some additional sustain. Set the amp controls with a little high cut, boosted mids, and a little added low end.

Put the amp on a chair or stool so that you can face your guitar into it when you want feedback. The position of the amp will vary according to the type of guitar you're using, i.e., the pickup sensitivity, how loud the control room monitors are, etc. (see Fig. 3.16).

There are two ways to initiate feedback: either by turning the face of the guitar into the pickups at the appropriate time, or having someone actually turn up the amp's

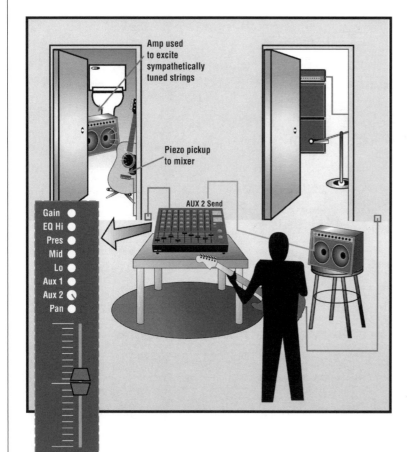

Here are two ways to use feedback to create unusual and different sounds:

1. Employ a combo amp (place it on the stool in the control room) to excite the strings. No sound is recorded from the combo; it's used only as a string exciter.

2. Use a speaker cab or a combo amp to excite the strings of a sympathetically tuned guitar (which is then fed to a mixer via the guitar's pickup) placed in proximity to the speaker. This is a great way to add eerie or ambient effects, especially if the music favors one chord or key. You can mic the combo as your main sound if you close-mic it and play loud enough that the acoustic can't bleed into the mic.

Fig. 3.16

Control-room feedback setup

volume in time with the music when the feedback point comes. This way an assistant "plays" the amp as you play the guitar. Again, no level change will be apparent in the final track, because this amp is not being recorded; it's merely acting as a string vibrator. You should practice with the track and your assistant, until you get the right performance down as well as establishing the right settings on the feedback-inducing amp. Even a subtle application of this works wonders. As Brundage points out: "There's a lot of magic that happens in that fringe area of feedback. Even a little sustain as the result of feedback will not only enhance a sound but will inspire a guitarist's performance."

Using feedback off of an amp is better than using the control-room monitors for two reasons: 1) you won't have to vary the monitor levels of the entire track just to induce feedback; and 2) the guitar won't get "confused" by the complete mix. Using the amp will allow the pickups to listen only to their own frequencies. Practice manipulating the frequencies that produce basic sustain and simple octave feedback before going totally "Steve Vai" with this trick. But once you're comfortable with that, by all means, get experimental.

CHAPTER FOUR

Effects in the Recording Studio

ELECTRIC GUITAR RECORDING: INLINE, INSERT, AND AUXILIARY PLACEMENT OF EFFECTS

When you perform live, you typically use your effects inline. You go from your guitar to your stompboxes to your amp, following a linear path, where the devices are ordered and (more or less) fixed. Figure 4.1 shows the signal path of a guitar to a tape recorder using effects in an inline configuration.

As you get more sophisticated in your approach to the signal chain, you begin to realize that certain effects sound better after the preamp (like reverb and delay), and some are designed to treat your signal before it reaches the preamp (like compression). Splitting your effects at the amp is good training for working in a studio, where there are several places to patch in effects.

To "split" your effects (that is, to put some before the preamp and some after), your amp has to give you access to the signal between the preamp and the power amp. This access point is called the effects loop (as described in Chapter 2), and is critical to achieving a modern, versatile sound if you use effects. This last condition is important to consider, because many quality amplifiers, including vintage models and reissues, don't include effects loops. And in many studio situations, you'll add reverb after the power amp because you're miking the speaker. But if you find yourself in a situation where you must deliver the total sound, effects and all, taking advantage of an effects loop is the way to go. Many multi-effects processors also have effects loops built into them, especially if they include a preamp stage. Look at Figure 4.2

Fig. 4.1

Signal path with inline effects

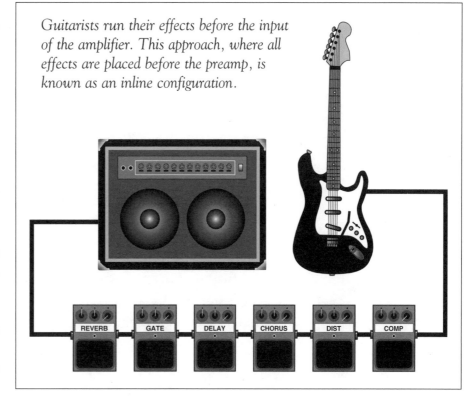

Guitarists run their effects before the input of the amplifier. This approach, where all effects are placed before the preamp, is known as an inline configuration.

REVERB GATE DELAY CHORUS DIST COMP

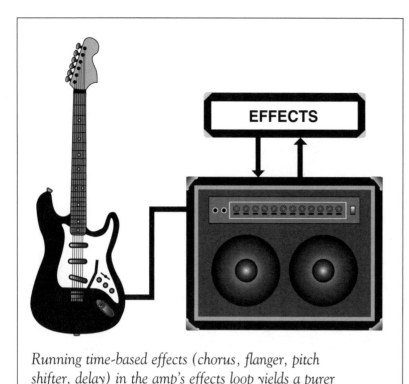

Running time-based effects (chorus, flanger, pitch shifter, delay) in the amp's effects loop yields a purer signal at the preamp.

Fig. 4.2

Amp effects loop

to see how a signal is split off at an amplifier's effects loop for optimal placement of a chorus effect.

When you record using a mixer, you have yet two more places to add effects. One is at the insert jack, which is like an effects loop in a guitar amp. It allows your post-preamp (the mixer's preamp, not the amp's) signal to be routed ("looped") out of the board to an external effect and then brought back into the channel to proceed through the rest of the strip (aux sends, panning, track assignment, fader, etc.). This is analogous to a serial loop, as it routes away the entire signal for processing. Effects such as EQ and compression are best used in the insert jack, as they should act on the entire signal and not a portion of it.

The other opportunity to add effects comes at the aux send section of the channel strip. This control routes only a portion of the signal out of the mixer (meaning some signal gets through dry, or with no effect), and so is analogous to a series loop in an amp. Effects such as chorus, delay, and reverb are best added in some proportion to the direct signal, so you should wire up your time-based effects in one of the aux send buses (see Chapter 5 for more on bus theory).

There are some key differences between the insert jack and aux send, other than where they occur in the mixer's channel strip. Consider that there is only one insert jack per channel and it applies only to the channel to which it belongs. There are, however, multiple aux sends (some boards have as many as six per channel), each capable of having a separate effect, and these are not exclusive to one channel, but are shared by every other channel on the board.

Many times you'll want to share an effect across several channels—say, to accommodate a grouping of instruments, like four horns, three backup singers, or two guitars. This way, each instrument has its own channel with level and EQ control, but shares a common effect so that they all sound like they were recorded in the same environment. You can vary the amount of the effect by turning one channel's aux send higher than the others, but all families of voices or instruments that should work together must have some amount of the identical time-based effect mixed in.

But if you have just one guitar and you want to add, say, delay, where should the effect go? You have four choices: inline (before the amp preamp), in the amp's effects loop (assuming you're using an amp), in the insert point of the mixer channel, or in an aux send bus. Generally speaking, the later in the chain you add the effect, the better its fidelity will be, so the classic application would be to put the delay at the aux send. However if you're creating a "total sound" for the engineer (even if that engineer is you), place the effect before you get to the mixer, either inline or in the loop, depending on the situation (effects before the preamp tend to yield a slightly less-defined, more vintage sound). All these choices will eventually become empowering and not confusing, as it may appear initially. As guitarists, you have an advantage over other musicians in that you're used to thinking of your effects in a modular sense, which is very much how a recording studio is organized.

EFFECTS DEFINED BY CATEGORY AND WHY

Most guitarists have an intuitive sense as to where basic effects should go in their signal chain. If you have two pedals, a distortion unit and a digital delay, you would naturally put the distortion before the delay (the guitar goes into the distortion, the distortion into the delay, and the delay into the amp). But the more pedals you use, the trickier it gets, and some truly bizarre gizmos—like a digital whammy pedal—might put you at a loss to explain just why effects go where they do relative to others in the chain. Additionally, some processors (such as EQs and reverbs) can go in different places in the chain, depending on the desired effect. Now you might be thinking, "Gee, I know in which order the basic pedals should go, but I guess I don't really know why."

Test your effect-ordering mettle by taking this quick quiz. What is the correct order of these 10 effects, from guitar to amp?

A.	EQ	1. __
B.	Distortion	2. __
C.	Chorus/Flanger	3. __
D.	Noise Gate	4. __
E.	Reverb	5. __
F.	Volume Pedal	6. __
G.	Preamp	7. __
H.	Compressor	8. __
I.	Delay	9. __
J.	Wah-Wah Pedal	10. __

Here now is the "correct" order: 1) G, Preamp; 2) H, Compressor; 3) B, Distortion; 4) J, Wah-Wah Pedal; 5) C, Chorus/Flanger; 6) I, Delay; 7) A, EQ; 8) D, Noise Gate; 9) F, Volume Pedal; 10) E, Reverb.

Don't deduct any points if you had the delay before the chorus/flanger; that one's a toss-up. Also acceptable but not as universal is to put the EQ just after the guitar or compressor (this is explained on the following pages).

Before we individually list the effects and discuss each one's specific function, it might help you divide effects into three categories, in the order they occur in the chain: Signal Conditioners, Time-Based Effects, Ambient Processors, and Other Effects (which may include a combination of the above categories). There are other ways to view effect families—such as Enhancers and Colorizers, or as Gain-Based and EQ-Based devices—but I've found the first way to be the most intuitive, especially when considering complex effects that may combine, say, time and EQ (e.g., phase shifters). Knowing the "proper" order becomes especially critical if you adopt a more recording-oriented approach where effects groups are split among the amp's effects loop and the mixer's insert and aux send sections, rather than the "live" approach, which has all the effects preceding the guitar amp's preamp stage.

SIGNAL CONDITIONERS

Signal Conditioners include all the gain-based and EQ-based effects. These generally don't try to change the basic nature of a sound, except to increase the gain and, theoretically, every aspect of the sound in exact proportion.

Preamps: These listen to the signal and boost it as faithfully as possible with as little coloring as possible. Usually, preamps have EQ and other controls, but it's essentially preamps that go first in the chain, as they must receive a signal with the highest possible integrity, even if their purpose is to create a distorted sound.

Compressors: These reduce the dynamic range of a signal by attenuating levels that exceed a certain point (threshold). Guitarists sometimes use compressors to increase sustain, but that's really an "overuse" of the effect (though it sounds great). The primary design of a compressor is to deliver a consistent level without significantly altering the signal's tone. With heavy compression, some high-frequency content can be lost, which can be put back in with EQ. Recording engineers love consistent signals, so be sure to inform them when you're giving them a compressed signal, as it may affect compression and limiting settings of their own.

Distortion: It's hard to imagine a distortion unit as a mere "signal conditioner," so dramatic is its effect on tone. However, its influence is limited to overdriving the gain stage of the signal. In other words, it doesn't change the basic content of the signal, it just pushes it past the breaking point of the circuitry's abilities to reproduce it faithfully. Distortion tends to compress a signal, so be aware of that when setting levels or running outboard compression

EQ: Equalizers can also be thought of as gain boosters, except that they apply it to only a portion of the signal, defined by frequency or frequency range. Graphic EQs are used for broad band applications, while parametrics can be dialed in to very specific ranges (usually defined by parts of an octave), and even to a single frequency, such as 440 Hz (the A above middle C, often used as a tuning reference). Except in "severe" cases, like a wah-wah pedal and a phase shifter, EQs don't dramatically change a signal's overall sound, and are often used for corrective measures (to rectify a frequency-reproducing deficiency in another component).

Wah-Wah Pedals: Wahs are active EQ circuits whose range is varied by means of a foot pedal. They apply a resonant-frequency peak that sweeps through the high-mid region (around 500 Hz–2 kHz), emulating somewhat the sound of a human voice. You can use a wah many ways: as a slowly opening and closing filter over a soaring lead solo; as the wacka-wacka disco effect popularized in the '70s accomplished by rocking the pedal while strumming muted strings; as a gently undulating modulation effect; or as a filter, with the treadle in a fixed position. Wahs would typically go after gain boosters, but Jimi Hendrix put his first, so there's a classic example of someone whose music wasn't hurt by not following the rules. A wah is one example of an effect that some recordists will use on a "re-amped" or previously recorded clean track. If your foot-rockin' chops are not up to snuff, consider recording a track of un-wahed guitar, then play back the track through the wah (focusing your efforts on just the wah—you can even use your hands) and record onto a new track.

TIME-BASED EFFECTS

A surprising amount of sonic variety comes from effects that alter a signal using time distortion. Time-based effects, by definition, combine the original signal with a time-manipulated version, and that's why these effects work well in an amp's parallel loop or from a mixer's aux send jack. You always want a portion of the original signal in the equation. Time-based effects take the original signal, sample it (through digital recording), stagger it in time, and combine it somehow with the original. You might not think of the swimmy chorus sound as being related to loop recording à la Brian May, but they're two ends of the same spectrum.

Choruses/Flangers: As far as ordering is concerned, these two effects are interchangeable. You probably wouldn't use them both at the same time in orthodox situations. Chorus is the more subtle of the two effects, usually consisting of a delay of 1–50 milliseconds, and is often used in stereo. Flangers are more dramatic, whooshy and vintage sounding. Put these after signal conditioners but before the delay and reverb.

Pitch Shifters: You'll hear these referred to generically as "harmonizers," but that's actually a trademark name under Eventide's control. A pitch shifter actually takes the second signal and detunes it slightly in increments of cents (hundredths of a semitone). Mild pitch shift settings yield chorus-like effects; drastic ones come in the form of musical intervals, like 3rds, 4ths, and 5ths. Intelligent pitch shifters will alter an interval to fit a certain key, so you can play in harmony with yourself (like the twin-guitar leads of classic southern rock bands).

Delay: With the advent of digital reverb, it's important to distinguish delay as a rather artificial effect compared to the more natural-sounding echo that reverb produces. Delay is a discrete, or separate, repeat of the original signal at a specified interval (in milliseconds) after the original. Delay yields a spacious sound when used with times higher than 100 milliseconds or so. Settings of about 125 and above produce "slapback," a popular rockabilly effect, and longer times (around 300 ms) yield a soaring, cavernous sound. Also included on a delay unit are Feedback (how many times the effected signal is fed into the delay channel), and Modulation (a filter sweep that adds a chorus-like sound), and, on a stereo delay, panning controls for a "ping-pong" effect. A delay goes at the very end of the chain, just before the reverb, unless it's substituting for a reverb, in which case it goes last.

AMBIENT PROCESSORS: REVERB AND DELAY

When used conventionally, reverb and delay act as ambient effects, and so are placed at the very end of the chain. The reasoning is that this is the most natural way we hear sound—in an environment which these effects are simulating. It doesn't make as much sense to add swirly chorus onto the tail of a long reverb as it does to add reverb to a chorused sound. If special effects are required, though—notably a rhythmic repeat in the delay or a gated reverb à la the Phil Collins snare sound—these units can be placed further up the chain. If you're using reverb as a studio sideman, you must clear it with the recording engineer, in case he has his own plans for ambient treatment.

If you are recording yourself, try to add reverb at the mixdown stage, as you may change your mind about the ambient treatment once all the instruments are in place in the mix. "Printing," or recording, with effects can't be undone once it's on tape. Often guitarists need to hear reverb to get the right feel, but most mixers allow you to "monitor" effects without printing them, which means you hear them through the headphones or speakers, but they don't go to tape. If you have only one reverb unit but need to use two reverb programs simultaneously (e.g., small room on rhythm guitar, large hall on lead solo), you may have to print with effects when tracking. You can press a stereo reverb into dual mono mode when two different effects are called for, but you'll have to make sure your unit is true stereo (separate ins as well as outs) and that the signal isn't "summed" (combined) along the way.

OTHER EFFECTS

There are other effects that may not fall neatly into one of the above categories, but we can at least place them in the chain. A **phase shifter** sounds a lot like a flanger, but is really more of an EQ-based effect than a time-based one. Nevertheless, it should go where flangers, choruses, and pitch shifters go—after signal conditioners and true-EQ-based effects. An **envelope-followed filter** (called "envelope filter" or "envelope follower" for short) is like an electronic touch-sensitive wah (play soft and it goes *wohl*, play hard and it goes *wack*), and so should go in place of it or adjacent to it. **Octavers**, or octave dividers, behave like doublers, except that the doubled signal is usually one or two (or both at once) octaves down. The same effect can be achieved with a pitch shifter, so put your octaver in the vicinity of other time-based effects. **Exciters** are EQ-based devices that are intended to sparkle up an entire sound, so put those at the end (but before the reverb to preserve the natural EQ roll-off effect programmed into a reverb's algorithm). If you use heavy effects, though, exciters can sometimes sound too "steely" if placed after the time-based effects because they interact with the chorused frequencies rather than the raw signal's. If that's the case, move your exciter up front. **Noise Gates** are designed to shut down the audio path until a certain level is achieved. This keeps noisy guitars from buzzing through quiet or silent passages. These typically go just before the reverb, because you want your guitar signal to cut off while the last ring-out of the reverb is still trailing away. Placing the noise gate after the reverb might cause an unnatural *shoop* sound as the gate slams shut the audio path during the reverb tail. **Speaker Simulators**, by the very definition of their role, should go at the end, just before the noise gate.

EFFECT ORDERING: THE ENTIRE CHAIN—A MAP

Figure 4.3 shows the entire effects chain, in a hypothetical correct order. Often you wouldn't have two similar effects on at once, but you might want to have them both available, so you can swap their order without making a difference. Placing all your effects inline, even when they aren't active can degrade your signal significantly—especially with inexpensive stompboxes–so a switcher (using a star network metaphor—as offered in units by Bradshaw and Digital Music Corp.—rather than a daisy-chain as an inline setup does) is a good idea if you use a lot of effects.

Fig. 4.3

The effects chain

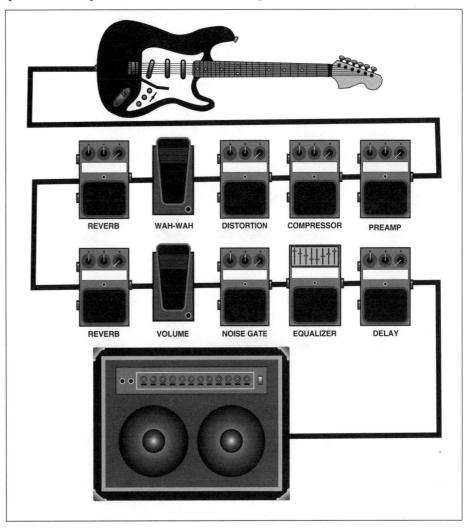

PRE VS. POST EFFECTS

Even if you use a multi-effects processor, it helps to think of effects in this inline stompbox way, as the different effects modules in the multi-effects unit can often be moved around. And when you split up your effects into pre and post placement ("pre" meaning before the preamp; "post" meaning after the preamp and before the power amp), you can move effects en masse, based on their family.

Follow the rule of thumb with effects ordering, which is to keep your signal conditioners in front of the preamp, and time-based effects, colorizers and other "total signal" effectors after the preamp. If you're a session player, you'll do this via your amplifier. If you record at home, you can do it either at the amp stage or at the mixing board. The advantage of doing it at the amp stage is that your signal gets created outside the board, and you can take that with you to any other board with predictable results (a mixing board does contribute to the signal's overall sound). The advantage of doing it at the board is for more flexibility and ease of operation.

MULTI-EFFECTS PROCESSORS

Effects ordering in multi-effects processors is usually pre-determined, but many allow you to change that order if desired. For example, if your multi-effects processor allows you to move the modules around in the "virtual chain," you should put the wah unit before the distortion if you're emulating the Hendrix sound (Robin Trower and Zakk Wylde also observe this setup approach). You might want to experiment with the EQ placement, say, before the distortion and after.

You can even combine your favorite outboard pedals with your multi-effects processor to get the best of both worlds. You might, for example, front-load your guitar signal via a popular preamp and distortion unit—such as the Mesa/Boogie Tri-Axis preamp and an Ibanez Tube Screamer—and plug that into the multi-effects processor for its killer stereo digital effects. To do that, you'd have to go into the multi-effects unit's programming mode and move all the gain-based signal conditioners to a place *before* the effects loop (or turn them off entirely), and then come into not the input but the effects return of the multi-effects processor. As long as you feed the correct ins and outs between each unit, you can mix and match.

One favorite trick is to go into a preamp and then into the effects return of a tube

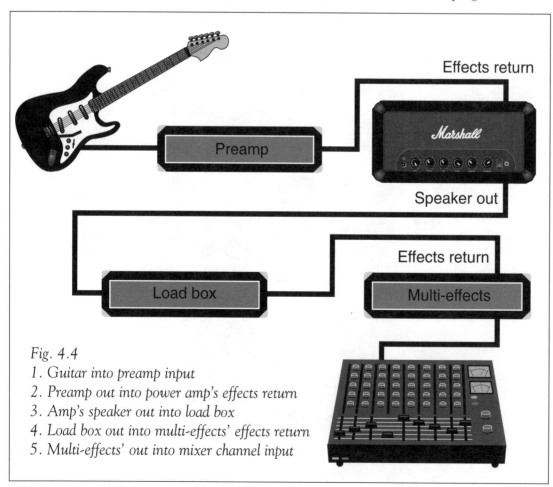

Fig. 4.4
1. *Guitar into preamp input*
2. *Preamp out into power amp's effects return*
3. *Amp's speaker out into load box*
4. *Load box out into multi-effects' effects return*
5. *Multi-effects' out into mixer channel input*

amp. This combines the tweazed-out preamp distortion with the warmth and natural response of a tube-driven power amp. You can then take the speaker output of the power amp and go into a load box/line-level convertor (such as the Marshall Power Brake or THD Hot Plate) and then route the output of that into the effects return of your multi-effects processor to get the time-based effects (see Fig. 4.4).

Whether you use stompboxes, a multi-effects processor, or a combination, thinking of effects in families will help you organize your pedals with regard to ideal placement in the chain for sonic integrity. And if a producer asks you to include an effect you hadn't planned on, or requests a combination of pedals you've never used before, you'll know in which order the pedals should go to get the highest signal-to-noise ratio and the most natural sound.

CHAPTER FIVE

Mixers: The Nerve Center of the Studio

If you've ever walked into a studio or even seen a photograph of one, you must have noticed one piece of gear standing out above the rest: the mixer. The mixing board is probably the single most important piece of gear in a studio, and it keeps track of all the sonic spinning plates. Without one, you could technically record to tape (assuming you matched your levels correctly), but you couldn't do much else. And while you can record without a mixer, you can't mix without a mixer (see Fig. 5.1).

Mixers not only provide the interface that allows guitars to go into a recorder, they combine the recorder's tape track outputs as well, so you can mix down to two-track stereo. They also provide flexibility and efficiency. Though flexibility and efficiency may not have a direct impact on your sound, they make recording go hundreds of times smoother, and over time make the recording process much more productive. Mixers unavoidably do have a sonic effect on your signal, but good mixers and good mixing technique should be virtually transparent in the overall sound.

Fig. 5.1

A recording mixer— note the eight submaster faders on the board's right side, just left of the master L/R fader

Knowing how mixers work will help make you more versatile when playing as a sideman at sessions, too. The engineer may never ask you about your signal, but you may recognize an opportunity to go direct into the board that might be overlooked if he's too busy troubleshooting another problem. Just being informed of your signal path's entire journey can't help but make you more sensitive to the recording environment as a whole. To make the mixer less daunting, we'll break it down into sections.

LEFT BRAIN VS. RIGHT BRAIN

Conceptually, it's easiest to think of mixers in two, albeit unbalanced, halves. The left half—the big one—houses the channels, and each channel is identical in design to the others. Understand one, and you understand all 8, 12 or 16, or however many channels that particular model boasts. The right side is where all the other stuff happens: signal routing, effects importation, auxiliary inputs, master volume, monitor mixes, sub-mixing, headphone mixes, and other arcane functions. It's the right side of the mixer where the bulk of the brain power resides. So ironically, even though the majority of real estate is taken up by the left side with channels, it is the right side that requires the most "imagination" to understand.

You tend to view the left side of a mixer as eight or 16 or 24 individual, vertically oriented modules. You don't usually scan sideways with your eyes on the left side of the board—except when viewing the volume faders at the bottom.

For example, say you've got all eight channels of your eight-channel board up and running, each with a different instrument. You decide that the rhythm guitar is muddy-sounding and too loud. To remedy the situation, you'd scan to find the rhythm guitar channel (usually labeled by you with marker or grease pencil on the "scribble strip"), and then move your eye up and down to determine what the problem is. It could be an EQ imbalance. It could be the effect send is too high. It could be the pan position is wrong. It could be the fader is up too high. You experiment by twisting the knobs (which are all in a vertical alignment) until you've corrected the problem. Then, after your adjustments, you may suddenly hear that the snare drum is now too bright. You'd then scan for its channel and take your eye up and down again, where you might discover the high-mid control is cranked too far to the right. In each case you didn't move horizontally; you considered each channel as a separate, vertical entity within a complete mix.

The right side of the mixer, by contrast, is best considered more globally, after you've gotten a basic "left side" sound. In other words, you usually focus on the right side of the board after you're happy with all the individual channel sounds. This is not to say that you won't go back to the left side of the board when mixing—you will, but one tends to take care of the left side first, then the right, then the left. That said, we'll start with the channel portion of a mixer, since it's easier and that's where you'll be plugging in and setting up your sound.

LEFT SIDE: THE CHANNEL BREAKDOWN FROM TOP TO BOTTOM

Though mixer controls are by no means standardized, most observe a certain top-to-bottom organization with respect to ordering the different components. So when you hear, say, an EQ problem, you instinctively look to the center of the board, whereas a pan problem would direct your eyes to the bottom of the board. Fig. 5.2 shows a typical mixer-channel layout. Some models are fancier and have more regions or knobs per region, and some units are more basic and have fewer knobs, but this represents the basic approach.

Trim: This controls the gain level of the preamp. For guitars, keyboards, and other line-level sources, you keep this control at the minimum (all the way left). For mics and piezo pickups this gets cranked to the right. The trim knob works in conjunction with the fader by "handicapping" signals so that differing input levels can be normalized here first, and then finely tuned with the faders.

EQ: The number of knobs and their function will vary, but a common arrangement in lower- to mid-priced boards is to have four controls: a high and low shelving EQ, and two knobs in the middle that work in conjunction with each other. One selects the frequency and the other provides a boost or cut at that frequency.

Aux/Effects: Here is where you can send out a signal to external sources, such as reverb, delay, flanging and other effects. How far you crank the knob determines how much effect your signal gets. By having one of the aux sends be pre fader (usually just marked "pre"), you can also use this level control to create a separate monitor mix, where the relative positions of all the channels' aux send levels—and not the faders—determine the mix. Moving the fader has no effect on the level of the aux send. That's the primary difference between a pre and post assignment in an aux send. A side note: What you wouldn't use an aux send for is to "mix" processors like compressors, gates, and noise reducers. Those go "inline" with the instrument or through the channel's insert points (discussed later).

Assign Switches: On a recording board, you'll see switches that route the signal to various buses, or output paths. (The word "bus" has nothing to do with the vehicle that carries school children; it's a corruption of Buss, the name of a German wire manufacturer.) Typically, these work in conjunction with the pan controls where tracks 1 and 2 are on one switch, 3 and 4 on another and so on. This way any channel can be assigned to any track (or several at once) by choosing the appropriate switch (1/2, 3/4, etc.) and the correct odd-even assignment (hard left=odd, hard right=even).

Mute/Solo: These switches allow the recording engineer to monitor any single instrument or any combination of instruments without affecting the master mix. A mute switch kills the sound of a channel in the monitors. A solo switch kills every sound but that channel. These are invaluable tools when trying to correct a problem on the fly or in the context of a mix.

Fader: This is a level control and it works in conjunction with the trim pot to control the overall level of the signal. The optimal loudness should occur when the fader is at about 7/8 of its travel, and this point is usually indicated as 0 dB (no boost or cut), and highlighted in some way for quick visual reference. If you're dealing with vastly different levels coming into the board, such as a powerful line level and a weak mic level, you'd use the trim pot to equalize them first, so that each signal is at equal strength when the fader is at 0.

CHANNELING YOUR ENERGIES

Setting up a channel sound can be done in isolation; you don't need to hear anything but the signal (your guitar, say) that you're trying to set up. You can adjust volume, EQ, effect level, pan position, and overall loudness, and each of these adjustments will make an immediate difference over your speakers or headphones. Set up each sound in isolation so that it sounds good by itself. This might be your rhythm guitar on channel 1, a bass on channel 2, drums on channels 3 and 4 (they should be processed

Fig. 5.2
A typical mixer channel control surface layout

in stereo, which requires two mixer channels panned hard right and hard left), and a lead guitar on channel 5. After you're happy with each sound by itself—including effect level and pan position—it's time to move to the right side of the board.

It's helpful to make your channel assignments more or less permanent, so that you don't have to turn every single knob from song to song or project to project. For example, you may really only use one lead vocal sound (always with the same mic and reverb program), so that channel can remain fairly unchanged because the EQ is tailored to your voice and the level is calibrated to the type of mic, etc. This helps you to leave the left half—the big one—of the board as a "set and forget" situation. You'll be thankful for that when you get into the topsy-turvy world of the mixer's right half.

THE RIGHT SIDE: MASTER AND SUBMASTER SECTIONS, AUXILIARY INPUTS, AUX SENDS/RETURNS, CUE SENDS

Over on the mixer's right side is where you'll be routing signals to tape, both for the multi-track machine (when tracking) and the two-track stereo machine (when mixing down). The faders at the farthest right are the master Left and Right bus (signal path that can accommodate more than one signal) faders, sometimes grouped onto one fader (as on Mackie boards, for example). These are usually used only in mixdown mode, because the submaster faders, immediately to the left of the master fader(s), are used for feeding the multi-track.

1. Left/Right Masters
On a live or PA board, you usually have only two buses—the left and right stereo masters. This means that of the, say, 16 channels on your board, there are only two choices as to where any signal can go: left or right (these go to a power amp and then to the speakers). On a recording board, however, there's an intermediate stage called the sub-mix or submaster section, usually consisting of four or eight buses. When you see ads for boards that say 24x8x2, it means 24 channels, 8 sub-mix buses, and 2 master—or left and right stereo—buses.

2. Submasters
By using the assign switches on the individual channels, you can route one or more signals to the submaster buses. Most often, it is the submaster outs that are routed to the tape inputs, and the master outputs that are routed to the master mixdown deck. Monitor outputs are routed to the control room speakers (via a power amp), and the pre-fade aux sends are routed to a headphone matrix (to set up an independent mix for in studio musicians to monitor from).

3. Aux Inputs
Also at the right side of the board are any auxiliary inputs for the submaster and master buses. These are for signals that require input and mixing to the submasters or masters, but don't need a whole channel's worth of control. This is a good place to add submixes (the stereo output of another mixer, say, from a drum kit), synth guitar (whose tonal and level changes can all be made on the synth itself), or a pre-recorded CD or cassette tape. Most submasters have insert points, meaning any channel assigned to a submaster can be processed by one external device.

4. Aux Sends/Returns, Cue Sends

Over on the right side of the board is also where you'll find the aux send master volume and aux return master volume. These determine how loud the signal is going out of the board (send) and how loud the signal is going into the master bus (aux return). Use the aux send jack to find the best level for your processor (where the loudest channel aux send knob sends the input meter just slightly into the red) and use the master return to actually blend the desired mix of effected signal. "Cue" is another term for an aux bus, usually used for monitoring or "cue" purposes. Many TASCAM Portastudio models feature a cue section.

THE BACK PANEL

Now that you've pondered the left and right sides of the mixer, consider that there is yet another "side," and that is the back panel. This is where stuff gets plugged in, but it also affects how you route signals around, similar to what we did internally with the bus assignments.

Figure 5.3 shows a typical back-panel configuration. Like the front of the mixer, the back panel also has a right and left orientation. The left side has the plugs, or jacks, for all the channels. The right side has jacks appropriate to the board's right-side controls. Let's tackle the channel side of the back panel.

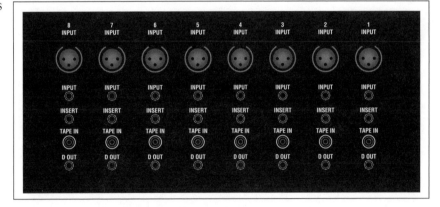

Fig. 5.3

The mixer's back panel

Input: As you might expect, this jack receives the instrument you want to record, be it a guitar, keyboard, drum machine, microphone, tape deck, or even the output of another mixer channel. If you have a three-pin, low-impedance microphone, you'll naturally want to have that corresponding jack as an available input option, as well as the more instrument-oriented quarter-inch jacks. However, many mixer manufacturers rightly assume that it's not necessary to supply every channel with an XLR jack, so they put XLRs only on a limited number of channels. This is an acceptable compromise in low- and mid-priced boards, as it keeps the cost down, and it's rare for home recordists and project-studio engineers to need more than four XLR mic inputs simultaneously.

Direct Out: This is a control that you won't find on a live (PA) board but is a great option to have on a recording board. This jack allows you to take the channel's output signal and route it directly to a tape recorder's input. For example, if you plug one end of a cord into channel 1's direct-out jack and plug the other end into your tape recorder's track 1 input jack, you can completely avoid the right side of the board. This is desirable for two reasons: 1) the less circuitry you run a signal through the better, and 2) you retain an intuitive one-to-one relationship between your mixer and your tape deck—channel 1 on the mixer is track 1 on the deck, channels 5 and 6 are tracks 5 and 6, etc.

Insert Jack: This is essentially an effects loop. It allows you to patch in signal processors, so that you don't have to use them "inline," which is the only other way to incorporate signal processing on individual channels. Many manufacturers put the send and return functions on one jack by using a stereo, or tip-ring-sleeve, configuration. This saves them from having to make a more expensive and real estate-hogging two-jack scheme, where the send is one jack and the return is another. The downside of the one-hole stereo scheme is that you need special Y cables that have a stereo plug on one end (which goes into the board), and two mono plugs on the other (one send for the input of your effect, one return for the output). These are easy to find and inexpensive, though you'll need as many of these as you have insert-jack effects running simultaneously. Still it's a clever solution and keeps the dimensions as well as the cost of the board down.

Tape In: This accepts the output of your tape recorder track. A simple switch on the front panel allows each channel to "listen to" either the instrument input or the tape track, depending on whether you're tracking or mixing. No more unplugging the instruments to put in the tape returns, and you get to keep your one-to-one correspondence of track 1 to channel 1, etc.

BUS THEORY, LOGIC, AND APPLICATION

Perhaps the most confusing aspect about a mixer for the guitarist is the "bus." Just what is that, and why the special name? How does a bus differ from a normal audio path, and what are some of the strategies for using buses? And how about those attendant words "send" and "return"? Why not just call them "in" and "out"? Let's tackle the somewhat elusive concept of a bus, and discuss its many functions in the world of recording.

"Bus" is an electrical term that carries over into audio applications. Technically, it's defined as a path that connects three or more circuits. A good way to think of it is as literally a bus—the kind that picks school children up from different locations and drops them off at a single destination such as a school. In the same way an audio bus is a path or line that can carry multiple signals (the 16 channels of your mixer) to a destination (the master stereo output). A mixing bus takes many signals and brings them to one (or two) locations.

DIFFERENT BUSES ON YOUR MIXER

There are three basic buses on any mixer. They are: aux, submaster and master (the master is sometimes referred to as left/right, main, or stereo). Any channel on the board can be assigned to any or all of these buses, and it makes no difference to the buses how many signals are onboard. Let's take the example of the aux send.

1. AUX SEND AND RETURN

Each channel has an aux send, and most boards have more than one per channel, even on a simple line mixer. When you turn up the knob labeled "aux send 1," you're sending a cloned copy of that channel's signal (let's say it's a lead guitar) to the aux 1 bus. This bus goes to a jack on the back of your mixer called "aux send 1," meaning that it's waiting there to be brought outside the mixer into an effects processor (typically reverb or delay).

So the knob titled "aux send" is really only a volume control that determines how loud you're setting the signal on the physical line (bus) that goes to the aux send 1 jack. To do anything with this signal, you must take it to an effects processor and bring it back into the board. The simplest way to do this is to plug a cord between the send jack and the reverb input, and then take another cord from the reverb's output and plug it into the correspondingly numbered aux return jack (though you could plug it into any return jack). Then you have to adjust the volume of the effects return to get the effect to be heard in the proper proportion to the dry signal. Simple, right?

You might be thinking, "Well, why not just plug the guitar into the reverb and plug the reverb output into the channel input? Why go through this convoluted aux-bus routine to get reverb on my signal?" Two reasons: 1) the aux bus picks up the signal after the preamp, EQ and fader, which is a better place to add time-based effects; and 2) using the aux send allows more than one effect to use the same reverb device.

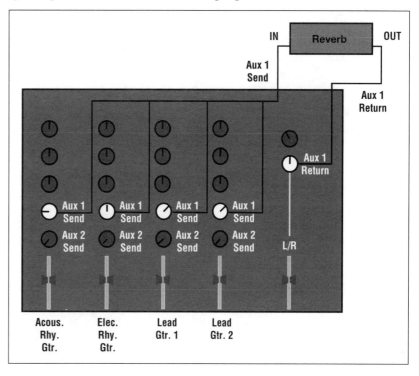

It is reason #2, however, that is the most significant here. If you have four instruments that all need the same ambient treatments you can use a bus to send all the signals to the reverb simultaneously, rather than using the "inline" method that would require four separate reverbs (all set exactly the same). In the bus method, any channel has access to the reverb. See Fig. 5.4 for an illustration of this concept.

Fig. 5.4

Aux sends let you assign multiple channels to one effect

The signals all join together at the top of the channel section, terminating at the board's aux send jack. Note that the knobs are all set differently, indicating the relative strength of the channel in the bus. You can tell that the acoustic rhythm guitar will have just a little reverb, the electric rhythm guitar will have more than that, and lead guitars 1 and 2 will have the most—in equal amounts with each other.

This combined effects signal gets sent to the reverb unit and then comes back to the board's aux return jack. From there, it is routed to a master volume control which sets the absolute level going to the stereo bus (indicated here by a single knob).

Turning up and down the aux return 1 knob affects only the reverb portion of the signal; the dry, unaffected signals still pass from the channels to the master bus (via the submaster or master bus). But routing the reverb signal separately allows you to both vary the mix of the individual channels and set the overall effect level.

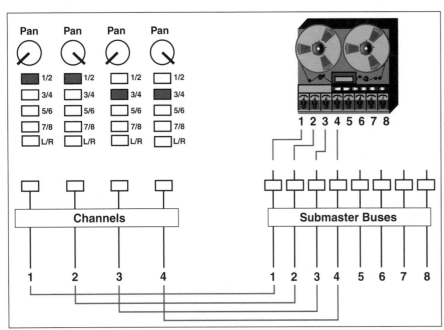

Fig. 5.5

Using the submaster to assign channels to tracks where channel 1 goes to track 1, channel 2 to track 2, etc.

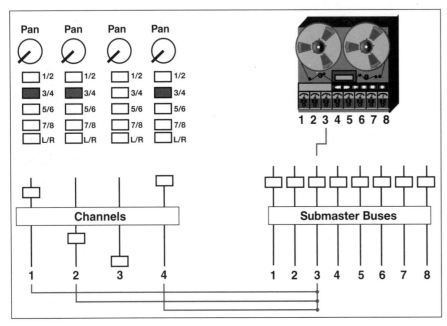

Fig. 5.6

Using the submasters to assign multiple guitars to one track for layering

2. SUBMASTER

The concept of the bus may be difficult to grasp at first, but it's at the heart of good mixing strategy. Again, a bus is a path or physical line that can accept more than one signal. Earlier, we touched on how this allows you to group two or more channels to the same fader (in the submaster section), which is not merely another channel fader, but a bus fader. This allows you to more or less permanently patch a submaster bus to a correspondingly numbered tape track input. For example, submaster bus 1's output would go to tape track input 1, submaster bus 2 to tape input 2, and so on. This way any channel—or any number of channels can go to any tape input via the submaster bus. All your routing is done with the assign switches; the submaster buses stay patched to the track inputs. Look at Fig. 5.5 to see how channels are conventionally routed to tape tracks via submasters.

Using a submaster is the only way to combine two signals to one tape track. Once you achieve a perfect blend among a three-channel setup of two mics on your amp plus a direct sound, you can assign them all to a submaster channel and control the level from there, rather than moving the individual channel faders (and attempting the impossible of moving three faders in perfect sync). The relative balance of the three channel faders never changes, only the overall level of the blend (see Fig. 5.6).

SEVERAL ILLUSTRATED APPROACHES TO THE MIXER

The mark of a truly flexible system is that there is more than one way to accomplish the same thing. Nowhere is that principle better illustrated than in the mixer. In our case, we want to take guitar signals and route them to the multi-track tape recorder's inputs. Let's explore just a few of the many different ways to do that.

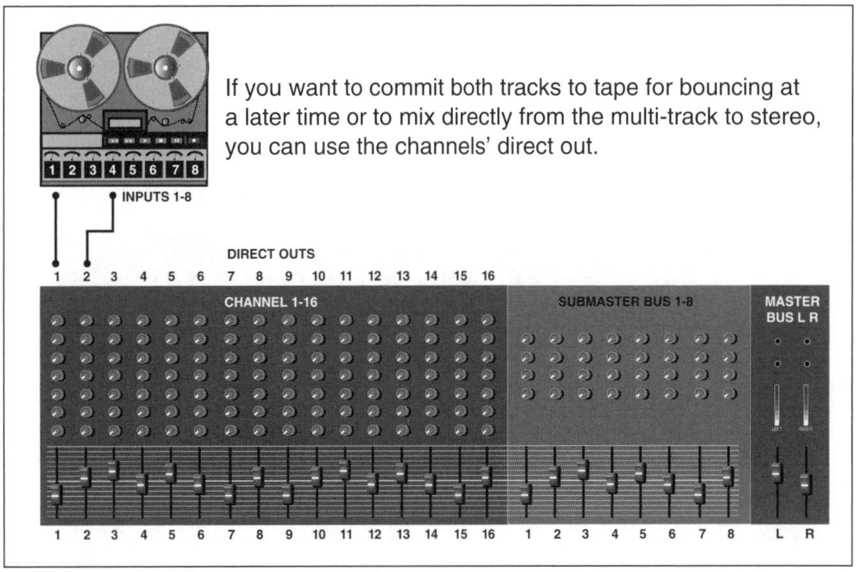

Let's say you have a close-miked cabinet in channel 1, and an ambient (room) mic in channel 2. You have two individual sounds that you can access instantly or combine in various ways for tonal variety. After you apply some EQ and reverb (via the channel controls), you have a choice as to how that signal gets to the recorder (i.e., analog tape, digital tape, hard disk).

1) You can record two separate tracks of guitars (tracks 1-2) onto the multi-track and at a later time bounce them to one, or route them to the left/right stereo bus at mixdown. For this approach, you should wire the direct outputs of the channels to the correspondingly assigned tracks 1 and 2 (see Fig. 5.7). This creates the shortest path from mixer channel to tape track and keeps each channel as a track, so that you don't commit yourself to a "pre-mix" which you can't separate later.

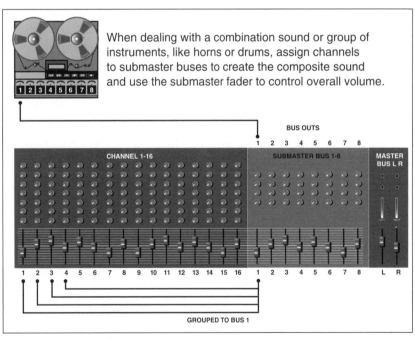

If you want to commit both tracks to tape for bouncing at a later time or to mix directly from the multi-track to stereo, you can use the channels' direct out.

Fig. 5.7

Using the direct outs to avoid unnecessary "board turf"

When dealing with a combination sound or group of instruments, like horns or drums, assign channels to submaster buses to create the composite sound and use the submaster fader to control overall volume.

2) You can combine the signals by assigning them to a bus. Remember, a bus is the name of a signal path that can accept more than one signal—like a multi-lane highway with numerous merging roads. You can experiment to find the perfect blend of channels and group them to submaster 1. Then if you need to make a level adjustment, you only have to move the submaster fader. That changes the volume but not the character of the sound. You can then have submaster 1 go to track 1 of your recorder (see Fig. 5.8).

3) This option might be described as the super-deluxe method. You can take the

Fig. 5.8

Here the submaster section is used to preserve the channel balance of a layered sound

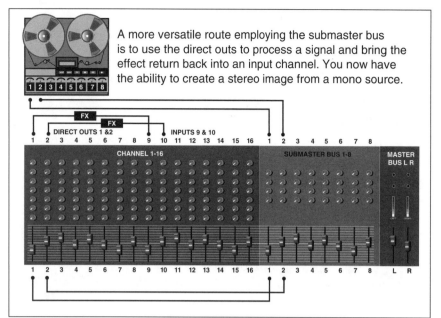

A more versatile route employing the submaster bus is to use the direct outs to process a signal and bring the effect return back into an input channel. You now have the ability to create a stereo image from a mono source.

Fig. 5.9

This method allows you to employ outboard effects via the direct outs

direct out of channel 1, feed it to an outboard processor and bring the output of the processor back into another input channel (like #9, for example). This allows you to do two things: a) get even more tone-blending variety out of one signal (you're now blending two channels of the same signal, each with different EQ and effects); and b) derive a stereo signal from a single source. You can then assign channels 1 and 9 to the left and right stereo buses or to the submaster section. You can do the same with the ambient mic in channel 2 (see Fig. 5.9).

For the highest sonic integrity, you want to take the path that treads the least amount of board turf. This keeps the signal cleaner and freer of electronic noise. But routing your channels to the submaster section provides greater flexibility and is usually worth the tradeoff in the noise increase acquired by going the submaster route.

If you're going to record a solo acoustic guitar album live in the studio with no overdubs, you can avoid a mixer completely by using a high-quality preamp and going straight into the recorder. But if you plan to have more than one instrument on a recording—and monitor the rhythm tracks while overdubbing a lead—you'll need a mixer. If these instruments never change recorder tracks (channel 1 always goes to track 1, channel 2 to track 2, etc.), then you can get away with the channel's back-panel direct outs (which are appearing on more and more live boards as well as recording ones). If you plan to blend signals or derive a stereo signal from a mono source, though, you'll need to use submaster buses and be aware of the different ways to route signals to the multi-track.

Regardless of which method you employ, with a little study you'll realize that the mixer offers you the most routing possibilities. Good mixer chops are probably the most important skills to have next to playing the guitar well and getting a good sound.

TRACKING VS. MIXING

Tracking is usually the most difficult and time-consuming stage of recording, because you're getting your sound together, searching for the right effect, overdubbing and double-tracking, and generally trying to produce good music. If you're out of time, or your intonation's off, nothing in the mixdown session will help that. But as you get better at tracking, you'll notice that mixing gets easier. You'll be able to measure your growth as a recordist by the ease of your mixdown sessions. The easier and more hands-off the mixdown, the better you've tracked.

Set your mixer up so that you don't have to repatch cables to switch from tracking to mixing. When mixing, you're listening only to the tape tracks (except if you're feeding a live signal to mixdown, such as MIDI-synched instruments or "virtual tracks"). Switch all your input channels to "tape" and, if you've wired your tape deck's tape outs into the correspondingly numbered channels, you should be on your way. You don't even have to unplug your input sources (mics, guitars, etc.).

If you're planning on using effects at mixdown, a good rule of thumb is that the same effect used at the mixdown stage as in the tracking stage will be applied more subtly. A compressor, for example, should be used only to smooth out any spikey levels that escaped processing in the tracking stage. The same soft touch applies to EQ. With all those open channels streaming into the stereo bus, you want to keep any extraneous gain to a minimum. EQ is non-discriminating; it boosts noise as well as program material.

This is the stage where you now assign every tape-track channel to a position in the stereo field. From now on, you must think in terms of stereo, and all the psychoacoustic aspects that go along with that. Mixing is easier than tracking in this regard, because you don't have all the "confusing" (the flip-side of "powerful and versatile") issues of bus, track, and effects assignments, tape vs. source monitoring, and input juggling. Now all paths lead to the stereo bus, and listening and adjusting becomes a much more intuitive task.

PLACING GUITARS IN THE STEREO FIELD

The phrase "placing it in the mix," can mean several different things depending on the context. It could mean where in the stereo field a sound sits. It could also refer to the front-to-back placement, which depends on two factors: the relative loudness of one sound to the others, and the ambient effect level (reverb) relative to the dry sound. Let's deal with the more basic of the two strategies, stereo placement, as it involves only the volume levels of the two speakers.

To place a sound anywhere in the stereo field you need only to have the sound assigned to one mixer channel with a pan knob. You can hear your sound go from hard left (sound coming from the left speaker only) to hard right (right speaker only) by slowly sweeping the pan knob from left to right. All you're really doing is changing the relative volume of the left and right channels, which gives the illusion of the sound traveling from left to center to right and various points in between. This is not stereo sound or stereo recording, but placement of a mono sound (i.e., one tape track) in the stereo field.

Hard left, hard right, and center (equal volume in both speakers) are pretty easy concepts to grasp. Where you have to put your thinking caps on is in those in-between places. Obviously, you can't physically have a sound emanating from in between hard left and center, but you can create the effect psychoacoustically. By having the majority of sound come out of the left speaker and just a little bit of sound from the right, you can create the effect of the location that is neither hard

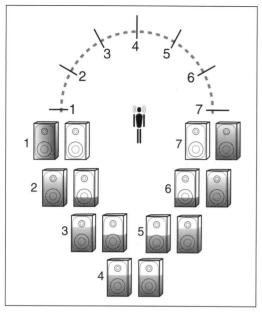

Fig. 5.10

7 steps in the stereo field

left nor center. Look at Fig. 5.10 which shows a seven-step stereo field. You can have any infinite odd-number positions to represent the stereo field above three (which would yield only hard left, center and hard right), but seven is a good working number. Underneath the seven semi-circular positions are the corresponding speaker loudness icons with the numeric position beside each figure. Notice that as you scan the speaker diagrams, you see the right level go down as the left rises, and vice versa—like a see-saw. But the effect to the ear is that the sound is moving from left to right—even to locations where there is no speaker.

So what's all this trickery got to do with music? It's quite simple: In order to create a proper illusion of musicians playing, you have to put them in relative horizontal positions in front of the listener. If you have three guitars playing three separate parts, you'll want to delineate them with respect to placement in the stereo field. For example, say you have one guitar playing full chords, another playing low-note roots only, and a third playing up-the-neck, high-string inversions. One method would be to put the chording guitar straight up the middle, the low-note guitar panned slightly left, and the high-note guitar slightly right. This allows the listener to hear each part in its own space a little better than if all three guitars were panned center. Fig. 5.11 shows how the listener would experience this psychoacoustically.

Sometimes you don't want to delineate the guitars, as in the case of layering or blending. Blending (such the close mic/room mic combination discussed earlier) requires the same pan assignment from each channel, which creates one thick sound at a unique location in the stereo field.

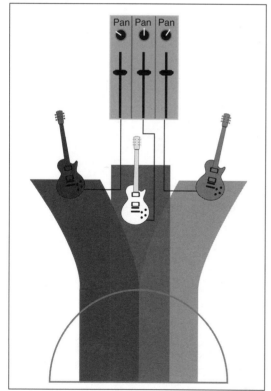

Fig. 5.11

3 guitars in a panning scheme

EXTENDING THE MIXER'S REACH: THE PATCH BAY AS CENTRAL SIGNAL ROUTER

As versatile as your mixer is for routing signals it can't change how devices are physically plugged in. If you want to "loop in" a compressor, you'll have to secure two patch cords and wire it either into the desired channel or the stereo bus, depending on your application. Normally this isn't a problem, but if your compressor sits in a rack and your mixer is against the wall, you'll be spending a lot of time on your knees or back with a flashlight, unplugging and plugging various devices into your board.

All this labor can be eliminated with the use of a patch bay. A patch bay allows you to take all the ins and outs of your various devices and bring them to one central location—the back of the patch bay. Then to make any connection between any input and any output, you, at the front of the patch bay, simply "jump" the connection with a short patch cord. Patch bays are great for processors that serve double duty, like reverbs, delays, EQs, and multi-effects processors. They're also good for devices that accept multiple sources, like cassette decks. Sometimes you'll want your cassette deck listening to the stereo bus of your multi-track (for mixing directly to cassette), sometimes to your DAT (for making dubs), and sometimes to your CD player (for dubbing your favorite commercially recorded CD). To unhook the cassette's input every time for each of these different applications is a real pain, but if you connect the "tape in" jacks of your cassette to the patch bay, you'll never have to look at the cassette's back panel again.

The output of your DAT machine is another candidate for a patch-bay assignment. When you're mixing to DAT from your multi-track you'll want to listen to the DAT through the monitors, which means the DAT's outputs must be plugged into the studio monitors' power amp. But if you want to record a DAT onto two tracks of your multi-track, you'll have to re-route the DAT's output to the mixer inputs. It only takes two or three devices that serve in different ways to make you realize the efficiency of a patch bay.

MONITORS AND POWER AMPS

The final consideration you should give to your mixer is what happens to the signal after you've performed all these amazing and clever routing techniques. You must be able to hear accurately the results of your labors. For this, you need a quality monitoring system. This involves two elements: near-field monitors and a power amp.

1. NEAR-FIELD MONITORS

Near-field monitors are not like the stereo speakers you buy at the consumer electronics store. Near fields are designed to give you a truer, "flat" frequency response, rather than a musically more pleasing one, which has "bumps" (accentuations) in the highs and lows. These bumps initially make the music sound at once more punchy and sparkly, but it's not really in the program material, but in the distortion of the output of the signal. This not only gives an inaccurate picture of what you've put into the speakers, it contributes to ear fatigue over time.

Studio monitors must be flat to guarantee the most neutral listening perspective from which to mix. Your music could be played on a Walkman, car stereo, boom box, home system, or even other near fields, and you may not have any control over how your music gets heard. Studio monitors are better at isolating electronic signals from each other, ensuring proper "imaging" (the independence of left and right signals). Their cabinets are also ideally designed for near-field work, which means they assume you will be in roughly an equilateral triangle relationship with your speakers. They are more heavy duty as well, as they're often expected to be driven hard for long periods of time.

2. POWER AMPS

To get the best results from studio monitors, you should pair them with a quality power amp. Using a home stereo receiver is not the best solution, as these usually don't have the power and quality of a dedicated power amp. "Dedicated" means it doesn't have other controls and functions, like EQ, and multiple inputs for various devices (tape decks, VCRs, CDs). As a serious recordist, all your EQ'ing and input selection is done on a mixing board and patch bay. You only need (and want to pay for) an amp that takes a mixer output and puts it through speaker outputs.

You can become expert at mixing and recording without ever having a good monitor system, but you won't improve your sound without devoting proper attention and care to these two important items that occur last in the recording process. Ultimately, all that matters is the final result, and you must consider not only the arrangement and balance of all the parts that took you so long to mix, but the overall sound and its impact on the listener.

CHAPTER SIX

Multi-track Recording: Two, Four, Eight, and Beyond

Recording musicians distinguish between the multi-track machine and the mixdown machine not so much for the number of tracks or quality of recording, but for its function in the recording process. It makes no difference to the listener whether you record and play back on a multi-track machine or a two-track machine, all things being equal (power amp, speakers, environment). The decision to record to multi-track first, before going to two-track, is made because you usually plan to overdub, edit multiple takes together (as in a solo), punch (record onto the master track itself), or have another track synched to your main track (a timing track, a reference, or "scratch," track). The multi-track is then mixed to a two-track to permanently capture the mixdown you performed with the multi-track. Even if you plan to record only one track, a multi-track machine allows you to keep several versions of the same passage or to retain a safety track at all times. A safety track is useful in case you make a bad punch (which is permanent except on random-access systems that have an "undo" function).

MULTI-TRACK SYSTEMS
TWO-TRACKS VS. STEREO

Strictly speaking, a two-track machine could be considered a multi-track recorder if it allows you to record separate tracks at separate times. Though DATs and cassettes won't let you do this, computer systems and older open-reel (also called "reel-to-reel") machines will, qualifying them as the most basic of multi-tracks. In this configuration, you're limited to two tracks of mono, but sometimes that's all that's necessary. You could, for example, record a click, timing, or other reference track on one side and a series of fills and solos on the other that could eventually be bounced onto a larger machine. By mixing down your two mono tracks of click plus music onto a hard-panned stereo DAT, an engineer can synch up your fills to an already existing mix (assuming the engineer can align your click track). So don't ignore those older machines. Sometimes they come in handy, and you can pick them up for a song at garage sales.

FOUR-TRACK REEL AND CASSETTES

Once you get to four and above, the advantages of increased tracks are obvious.

Fig. 6.1

From the entry-level Fostex XR-3 (left) to the full-featured Yamaha MT8XII, cassette four-tracks are still some of the best multi-track deals going

Consider that for every instrument you want to put in stereo, two discrete tracks are required. Four tracks first appeared on open reel machines (such as the venerable TEAC 3340 and 3440 models) and to this day can be found on cassettes, MiniDiscs and hard-disk-based machines. Four tracks are considered the minimum for today's multi-track requirements, and you can go quite far with these machines. For example, designate one track as a "synch" track that drives a sequencer, which then plays all the MIDI instruments in your studio. This is known as "virtual tracking" because these instruments never get committed to the multi-track; they go "live" directly to the mixdown deck. Using the synch-track approach, a four-track can drive a whole studio's worth of MIDI instruments and still leave you three open tracks for vocals and guitar.

Four-track cassette recorders suffer not so much from the restricted number of tracks, but by their lack of sonic quality. Narrow tape width, the absence of constant tape tension in the transport, and slow speed yield less than professional results. But now MiniDisc and hard disk systems have all but superseded four-track cassettes in the quality department (but haven't killed them totally in the price, convenience or reliability arenas).

MINIDISC

Like cassette-based four-tracks, MiniDisc recorders offer compatibility among different manufacturers. The MiniDisc itself already exists as an independent medium, which helps stave off obsolescence. And MiniDisc machines offer random access editing, which means they act more like a computer-based recorder than a linear, tape-based one. With random access you can undo a bad punch, copy song sections from place to place (allowing you to sing a background chorus only once and place it in all four choruses of the song), and create playlists (instantaneous and seamless playback of various song segments from different disc locations).

Fig. 6.2

MiniDisc multi-track recorders retain the look and feel of their cassette counterparts, but offer the advantage of digital sound quality and editing power

EIGHT-TRACK SYSTEMS

Eight-track machines are where you first enter professional territory, with respect to hardware. Clever four-track users can get their tracks onto professional projects, but the pro world does not consider anything less than an eight-track appropriate for outfitting a commercial or project studio. The greatest variety of formats is available for the eight-track standard, so let's explore them.

Open-reel machines still exist, both in the old TEAC 38, 48, and Otari Mark III/8, as well as the new TASCAM TSR-8 and others. By far the most popular current eight-track format is the MDM, or modular digital multi-track, as exemplified by the Alesis ADAT and TASCAM DA-88. These are two of the "classic" MDMs, and both now have siblings to these well-known models. The ADAT works with S-VHS tape and the TASCAM works with Hi-8 tape, but both are tape based, and operate in the normal linear fashion recordists are accustomed to. Various stereotypes still circulate about the advantages and disadvantages of one over the other, but both offer high-quality digitally encoded sound in a video tape format. As with the "Mac vs. Windows" debate, subsequent upgrades narrow the gap between the feature sets of each system.

Fig. 6.3

The Alesis ADAT (top) and TASCAM DA-88 are two examples of the wildly popular multi-track digital-tape format known collectively as MDM, or modular digital multi-track

MODULAR DIGITAL MULTI-TRACKS

MDMs are decks only, meaning they don't provide any mixing capabilities (though they allow you to route signals from one input to another, which saves re-patching). If you use an MDM, you'll need an external mixer. MDMs are quite portable, being only 3 RU (rack units, each about 1¾") high, so several of them can easily fit in a rack case. Perhaps their biggest advantage is not small size but the fact that they can be synched together, up to 16 machines, for a potential total of 128 tracks. Most people use only two or three machines for 16 and 24 tracks, respectively. The "modular" in modular digital multi-track has three advantages then: portability, easy synchronization, and the ability to add or subtract machines as your needs demand.

Although MDMs are by far the most popular digital recording format, there are some disadvantages. Though they're quite portable, you still need a mixer to operate one, which cuts down somewhat on the ease of operation. And even though it's a digital recording process, an MDM is still tape based, which necessitates a linear approach to recording. Because tape is dragged across a head (and in the case of videotape, wrapped 270 degrees around a cylindrically shaped drum), many of the mechanical problems that plagued analog tape—head wear, crinkled or damaged tape, dropout, slow access—persist in the digital domain. Perhaps the biggest disadvantage in this digital age is the fact that MDMs don't operate by random access. You can't cut and paste tracks or musical sections, you can't reorder segments, and you can't access a song selection by typing in a location point (you must physically rewind or fast-forward the tape to that point).

WORKSTATION-BASED HARD DISK SYSTEMS

Stand-alone hard disk recorders are like MDMs except that they record to disk instead of tape. You still need a mixer to interface instruments with the recording mechanism, but you have random access operation and editing, which is a big plus

Fig. 6.4

Hard-disk recorders, like the Akai DR4d, resemble MDMs in size and modularity, but because they are disk-based, they have an advantage when it comes to digital editing

(see Fig. 6.4). The sound quality between hard disk recorders and MDMs can be equivalent, so it comes down to personal work routines and other ergonomic factors. Storage on hard disk recorders is always an issue, since digital audio is so memory intensive. If you record to hard disk instead of tape, you'll constantly be offloading data from the internal hard disk (where you must record) to external media, such as Jaz and Zip disks (except in some cases, where you can record directly to the removable medium). But stand-alone hard disk systems do offer fast and easy operation.

The self-contained workstation (sometimes referred to as "DAW," for digital audio workstation) includes a mixer as well as onboard disk-editing functions for true random-access operation. The Roland VS-880 (see Fig. 6.5) and Akai DPS12 are two examples of all-digital audio workstations, where the mixer and the audio recording mechanism operate in the digital domain. The Fostex DMT-8VL has an analog mixer and a digital recorder, and so is more like a conventional configuration of, say, a Mackie mixer and an ADAT (a very popular setup) except that it's self-contained.

COMPUTER-BASED HARD-DISK SYSTEMS

Computer-based systems are perhaps the most evolved of all the recording media because they combine hard-disk recording with a graphical interface (a color computer monitor) for editing and easy data viewing. If you work extensively with MIDI and audio data, you will find yourself on a computer and happy for it. If you don't use

Fig. 6.5

The Roland VS-880EX is an example of an all-digital self-contained recording workstation, featuring a digital mixer, built-in effects, and a hard-disk recorder. Optional software even lets you burn your own CD

MIDI, recording on a computer can present some hassles. Obviously, you must turn on a computer every time you record, and many people—especially guitarists—have a problem with this. It can seem as if the recording process is one step removed.

The more real consideration is that a computer is acoustically noisy, because of the cooling fan, so the unit must be isolated from any open mics. This can be a problem for one-room recordists who don't have a separate machine room or control booth. There's a nagging reliability problem too. When you record on a computer, there's always the tense moment after you press "stop," where you wait for your music to be written to disk. And since you are using a computer, you must become computer literate—upgrading RAM, seeking out the best removable storage deals, envying more powerful systems—a vocation many musicians resist out of principle if not practicality.

But all this grousing can be allowed because, like it or not, the future moves inexorably toward computer usage for musical activities. Guitarists may like to "slam" analog tape to yield a pleasing, compressed sound, but when you go to sequence your master CD, you'll appreciate the powers of a computer for assembly, gain normalization, imaging, and editing. Analog hold-outs will probably use the editing power of computers to tweak and edit individual tracks, and then reserve the final mastering stage for an analog medium.

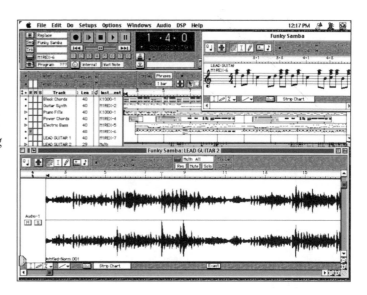

MIXING DOWN TO STEREO

After your tracks are all recorded, you'll need to mix them down to stereo. This creates a permanent record of your efforts and allows you to produce multiple copies for general distribution. Mixing takes years of experience to perfect, and many people treat it as a completely separate activity. Many will even hire a different engineer, use a separate facility, or both. Tracking, by contrast, follows a more logical and practical approach: Get a good sound, watch your levels, use a couple of tricks, and you're all set. But to mix those tracks, that's where craft leaves off and art begins. It is in your mixing technique where you'll establish your identity and exhibit your tastes in how music should sound—at least to you.

Fig. 6.6

A computer's processing power and graphical interface are ideal for digital editing of both MIDI and audio data

Always keep in mind who your target audience is, as it may affect the way you approach the mixdown. For example, if you're creating a demo to show off your guitar playing, you might want to consider mixing the guitar a little hotter than if you were mixing a songwriting demo. Historical context is another factor. If you're going for a retro sound, don't give the bass and drums the prominence they get in today's music. But try to keep the setting from sounding too artificial, no matter what the context. If you were showing off your ability to play in a classical guitar quartet, for example, it would be inappropriate to bring your guitar up so high that it overpowered the rest of the ensemble—especially if the music dictated even dynamics from the four guitars.

TWO-TRACK MASTERING: VARIOUS FORMATS

You can mix down to a wide variety of media formats: cassette, open reel, DAT, video tape, MiniDisc, CD, hard disk, or even two spare tracks on your multi-track. Most of the time, you'll mix your master to DAT, CD or hard disk, as these are high-quality digital formats that can then be transferred to another format, such as cassette or video

Fig. 6.7

Although DAT recorders never caught on with consumers, they reigned unchallenged in the professional arena as the mastering medium of choice until affordable CD recording came to the desktop. Pictured here are two models: the portable Sony PCM-M1 (top) and the standard-sized TASCAM DA-20MkII

tape without much "generation loss" (the inevitable signal degradation that comes when transferring from medium to medium). If you must create two master mixes—one that will be used for CDs and another for cassettes—you can opt to perform two separate mixdowns, which will produce two masters. This way each mix can better reflect the media for which it was intended. (Cassettes may require higher compression and a slight boost in the high frequencies, for example.) In general, though, the mixdown medium should not affect the way the music will ultimately sound, only the approach.

MASTERING TIPS
1. COMPRESSION ON MIXDOWN

Whether or not you've had to use it when tracking or as a specific inline guitar effect, most people employ some degree of compression for the mixdown. A good compressor (and good compression technique) helps to even out any errant level jumps that might peek through, and gives a mix a smoother, punchier sound. In this context, you will use a compressor as a studio processor, rather than as a guitar effect to produce sustain. Like plumbing, if it's done well, no one notices. It's only when it screws up that disaster occurs.

For compressing on mixdown, you'll want the best compressor money can buy (or rent). You can use mid-priced compressors to protect your tracks from distorting during tracking, but it really pays to employ a high-quality compressor during the mixdown stage for the most subtle and musical results. You typically put the compressor into the stereo L/R insert points, so that the entire signal gets routed to the compressor. You also must remember to select the "stereo link" option on the compressor, which ensures that both channels are attenuated even if there's a spike in one channel only. Failure to do this might cause an "imaging" problem, where one side attenuates when the other doesn't, and the listener perceives a shift in the stereo spectrum.

If you have two compressors at your disposal, use one as a limiter. Place the lower-quality one first and use it as the limiter. That way, the device is pressed into service only when there is a peak that could either result in distortion or tie up the higher-quality compressor with limiting duties, when it should really be used only to smooth out the mix. If your limiter is first in the chain, the second compressor never "sees" any spikes, and you can tailor its parameters for the more uniform signal coming its way.

2. SONIC ENHANCERS OR EXCITERS

If you're going to add a sonic enhancer (also called an exciter), the mixdown stage is a good place to try it, especially if you're going to cassette. While the use of enhancers can sometimes make a mix sound "candy coated," they're very effective over short listening periods in less than optimal audio conditions. So if you know your three-minute demo is going to be listened to over a car-stereo cassette with probably dirty heads (who cleans these regularly?) cruising down a highway at 65 mph (increasing the ambient noise in the listening environment), you may want to employ the enhancer.

A good check to perform is to "sum" your mix to mono to see if this significantly hurts it. To do this, take your left and right bus, pan them up the middle and listen to the results over headphones. Go back and forth between summed mono and panned stereo to hear where you're losing strength. If it's drastic—and you're not sure how your tape will be heard—you may want to adjust your mix to better resolve the disparity between stereo and mono. Practice this technique over a single monitor speaker too. The wider things are panned, the more they will cancel out when summed. One trick is to pan everything center and place only the effects in stereo. This way, a mono mix sounds the same as the stereo, except that the effects are slightly compromised. The theory is that if it's played on a mono system, chances are the surrounding environment isn't conducive to discerning the stereo effects anyway.

MIXING FOR MULTIMEDIA AND THE INTERNET

In most situations you want to mix down to the best medium possible—usually DAT or CD, though sometimes 1" or 2" analog tape is desired. In the twin arenas of multimedia and the Internet, though, fidelity is readily swapped for the more precious commodities of storage space and bandwidth. And so mixing to these two digital formats requires a "dumbing down" of the signal, audio-wise. Though it's an ever-improving situation (due to better compression schemes and real-time broadcasting), the fact remains that CD-quality digital audio files are simply too big and cumbersome to be transferred, broadcast, and processed effectively by today's computer technology.

Multimedia is a fast-growing field that needs music as much as it needs video, text, and still images. But in order to process all those media simultaneously, it's usually the music that's asked to compromise. Like it or not, we live in a more visual-critical world than an audio-critical one. The ear will forgive—and can even be tricked by—schemes that would never be accepted by the eye.

And so, if you know the end result for your music is a CD-ROM or the Internet, check your mixes by reducing them to digital form, with a 22 or 11 kHz sampling rate, 16- or 8-bit resolution (depending on the limitations of the technology you're working with), and a mono format. Then work backwards—by creating a mix and listening to the results in a reduced-quality format—to determine the best approach to dynamic range, EQ, and effects applications.

The Internet shares many of the same limitations as multimedia. People hearing your music will also be dealing with the digital domain and multimedia playback equipment, which is less than ideal, compared to the reasonably equipped home studio. But the whole idea of the Internet—at least as far as music is concerned—is more about expedience than quality. The purpose is to disseminate information as quickly and as easily and as widely as possible.

An example of this is putting your demo on your web site. You want to make it as easy and painless as possible for surfers to hear your music. To do this, you must make the sound files small, so that they'll download in a short amount of time. A file with an 11 kHz sample rate is half the size of the same file with a 22 kHz rate, and one fourth the size of a file at the full resolution of 44.1 kHz.

At left is a chart that shows the relative disk space a one-minute sound file occupies.

Bit Depth	Sample Rate	Mode	Mb/minute
16	44	stereo	10
16	44	mono	5
16	22	stereo	5
16	22	mono	2.5
16	11	stereo	2.5
16	11	mono	1.2
8	22	mono	1.2
8	11	mono	0.67

As you can see, it's fairly straightforward: reduce the sampling rate by half, and your storage requirements drop by the same proportion. The same is true for stereo vs. mono. A mono file is always one half the size of a similarly formatted stereo file.

Two observations. If you're trying to save space, the first thing you should do is dispense with stereo mode and go with mono. Right there you save 50 percent of your storage requirements, and once you go below the CD standard of 16 bits/44.1 sampling, you're probably in demo mode rather than audiophile mode. The other point to remember is that bit depth is more important than sample rate, so all things being equal, go with higher bit depth and lower sample rate rather than vice versa. In other words, lines 6 and 7 in the chart both require 1.2 megabytes for one minute of audio. But 16 bits at 11 kHz yields a better sound than 8 bits at 22 kHz. In general, the best quality to file-size ratio boils down to these two formats:

Bit Depth	Sample Rate	Mode	Mb/minute
16	22	mono	2.5
16	11	mono	1.2

OTHER MASTERING CONSIDERATIONS

True mastering is not simply the mixdown stage, but what happens when you take your final mix to mastering session, run by a mastering engineer. Here, your mix will be put on display, up for ridicule (or so it will seem), and under a microscope. A mastering session is a very sobering experience, because a good mastering engineer will point out weaknesses in the mix, and provide you with solutions (via an A/B demonstration). Typical problems include stereo imaging, EQ and levels.

Gain normalizing is one of the most difficult aspects to control especially over several pieces of music all recorded at different times, using different machines, and with varying orchestrations. A mastering session will look at the loudest and softest signals in each song, compare them to each other, and then "normalize" them, so that there is a dynamic consistency among songs as well as within songs.

Additionally, some songs may just seem louder or softer than others, even after normalizing, and you might want to change the overall level of a song, beyond the smoothing of peaks. The mastering session is the place for those adjustments as well.

Sequencing is how you put your work together and includes fade-out times and the time between songs. Generally, you'll want a shorter time span between songs if the previous song ends in a cut-off (2–3 seconds is a good range). Songs that fade out are better suited to longer pauses (3–5 seconds). If you're recording on a hard disk, you can often do your own sequencing and transitions, but the mastering session is traditionally where these types of decisions are made. If you record using a CD burner and software, you can specify the time in between songs, perform cross-fades, and even give a song a "pre-roll," where the numbers count down (e.g., *-3, -2, -1*) before a song plays.

CHAPTER SEVEN

Computers in the recording Studio

The computer has become an almost indispensable tool for modern life, especially for people involved in any kind of technological endeavor. If you're a writer, a computer improves upon the typewriter by allowing you to cut, paste and re-work your prose in flexible ways (to say nothing of the improved printing capabilities). If you're a graphic artist, a computer lets you draw straight lines and create geometric shapes with just a few keystrokes, vastly cutting down the time it takes to automate these simple but time-consuming tasks. The advantage for musicians is the same as it is for graphic artists: processing speed and the ability to use the screen for visual feedback and editing chores (see Fig. 7.1).

Guitarists can exploit the powers of the computer the same way that any other creative person does—by having it handle routine but essential aspects of music-making. A computer can't do your creative work for you, but it can sure make getting your inspiration to tape a lot easier.

There are three principal ways musicians use computers: hard-disk recording, MIDI and engraving (also called scoring or notating). Though there's overlap between all three, recording guitarists need to be familiar with the first two. We'll start with hard-disk recording for the computer, because, conceptually, it's most easily understood.

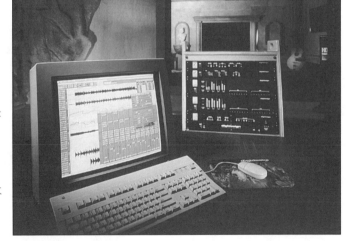

Used in its simplest capacity, a computer can substitute for a tape recorder. Plug your mixer outputs, or any similarly prepared signal (from, say, the outputs of a preamp or guitar effects processor) into the jacks sticking out of the back of your computer. Use the screen for all your transport controls (record, stop, play, rewind, fast-forward). Plug the outputs from the computer back into your mixer, and listen to your results over headphones or studio monitors. No surprises there, but as we'll see, there are many more functions that make a computer superior to a standard tape recorder.

Fig. 7.1

A computer's large screen and ability to automate routine tasks make it an important recording tool

HARDWARE

If you're going to use a computer to record, the first thing you have to consider is what kind of computer you need. As long as the audio standard remains stable at the CD standard of 16-bit resolution with a 44.1 sampling rate, computer prices will continue to come down as systems get more powerful. A 266 mHz Pentium or PowerPC with 64 megs of RAM and a 2-gig hard drive is sufficient for just about any audio project involving eight tracks or less, especially if you plan to record those eight tracks two at a time (the overdub approach).

Depending on the system you choose, you may not have to do anything else to your computer. Virtually all computers today come with sound-recording capabilities, either through a "bundled" (included for the system's purchase price) soundcard and software, or in the case of the Macintosh, built in (the jacks are built right into the back of the computer itself, instead of on the soundcard). Third-party software will typically work on any system, so you don't necessarily have to use the software that came with your hardware.

The separation of hardware and software for the computer makes it easier to deal with computer recording. The hardware will determine the limits of your recording—how many simultaneous tracks you can record, whether you can import a digital signal—and software gives you the choice of different interfaces and file formats.

Often there are several packages that will have more than enough power to suit your needs. Which one is right for you might depend on aspects other than sheer power. If you're going to be swapping files with a partner or client, you might choose to get on his or her system. Another consideration might be the upgrade path. Many pro-level packages offer lower-end programs that will satisfy your current needs and get you familiar with their interface design, so that when you upgrade, you're well through the learning curve. Finally you just may prefer the look and feel of one product over another. If you're self-contained—that is, you're not concerned with file interchange or inter-platform compatibility (i.e., making sure your file will play on different programs and computers), make look and feel and personal preference your top criteria.

Systems

All multimedia computers have sound-recording capabilities. If your computer has a CD-ROM drive, you can get software that "captures" digital audio right off the CD inside the drive—which is pretty convenient. Though inexpensive soundcards and the Mac's built-in recording won't rival more expensive systems, you can appreciate many of the benefits of computer-based digital recording without ever buying any additional hardware or software. After getting your feet wet with your computer's onboard or included lower-end card, it's time to consider more professional solutions.

SOUNDCARDS

Typical entry-level cards have a stereo input and output, supplied by two 1/8" or 1/4" jacks, or four RCA plugs of left and right in and left and right out. These plug right into slots in the back of your computer, and are designed to be installed by the user. Better cards will have, in addition, two digital RCA—called coaxial, or "coax" (pronounced "CO-ax") in digital parlance—jacks, one for stereo input and one for stereo output. These allow you to import digital audio (say, from a DAT machine) without ever entering into the analog domain, thus saving a generation of degradation. Every time you convert or run through the analog domain, you suffer a generation loss. You pick up noise, and fidelity is reduced somewhat. But keeping things in the digital domain avoids all this, so a card with digital I/O is very desirable.

With digital I/O (pronounced "eye-oh"), you can take your DAT's digital output and go into the digital computer (through its digital input), perform any adjustments, and "fly" (a straight transfer with no processing involved) the results back to an unused section of DAT tape (you'll want to keep the original section in case you screw up) via the computer's digital out and the DAT's digital in. Unlike analog channels, one signal carries both the left and right data, so on a stereo card (and DAT) you need only one out and one in.

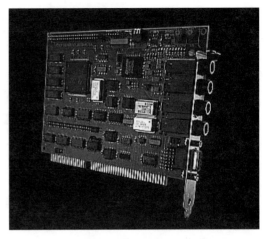

Fig 7.2

A soundcard installs easily into the back of your computer. The jacks remain exposed, allowing you to plug in your audio equipment

INTEGRATED SYSTEMS

As you get into more sophisticated systems an additional hardware interface may be required in the form of a rackmount unit that handles audio I/O duties. Out of the rackmount unit will come a special cable that carries all your multi-track signals to the computer via an installed PCI card. Other systems, such as Event Electronics' Layla and Emagic's Audiowerk8, come with a special multi-in/multi-out card and software packages that utilize the card's special configurations. These cards can also work with standard software programs as well, such as Cubase VST, Cakewalk, Digital Performer, Studio Vision Pro, etc. Korg makes the 1212 I/O and Yamaha makes the DSP Factory, both of which can be accessed by a growing number of software supporters. Ensoniq includes in its PARIS package control surface hardware, making it a truly integrated system that includes software, audio interface hardware and a control surface so you don't have to resort to mouse movements to mix. Pro Tools is the leading computer-based hard-disk audio recorder, and it offers an optional control surface as well, or you can

Fig. 7.3

Some computer systems require hardware in addition to a soundcard. Digidesign's Pro Tools comes with software, rackmount interfaces for audio connections and a computer soundcard

use a third-party device, such as Mackie's HUI (human user interface). Keep in mind you can control any software program's MIDI function through a MIDI controller or a mixer that sends MIDI controller data (see "Real-time Parameter Control" under "MIDI Applications").

SOFTWARE RECORDERS
DIGITAL AUDIO/MIDI SEQUENCERS

Most software recorders can function over a variety of hardware interfaces. Some of the standard "big guns" of MIDI-sequencing/audio-recording software include Cakewalk Pro Audio, Digidesign Session and Pro Tools, Emagic Logic Audio, Mark of the Unicorn Digital Performer, and Opcode Studio Vision Pro. The audio-only category (with limited or no MIDI support) includes BIAS' Peak, Digidesign's Pro Tools, Sonic Foundry's Sound Forge, and Syntrillium's Cool Edit Pro. All of these give you increased features, depending on your specific hardware configuration.

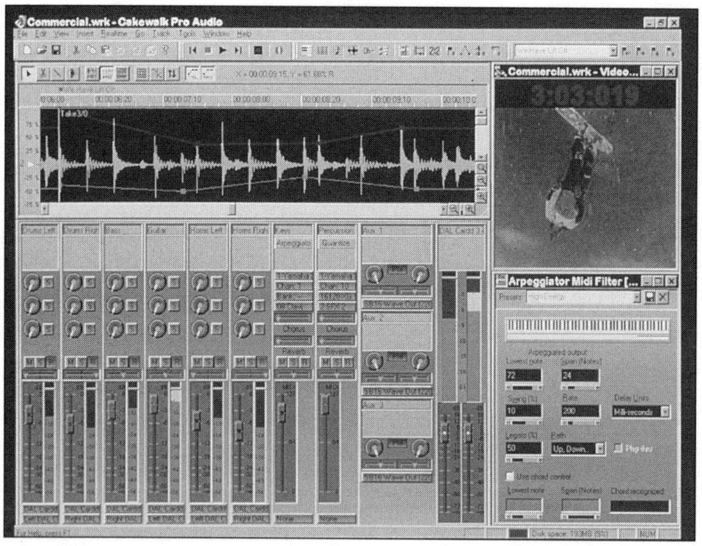

Most software recorders offer MIDI integration, which means you can combine MIDI sequencing and audio recording on the same screen. Even if you don't drive any modules with MIDI (like drum machines, samplers and synthesizers), having a MIDI timing reference can be valuable, especially if you require any exact-timing or synching requirements (see Chapter 10, "Scoring To Video").

Computer-based recording not only allows you to cut, copy, and paste data (creating different arrangements of the same song, for example), it provides you with a means for changing the sound itself. You can do this two ways: with a wave-form editor, and with effects. A wave-form editor allows you to actually shape the sound. You view the sound graphically and with a mouse, pencil icon, or other tool, actually go in and manipulate the shape of the sound itself (both in the visual and audio sense—you're changing the wave-form's shape on the screen, which in turn makes it sound different when played back).

Fig. 7.4

Wave-form editing on Cakewalk's Pro Audio. Note the QuickTime window. Because they can import movies, audio/MIDI sequencer programs are powerful tools for scoring

Typical operations include cutting out unwanted artifacts (such as vocalists' pre-entrance breaths and lip smacks, and guitarists' string noise and pickup buzz before or after their solo), reducing level spikes, and correcting pitch. Effects work in the same way your analog-based ones do: They put the original signal through EQ, reverb, delay, chorusing, pitch shifting, etc. Here it's done digitally, though, so it becomes a permanent part of the wave form after you've finished. Because of this, it's best to use wave form editing for corrective measures, like tuning an off-pitch note, deleting a vocal artifact, or normalizing volume peaks.

While many people prefer the sound of their outboard, analog-based effects for things like reverb and EQ, there's no denying that computer-based wave-form editors have their place, and they're improving all the time.

HARD-DISK MASTERING: ASSEMBLY, SEQUENCING, PROCESSING, NORMALIZATION, DAT MASTERING IN THE DIGITAL DOMAIN

The advantages of computer-based recording are most apparent in the mastering stage. After you've recorded your music on a multi-track, mixed down to the medium of your choice, and are ready to master, few can argue with the advantages of a well-outfitted computer. Since they work graphically, many people like to perform mastering-type operations like sequencing, level matching, and corrective EQ on a computer. For example, let's say you wanted a slow, even, 20-second fade-out at the end of a song. That would be very hard to do manually—with your fingers trying to pull down the faders at an even rate over 20 seconds. But with a computer, you just "zoom out" to make the last 20 seconds of your music visible on the screen, take a pencil icon and draw a 45 degree line from top-left to bottom-right, and voilà—you have a smooth, linear fade. Don't like the results? Choose Undo from the edit menu and try another approach.

It is quite common to use the computer only in the last step of recording—just to apply mastering-type touches to your project. After you mix down to DAT or CD from your multi-track, you can fly your mixdown into the computer within the digital domain, perform large- and small-scale adjustments that benefit from the computer's graphic interface, and then fly your work back to DAT or CD, also in the digital domain. This contribution alone is worth the price of the computer—especially if you can find other uses for it in your life.

MIDI APPLICATIONS
PROGRAM CHANGE

MIDI is another area where guitarists can enjoy the benefits of computer power. In addition to creating sequences (in the form of drum parts, rhythm accompaniments, etc.) from a MIDI-pickup-equipped guitar, MIDI can be used to change presets on your multi-effects processor faster than you could perform them by hand (or foot). Many guitar amps also feature channel switching that can be executed through a MIDI command, which is great if you're recording live while playing along to a MIDI track.

REAL-TIME PARAMETER CONTROL

Real-time parameter changes can be effected through MIDI too, such as varying the pulse of a tremolo in exact synch with the tempo. If you perform with a MIDI foot controller—such as a digitally based wah or volume—you can capture those movements by recording the MIDI data as well as the audio result of your "foot performance."

MIDI can also be used in mixing. A digital mixer (such the Mackie Digital 8•Bus, TASCAM TM-D4000, TM-D1000, or Yamaha 02/R, 03/D, 01v) sends MIDI data out from the faders as well as internal volume control. By using your mixer's faders to control your sequencer's software faders, you work in a much more intuitive environment than when using a mouse. Plus, your fader movements will be smoother using a hardware controller rather than a mouse and a screen fader. On the playback side, digital mixers will accept MIDI volume change, and automated mixers will even move the faders along to the sequencer's fader moves!

Even if you don't have a digital mixer, you can use a MIDI-controllable fader to control your software. If you patch the MIDI fader into the insert points of your analog mixer, you can enjoy the benefits of automated volume control for a fraction of the price of a digital mixer. This is especially important to know for guitarists, because guitar signals tend to be very noisy, and fader and mute automation is a much easier solution than introducing (and endlessly tweaking!) noise gates into the guitar's signal chain itself.

DATA DUMPS AND ARCHIVING

Any "data dumps" (saving of setups and parameters) that you want to execute (such as programs you've created on your multi-effects processor) can be sent over MIDI to an editor/librarian program for permanent storage and further editing. Many studio processors have MIDI jacks built in, and though you may not use them much, it's good to know they're there. If you have a lot of custom programs on your reverb or multi-effects unit, you should back them up via MIDI into a librarian. That way if your machine gets "zapped" (incurs a voltage spike which erases or corrupts the data), you can always get your programs back via the computer.

MIDI guitars are even capable of saving and loading such data as sensitivity, MIDI channel, and pitch bend settings. This is handy if you want to switch your guitar from a soft touch to a more percussive setup, or have all six strings sent to separate MIDI channels (such as when you're working in the tablature window of a scoring program) instead of one or two.

MIDI MACHINE CONTROL

MIDI is useful for putting all your machines under a central controlling interface, using a system called MMC (MIDI machine control). Here, you can operate, say, your ADAT's transport controls (play, stop, rewind, etc.) with a virtual transport on the computer screen. The advantage of this is that it's visual. You can't tell by looking at the numeric display on your ADAT where the third chorus begins, but you can with a computer's track window (assuming you've put in markers). Of course, any sequences synched to the ADAT will play back too (actually, it's the ADAT that's synched to the sequence, a term known as "chase lock," meaning the ADAT will "chase" and lock on to the computer-generated MIDI sequence). A computer window will allow you to toggle back and forth between real time (hours, minutes, seconds, frames) and musical time (bars, beats), which is handy during a scoring session.

SMPTE

SMPTE is an acronym that stands for Society of Motion Picture and Television Engineers, but is commonly used to mean the timing standard established by that group. SMPTE works in hours, minutes, seconds, and frames (which are grouped in several schemes, from 24 per second to 30 per second). When working in absolute time, like the length of a film and its component scenes, it's easier to use real-time increments, as SMPTE does. But in musical time, it's easier to use tempo (beats per minute), meter and rhythms. You can convert musical time to real time, but it's cumbersome to do so by hand, so a computer usually does it for you. If you're working with a video that has a master timing reference "burned" (recorded onto one of its audio tracks) to it, you take that audio signal and use it to "slave" your computer to it. Your computer converts the SMPTE to MTC (MIDI Time Code) to allow you to think in more musical terms. Even if you never sequence a note, you will need to use a SMPTE-to-MTC converter (usually in the form of a sequencer) to find your way around a scoring project. For more on scoring and SMPTE, see Chapter 10, "Scoring To Video."

AUTOMATION

In addition to your processors (reverb, delay, multi-effects) responding to MIDI commands, many mixers allow some time of MIDI integration too, such as channel mute and MIDI volume. So using a MIDI sequencer and MMC can access functions on your mixer that aren't normally available to you. Having MIDI mute unused channels—instead of manually muting them yourself—and control volume faders is a big help in keeping your audio path clean and automating an important operation.

The advantage of using a computer system is unchallenged power and ease of use. The disadvantage is that you have to have your computer on all the time to record. Computers are noisy and must be isolated from open mics. They need to be maintained and upgraded regularly. You must back up religiously, and offloading and archiving data is an added burden. Some people don't necessarily want to make the computer the central focus of a recording session, and that is why self-contained workstations and MDMs are still popular. But you cannot beat a computer for flexibility, and for some situations—like film and video scoring, or MIDI-dependent projects—a computer is the only way to go.

PART TWO:
APPLICATIONS FOR
THE RECORDING
GUITARIST

CHAPTER EIGHT

Dial A Sound

How to re-create 14 classic setups of the guitar gods

As guitarists, we're constantly seeking our own sound, our own unique voice. But the rest of the world often seems more comfortable with pigeon-holing us into a sound or style that they already know and can call for by name. That's why producers often resort to giving instructions like "Give me a raunchy, blues sound, a la Billy Gibbons," rather than "Give me something wholly original and that I've never imagined before."

It's not that producers are unimaginative or that they deliberately want to ape another guitarist's sound; it's just that categorizing sounds saves a lot of time and gets you to a point of departure. Often you'll hear of producers requesting that a guitarist get an "early Van Halen sound," or a "Hendrix rhythm sound a la 'Little Wing,'" or a "Dimebag Darrell over-the-top-tweazed-out-solid-state-distortion" sound. These are perfectly legitimate requests, and will come as often as the ones involving instruments and amps—as in, "Give me that Les Paul through a Marshall, will ya?"

With that in mind, I've selected 14 well-known guitarists, from slide master Sonny Landreth to neo-classical god Yngwie Malmsteen, and presented their rigs and how they use them. Keep in mind that the following setups are only guides to one guitarist's particular sound. They are by no means the only sound that particular guitarist produces, but it is one he has used for a significant portion of his recorded work, and one we associate with being his "classic" sound.

Dimebag Darrell

Heavy metal poster boy Dimebag Darrell doesn't make any apologies for his tweazed-out solid-state distortion sound. Like Hendrix, Darrell goes first into a wah pedal (either the Dunlop or the DigiTech are on, but not at the same time), and then into another pitch shifter (the PS-3) before hitting the gain-shaping distortion box, the Boss DS-2. After going into an MXR pedal-based graphic EQ (set in a "V" shape, as all good metal guitarists do), Darrell passes his signal through a rack containing a parametric EQ (for any final tone shaping before the amp stage), an MXR Flanger/Doubler (his only time-based effect), and then through the Rocktron Guitar Silencer as his noise gate. The gain on Darrell's amp is rarely set to anything but 10, and the presence and bass are goosed while the treble and mids are cut, to keep the sound from becoming too brittle.

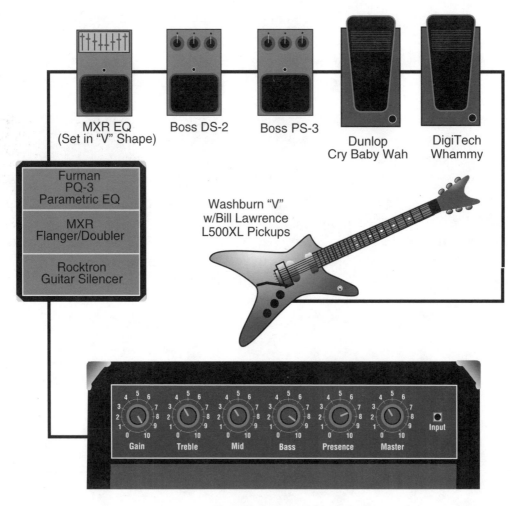

Randall Century 200

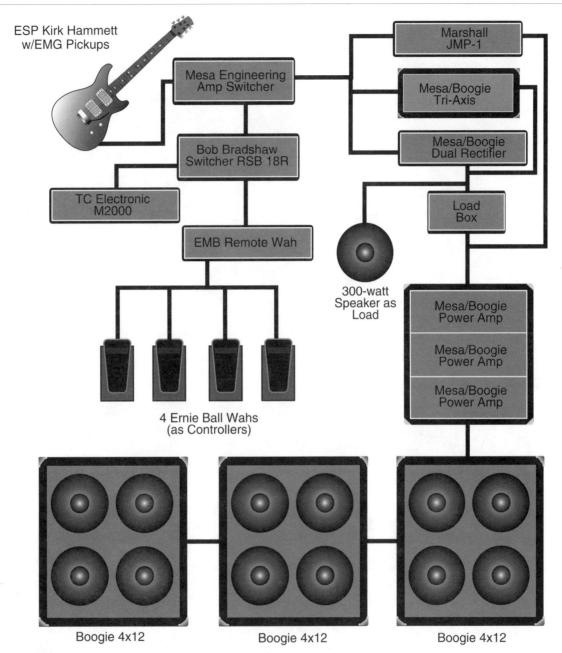

ESP Kirk Hammett w/EMG Pickups

Mesa Engineering Amp Switcher

Marshall JMP-1

Mesa/Boogie Tri-Axis

Mesa/Boogie Dual Rectifier

Bob Bradshaw Switcher RSB 18R

TC Electronic M2000

Load Box

EMB Remote Wah

300-watt Speaker as Load

Mesa/Boogie Power Amp

Mesa/Boogie Power Amp

Mesa/Boogie Power Amp

4 Ernie Ball Wahs (as Controllers)

Boogie 4x12   Boogie 4x12   Boogie 4x12

Kirk Hammett

The unique setup of Kirk Hammett's wah pedals are the result of Metallica's performing logistics. The band usually sets up different "performing stations" when they play, and at various times during the concert, they simply rotate around to the next area. But this presents a problem when you have to have access to your effects at all the various locations. So Hammett devised a rig where the wah pedals act as mere controllers (allowing for longer, low-impedance lines to run between them), while the brains of the wah sit in the rack offstage. Hammett uses two preamps, the Marshall JMP-1 and the Mesa/Boogie Tri-Axis. These feed Mesa power amps which drive three Boogie 4x12 cabinets.

Hammett also uses a Mesa Dual rectifier, but instead of relying on one head to drive three cabs (or employing three amp heads), he will load down the speaker out with a 300-watt speaker (which is buried offstage somewhere) while a load box takes the line-level signal and delivers that to the three power amps. This has the effect of normalizing the amp output with the preamps' output and gives a relatively consistent signal among all three tone-shaping devices.

Jimi Hendrix (then and now)

Jimi Hendrix's tone is possibly the most emulated of all time, so many manufacturers have devoted considerable resources to re-creating the gear that helped shape Hendrix's tone, but is no longer available (or is too rare and expensive to come by easily).

First, a look at Hendrix's original setup. Hendrix went first into a Crybaby or Vox wah and then into a fuzz. He used primarily two, an Axis Fuzz and the Roger Mayer–designed Fuzz-Face. From there he went into a Uni-Vibe and Mayer Octavia, before going into a 6550-equipped Marshall.

For the modern Hendrix sound, the Dunlop Crybaby is the wah of choice, and then distortion units by Fulltone (Fuzz) or Prescription Electronics (Experience Fuzz) are considered *de rigueur*. Fulltone makes the Deja'Vibe that closely emulates the original for a fraction of the price. For that square-wave octave sound, the Boss OC-2 does a nice job.

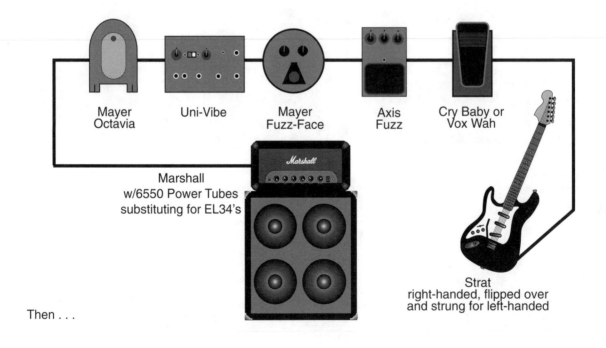

Mayer Octavia   Uni-Vibe   Mayer Fuzz-Face   Axis Fuzz   Cry Baby or Vox Wah

Marshall w/6550 Power Tubes substituting for EL34's

Strat right-handed, flipped over and strung for left-handed

Then . . .

. . Now

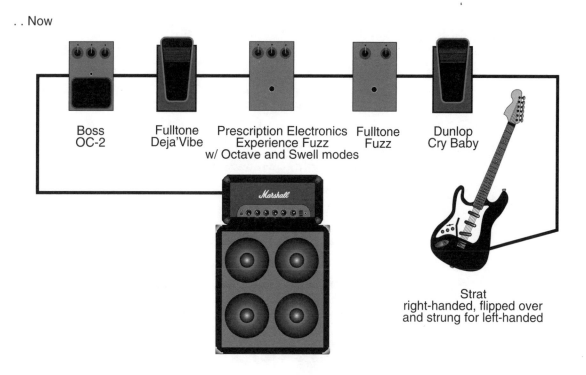

Boss
OC-2

Fulltone
Deja'Vibe

Prescription Electronics
Experience Fuzz
w/ Octave and Swell modes

Fulltone
Fuzz

Dunlop
Cry Baby

Strat
right-handed, flipped over
and strung for left-handed

Much has been made of the fact that Jimi played a right-handed guitar flipped upside down and strung left-handed. This means that as a left-hander himself, Jimi played the guitar conventionally, but there were several key differences in the imposition of his instrument. 1) The string tensions were all different, because Strats normally have the first string as the longest. By reversing the strings on the Strats inline tuner configuration, the sixth string became the longest and the increased tension on the thickest string changed the resonant properties of the guitar significantly. 2) The pickups were angled the "wrong" way, with the bridge pickup slanted toward the neck instead of the bridge. This placed the first-string pole-piece well up from the bridge instead of right next to it, as on a normally strung guitar. (The pole-piece heights were all different as well.) 3) The bar and the controls were above the right hand. While this may not affect the guitar's tone per se, it affects the way a performer approaches the instruments, and we know from listening to Hendrix's music, this was perhaps the most influential element on his tone of all.

Allan Holdsworth

"I don't like distortion so much as I like sustain," Holdsworth has said, and his setup shows that he is more after an organic sound than an artificially induced fuzz effect. Holdsworth runs straight into the amp (a Mesa Dual Rectifier) and accesses all his time-based effects from the amp's loop. The effects Allan uses offer great flexibility in terms of LFO routing and processing power. After the signal comes back into the amp via the return, it's outputted to a load box of Allan's own invention, called "The Harness." In addition to stepping down the speaker signal to a line level, Allan's added some magic of his own with filters and EQ circuitry. The line-level signal then goes to a Carvin power amp and is outputted to two 2x12 Boogie cabs.

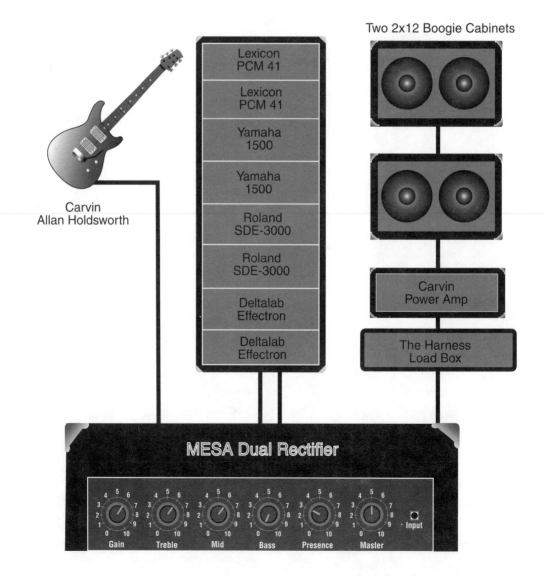

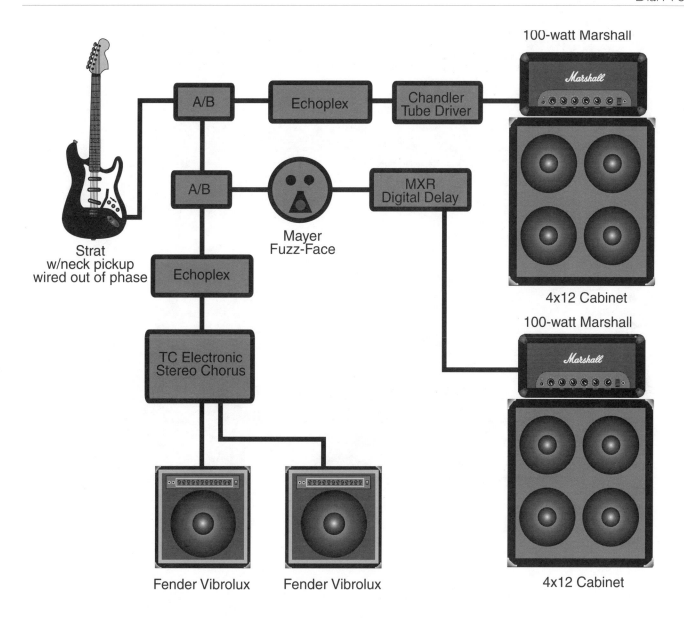

100-watt Marshall

A/B

Echoplex

Chandler
Tube Driver

A/B

Mayer
Fuzz-Face

MXR
Digital Delay

Strat
w/neck pickup
wired out of phase

Echoplex

4x12 Cabinet

100-watt Marshall

TC Electronic
Stereo Chorus

Fender Vibrolux

Fender Vibrolux

4x12 Cabinet

Eric Johnson

Eric Johnson is a tone purist and therefore runs a fairly straightforward setup. He gets almost all of his tone from the amp, invoking a Chandler Tube Driver judiciously and mostly for increased sustain rather than distortion. Johnson employs two A/B boxes, which gives him a choice of three separate audio paths to choose from. The first path goes to a tape-driven Echoplex and then into the Chandler Tube Driver and into a 100-watt Marshall head and cab. The second path goes to a Mayer Fuzz-Face and then to an MXR Digital Delay before also going to a 100-watt Marshall head and cab. The third path begins with an Echoplex (like path #1), but is then split by a TC Electronic Stereo Chorus (mono in/stereo out) and output to two Fender Vibrolux amps.

John Jorgenson

Most country guys—even ones with the sound-shaping chops and impressive producing credits of John Jorgenson—still prefer to adopt an all-pedal setup. Since you can't have presets on a Tube Screamer, Jorgenson keeps two of them (a vintage TS-808 and a TS-5) inline, each set for a different function. The time-based effects follow as you would expect: chorus, delay, and reverb. John uses an outboard digital reverb (albeit in pedal form) because the Matchless amps he uses don't usually sport a separate reverb.

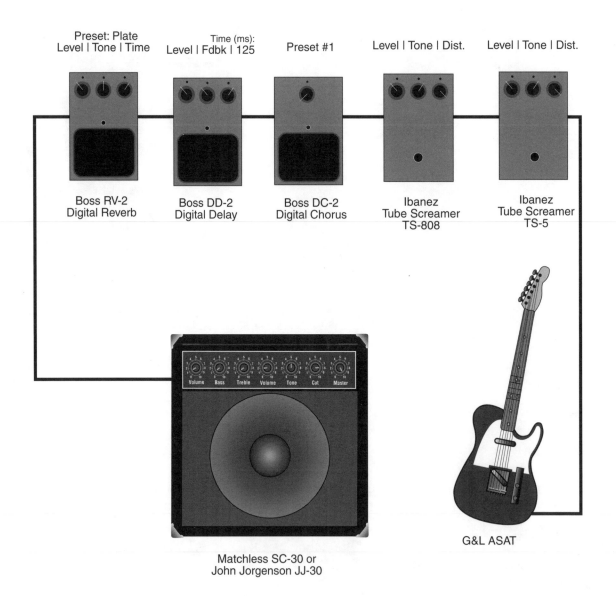

Preset: Plate
Level | Tone | Time

Time (ms):
Level | Fdbk | 125

Preset #1

Level | Tone | Dist.

Level | Tone | Dist.

Boss RV-2
Digital Reverb

Boss DD-2
Digital Delay

Boss DC-2
Digital Chorus

Ibanez
Tube Screamer
TS-808

Ibanez
Tube Screamer
TS-5

Matchless SC-30 or
John Jorgenson JJ-30

G&L ASAT

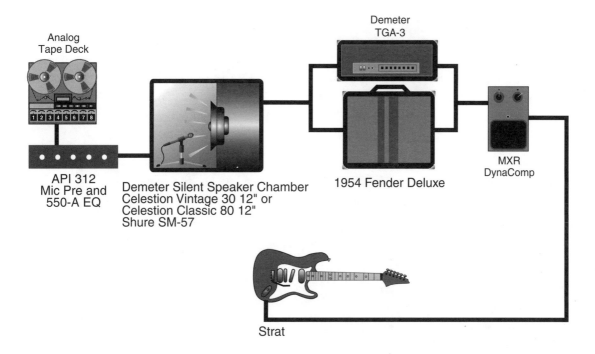

Analog
Tape Deck

Demeter
TGA-3

API 312
Mic Pre and
550-A EQ

Demeter Silent Speaker Chamber
Celestion Vintage 30 12" or
Celestion Classic 80 12"
Shure SM-57

1954 Fender Deluxe

MXR
DynaComp

Strat

Sonny Landreth

Slide guitarist Sonny Landreth has one of the most unique sounds working, partly because he employs an actual miked speaker in his setup. He uses an isolated speaker with an enclosed mic and often employs an honest-to-goodness Leslie cabinet (no simulators in this man's rig!). A healthy overdrive and a mature and evolved vibrato technique round out this singular slide artist's setup.

Known for his monstrous slide chops and widely varied repertoire, Landreth is also a purist when it comes to sound. He goes through an old red MXR DynaComp to get a smooth sustained sound, and then into either a Demeter TGA-3 or a 1954 Fender Deluxe amp. From there, things get interesting. The speaker out goes to a Demeter Silent Speaker Chamber, which is an iso-cab housing a Celestion Vintage 30 or Classic 80 speaker and a mic. The mic is either an SM-57 or a custom-specified mic supplied by Demeter. From there the signal gets treated to an API mic pre with EQ and delivered straight to analog tape.

Yngwie Malmsteen

Much of Malmsteen's expressive phrasing technique can be attributed to his scalloped-fretboard Strat, where he can control vibrato to a great degree because of the increased distance between the string and the fretboard that the scallop creates. By pushing down on the string as well as pulling it from side to side, Malmsteen creates some of the most expressive notes around—especially when he employs near-infinite sustain. That sustain is created by two maxed-out 50-watt Marshall heads, one outputting a dry sound, the other outputting the effected sound. Note that one amp feeds a cabinet wired at 16 ohms, while the other feeds two 8-ohm cabs in series, so that the speaker output is equivalent. Malmsteen is one of the only guitarists to use a sonic enhancer (a BBE Sonic Maximizer) in creating his sound, which he credits to giving a little more sizzle and definition to the top end.

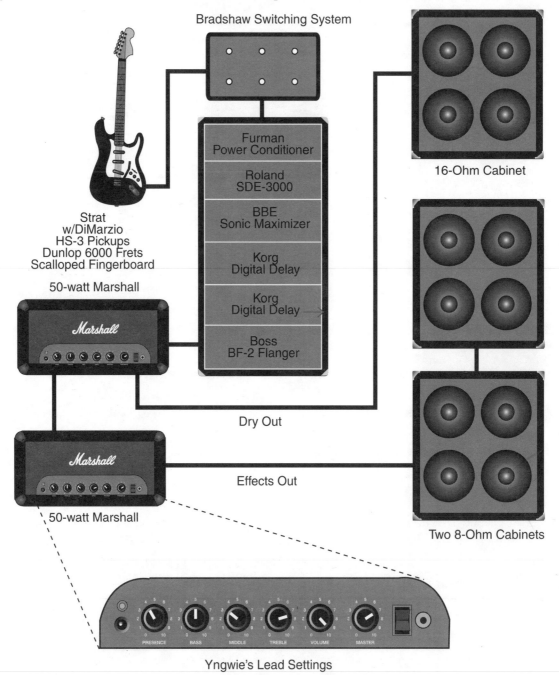

Bradshaw Switching System

Strat
w/DiMarzio
HS-3 Pickups
Dunlop 6000 Frets
Scalloped Fingerboard

50-watt Marshall

Furman
Power Conditioner

Roland
SDE-3000

BBE
Sonic Maximizer

Korg
Digital Delay

Korg
Digital Delay

Boss
BF-2 Flanger

16-Ohm Cabinet

Dry Out

Effects Out

50-watt Marshall

Two 8-Ohm Cabinets

Yngwie's Lead Settings

PRESENCE   BASS   MIDDLE   TREBLE   VOLUME   MASTER

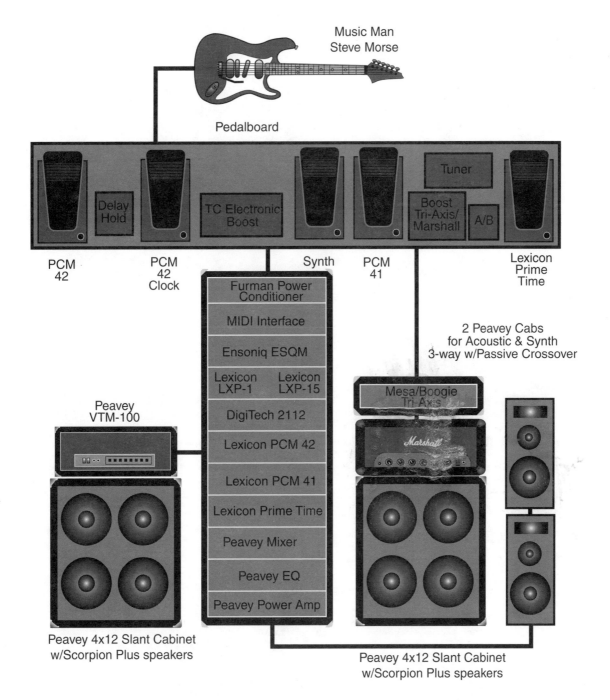

Music Man
Steve Morse

Pedalboard

Delay Hold

TC Electronic Boost

Tuner

Boost Tri-Axis/ Marshall

A/B

PCM 42

PCM 42 Clock

Synth

PCM 41

Lexicon Prime Time

Furman Power Conditioner

MIDI Interface

Ensoniq ESQM

Lexicon LXP-1   Lexicon LXP-15

DigiTech 2112

Lexicon PCM 42

Lexicon PCM 41

Lexicon Prime Time

Peavey Mixer

Peavey EQ

Peavey Power Amp

Peavey VTM-100

2 Peavey Cabs
for Acoustic & Synth
3-way w/Passive Crossover

Mesa/Boogie Tri-Axis

Marshall

Peavey 4x12 Slant Cabinet
w/Scorpion Plus speakers

Peavey 4x12 Slant Cabinet
w/Scorpion Plus speakers

Steve Morse

With his three-pickup Ernie Ball Strat hybrid and an arsenal of effects and amps, Steve
Morse is ready for any kind of sound—fusion, new age, blues rock, hot country and
classic metal (with his Deep Purple gig). Morse first goes into a pedalboard, which
has two boost switches, one that feeds his Peavey VTM-100 amp, and the other
that goes into his Mesa/Boogie Tri-Axis preamp. A series of volume pedals to bring
in and out various elements, such as the synth guitar volume, delayed sounds
generated by the various Lexicon devices in his rack, and an arpeggiator or clock to
his Lexicon PCM 42. Morse favors Peavey 4x12 cabs for his straight guitar sound,
but he also has two full-range three-way speakers for the acoustic and synth outputs.

Joe Satriani

Joe Satriani sets up his signal chain in a fairly orthodox manner, with the wah first, the distortion second, and the the time-based effects following after that and then finally into the front end of a Marshall 6100 head, with 6550 power tubes substituted for the more-common EL34s. Satch's setup is suspiciously Hendrix-like, with the wah in front and then a Fulltone Ultimate Octave later on in the chain. But Satriani also makes expert use of delay (something Hendrix didn't experiment in much), using three different delays. First is the Boss DD-3, which feeds into a two Chandler Digital Delays in series.

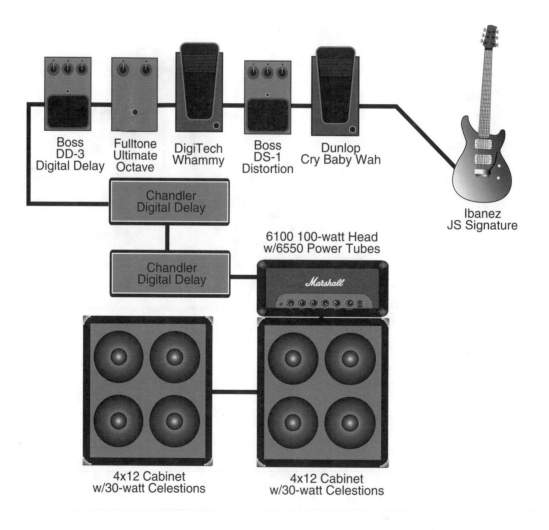

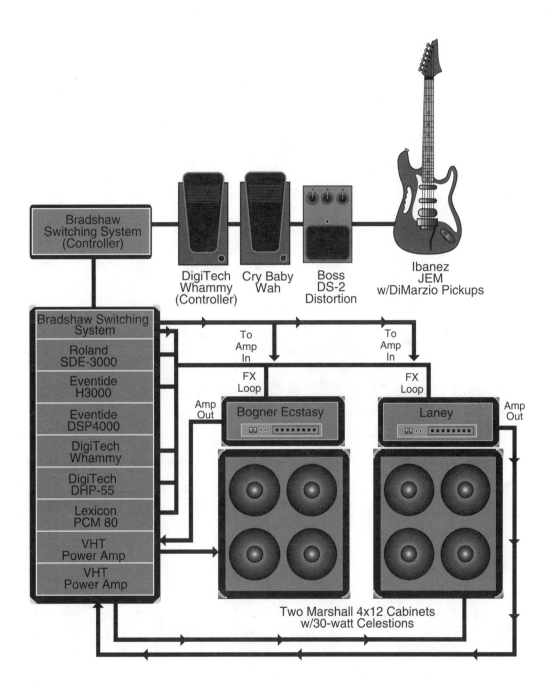

Bradshaw
Switching System
(Controller)

DigiTech
Whammy
(Controller)

Cry Baby
Wah

Boss
DS-2
Distortion

Ibanez
JEM
w/DiMarzio Pickups

Bradshaw Switching
System

Roland
SDE-3000

Eventide
H3000

Eventide
DSP4000

DigiTech
Whammy

DigiTech
DHP-55

Lexicon
PCM 80

VHT
Power Amp

VHT
Power Amp

To
Amp
In

To
Amp
In

FX
Loop

FX
Loop

Amp
Out

Amp
Out

Bogner Ecstasy

Laney

Two Marshall 4x12 Cabinets
w/30-watt Celestions

Steve Vai

Everything starts out conventionally enough in Steve Vai's rig, with a distortion pedal, wah, and whammy pedal, but a switching controller steps in to turn this setup into something ingenious but unconventional. The switching system selects between the various time-based effects in the rack while sending the pedal-driven signal to the amps' input. The amps' effects loop brings in the effects via the send and return jacks, and the amps' slave outputs go into two VHT power amps.

Eddie Van Halen

He's come a long way from his days when he would just plug a "Frankenstein Strat" into an MXR Distortion+ and a Phase 90. Actually, the Phase 90 is still in his rig, but the setup has become a little more sophisticated. Eddie gets all of his distortion from the amps, whether they be Marshalls or the Peavey 5150s created especially for him and which he endorses. The amp switcher can select the path between Marshall and Peavey, and the time-based effects (which include Eventides, Rolands, and Lexicon) all come via the amps' effects sends.

After going from the amp preamps to the effects sends to the effects rack, the signals are not returned, so the power amp section of the Marshalls and Peaveys never get used. Instead the signals are sent to three pedals (a Cry Baby wah, a Boss OC-2 octaver, and the above-mentioned Phase 90) before going into a rack containing speaker simulators and power amps. The speaker simulators are necessary to take the high-end edge off of the line-level signals from the Marshalls' and Peaveys' preamp sections. After being simulated, the line-level signal is delivered to the power amps and sent to three 4x12 cabinets.

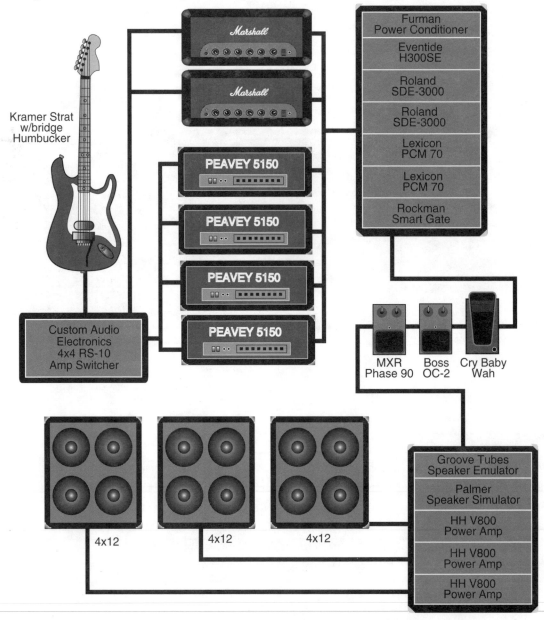

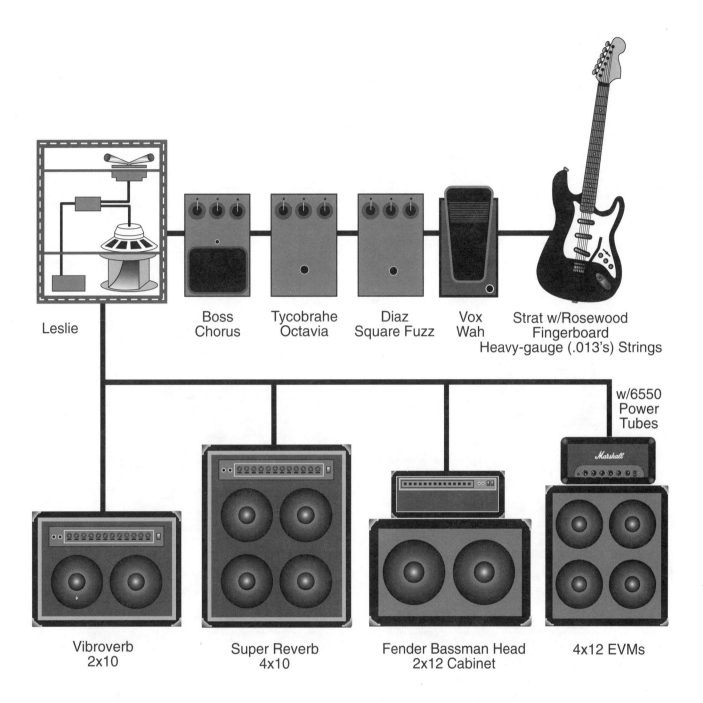

Leslie · Boss Chorus · Tycobrahe Octavia · Diaz Square Fuzz · Vox Wah · Strat w/Rosewood Fingerboard Heavy-gauge (.013's) Strings

w/6550 Power Tubes

Vibroverb 2x10 · Super Reverb 4x10 · Fender Bassman Head 2x12 Cabinet · 4x12 EVMs

Stevie Ray Vaughan

He was a little bit blues and a little bit rock and roll. His setup showed a nod to
   Hendrix, with the Vox wah in front and the Diaz Square Fuzz and Tycobrahe
   Octavia in the chain. Vaughan also employed a Boss chorus pedal and a real Leslie
   before driving an armada of Fender-made amps. Vaughan also played through a
   Marshall, configured with 6550 power tubes instead of EL34s.

Carl Verheyen

Carl Verheyen uses a combination of devices, from pedals to rack-mount gear, but he essentially runs two paths: clean and distorted. For his distorted sound he goes through his pedalboard (which contains such front-end devices as a Cry Baby wah and an Ibanez Tube Screamer and then into either a Marshall head or a THD modded Plexi. The speaker outs of both heads are run through a load box (the THD Hot Plate) to convert them to line level. At this point the signals are carrying all that wonderful amp distortion, both from the preamp and power amp stages, but are at line level where they can be further processed by a Lexicon PCM 41 before being amped up by a solid-state power amp and driving the speaker cab.

Carl approaches his clean sound a little differently. After the pedalboard, Carl first goes through a tube-driven Fender reverb unit (which provides a gain boost). He then takes the signal in mono through a Chandler Digital Delay and takes the output through a stereo delay (mono in/stereo out). The right and left outputs each go to matched Vox AC30s. Carl considers his clean sound, as outlined here, to be one of his trademarks.

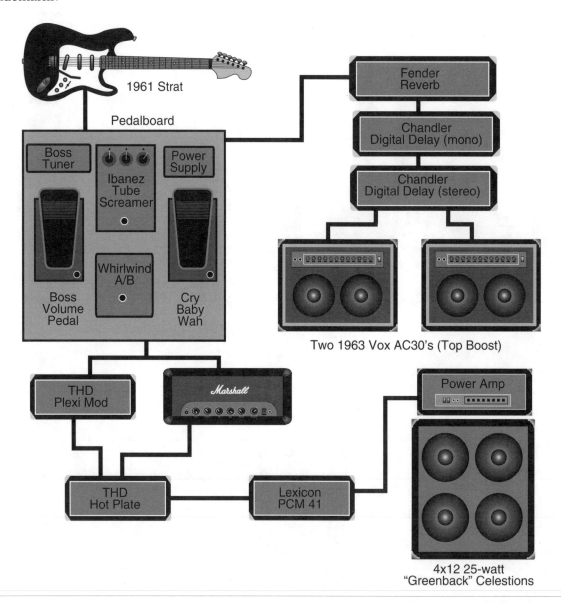

CHAPTER NINE

Tricks & Tips

TRICKS AND TIPS FOR THE RECORDING GUITARIST

This chapter is a collection of guitar tricks and studio techniques that fall outside the normal practice of recording. In no particular order, I've listed some of my favorites, the ones I keep returning to when a conventional approach or lack of resources (both hardware and creative) leave me still searching for solutions. These tips range in scope from simple advice, like soaking your left-hand calluses in hot water to reduce string noise, to the more esoteric practices involving your hardware, e.g., using a mixer channel's aux send to generate non-recorded, control-room feedback. So here they are, presented in a non-linear no-particular-order format. Check out some of these tricks to make sure they work for you or with your particular setup. Again, these are beyond the realm of normal recording techniques, so feel free to experiment and come up with your own variations. One person's mistake is another's inspiration.

USE YOUR STUDIO MULTI-EFFECTS PROCESSOR INLINE

A rack-mount processor can often serve double-duty as an inline guitar effect if you convert the guitar signal to the proper level and impedance.

There are many times when you'll be fooling around with your multi-effects processor and come up with a killer flanger-delay-ring-modulator-reverb patch. The trouble is, that patch is typically optimized as a mixer effect—meaning it's used on an aux send where it receives a line level. If you wanted to take that same effect with you, to a session where you're a sideman and presumably don't have access to the mixer, you'd have to put the effect in your amp's effects loop or use the processor inline. If the amp doesn't have an effects loop, or if you simply want to plug your guitar directly into the processor, you have two choices.

The first is to re-program the unit's input stages to receive the weaker guitar signal. This involves setting up a "mirror" patch where all parameters are the same except for the input gain (you can simply copy the edited patch to an open memory slot and rename it). But even this isn't completely successful, as the impedance is still mismatched, and impedance is frequency dependent—meaning that even if you optimize the level (i.e., tweak it to where it's above the noise floor but below the clipping stage), there will still be a tonal imbalance.

So the better way is to use a direct box or preamp. By converting your guitar signal to a line level via a preamp or direct box, you can give your multi-effects processor a signal with an optimal level and impedance. Many direct boxes don't offer a line-level output in the form of a quarter inch jack, so make sure to either get an adapter, or opt for a box that sends a line level (balanced or unbalanced, either is okay) out via a quarter-inch jack (such as the ART Tube MP).

Many multi-effects processors, especially ones designed for guitars, have mirror banks set up that contain the same program names but are optimized for either the front end (into the amp's preamp), effects return (post preamp), or direct recording (into the board with the unit's speaker simulator engaged). Find out if your multi-effects unit has these options. A processor designed for guitar will have solved the input-level matching problem, but you still want to make sure that the program you've created uses the "guitar input" algorithm rather than the "effects send" algorithm. If you find you've created your masterwork in the "wrong" mode, just use a direct box or other outboard preamp and plug directly into the multi-effects' Loop Return jack.

USE JUST THE DELAYED SIGNAL OR REVERB OF ANOTHER GUITAR PART

Here's a neat trick that's subtle enough to turn the heads of the attentive, but won't distract from the musical impact of the principal signal. Start by recording a melodic line onto one track. Then double the line by playing it onto a second track as an overdub, but take care not to play it exactly like the original. Take a few liberties with the tempo, the articulation (slide into a note instead of striking it, etc.), and maybe even the choice of a note or two (but do this sparingly, as it will come back to "haunt" you). Then run the second part through a delay or reverb and have only the effected signal sound against the original guitar track.

Typically you'd use the little-understood pre aux send for this. The "pre" in this case refers to the fact that the level going out to the aux send jack is not influenced by the channel's fader. It's pre-determined at the channel's trim control. Moving the fader up increases the dry-to-wet ratio and moving the fader down decreases it. Move the fader all the way down and you're left with just the ghostly effect sound. This is precisely what we want here. The pre aux send effect with the fader at zero lets just the effect of the doubled guitar through. Combined with the original track, it sounds like "wrong-note reverb" where the effect is misbehaving and deviating from the original signal. This technique is great for atmospheric effects.

USE A MIDI VOLUME FADER TO SQUELCH NOISY GUITAR TRACKS

If you use any sequenced tracks when recording, even if it's just for a drum machine part, consider employing MIDI for your audio channels too. The best use of MIDI for audio can be found in the device known as the MIDI-controlled volume fader (such as the MixMaster by J.L. Cooper Electronics). Just plug how ever many channels your volume fader comes with (4 or 8 is typical) into the insert points of your mixer. Now your sequencer, through MIDI commands, can control your mixer's volume controls through automation. This beats having to put multiple gates on all those noisy guitar channels, or trying to constantly ride the faders and mute buttons.

PROCESS YOUR PIEZO AND MAGNETIC OUTPUTS DIFFERENTLY

Many guitars come wired with both a piezo pickup and magnetic pickups (the Parker Fly, Hamer Duotone, Brian Moore C-90, and Godin LGX are but a few). This presents many blending and processing abilities, but you can actually use the split signal to create the illusion that two guitarists are playing. For rock and electric-blues playing, take the magnetic output and run it through a wah-wah, while leaving the piezo output fairly dry and unprocessed. This will create the illusion of an acoustic guitar doubling the wah part.

SOAK YOUR LEFT HAND IN HOT WATER TO SOFTEN THE CALLUSES

On very exposed acoustic guitar parts, your left-hand calluses can sometimes make unacceptably loud *skritching* noises as you change positions. A little bit of this noise is natural, but sometimes it can be distracting, especially to producers not used to hearing acoustic guitars so close up. Soaking your fingertips in hot water until they turn slightly pruny will help cut down on the noise.

USE FLATWOUNDS ON YOUR DOBRO TO ELIMINATE BAR NOISE

Speaking of noise, a metal or glass slide will often make an unacceptable level of noise as you drag it over wound strings. As in the callus tip above, a little is acceptable, sometimes it gets to be too much, especially if the music is not raunchy and blues based, but more atmospheric in nature. Flatwounds may not have the brilliant character of wound strings, but they are far more quiet when moving the slide around. A compromise is to use half-rounds, which retain some of the brilliance of fully round wound strings (and sound more "acoustic") but are not quite as noisy.

MAKE YOURSELF A SLIDE CADDY

If you record a lot with a slide, you'll find you sometimes have to set it down and pick it up in a hurry. If you set it down too quickly on a music stand, it can make a clank ruining a take if there are open mics around. Or if you play with a glass slide and it rolls off the stand or your amp, it can break against the wood floor or the metal mic stand base. Placing it in your shirt pocket might be good for getting rid of the slide, but you'll have to fumble to get it back. If you use a music stand, place some felt on the lip so that you can jettison and retrieve your slide quickly without making noise. If you go stand-less in the studio, make a little slide caddy out of pipe cleaners (a circular base with an upwards-pointing center shaft should do it) that sits on your amp or nearby ledge so you can grab your slide in quarter-rest's time.

Use Slides with Open Tunings for Rhythm Parts

If you drop your low E to D, you can make a power chord (root-5th-root) by fretting straight across the lower three strings. For example, in drop-D tuning, playing the 6th, 5th, and 4th strings at the second fret produces an E5 (E-B-E) chord. Use a slide to get a super legato sound when playing chords. Unlike fretting, the strings never stop vibrating as you change frets. Sliding between chords with no break in sound can be especially effective on slower numbers where the portamento (continuous pitch change) is pronounced, and for faster passages, the sliding sound provides a sort of sonic "glue." Also, a slide lets you create a wider vibrato and faster vibrato than is possible with just the left hand alone. If things get too "rattly," try putting on half-round or even flat-wound strings.

Mic the strings of your electric guitar

This trick is not applicable if you have a split-signal, piezo-plus-magnetic configuration. But if you don't have a split-output pickup configuration and want to get some acoustic snap from your electric, mic the strings of your electric guitar acoustically. If you're in the control room, close mic the strings of your electric with a small-diaphragm condenser at a distance of only a few inches. You have to be sure there's no other noise, like phones ringing, clients talking, and of course control room monitors blaring. Run the miked signal to its own track and then mix judiciously with the principal electric guitar sound. You'd be surprised how this sound, anemic on its own, adds a whole new dimensionality to your sound.

CAPO CAPERS
Create Low Drones by Capoing Just the Top Four or Five Strings

To do this you need the type of capo that works as an open clamp (like the Shubb) rather than the elastic wrap-around kind. Attach the capo with the opening of the clamp facing the lower strings of the guitar (that is, put the capo on from underneath), except don't cover the bottom two strings (low E and low A). These will remain open and act as your drones (meaning you won't fret them). If you capo the first four strings at the 9th fret and play in the key of C, you have the lower two strings acting as your root (A) and your dominant (E). This gives you an incredible range and is good for loop-based, diatonic music.

Doubling an acoustic guitar is a great way to add color to a rhythm part. If I'm in a situation where I know there are some available tracks (and who isn't these days with the virtually unlimited track space afforded by MDMs and hard-disk recording), I try to double tracks rather than merely running a stereo effect. It's so much richer, interesting, and less processed-sounding. Plus I get paid double scale.

When I know I can double my parts, I can fashion them as a unit, rather than playing one self-contained part that I later try to fill in the gaps to (if there are any). This is one of my favorite tricks. If you try it, and you're a sideman, be sure to establish this with the producer beforehand. Tell him you have orchestrated a multi-part arrangement that will sound good as a whole, but requires the inclusion of each part.

ENHANCED 12-STRING

You can effect the sound of a super-duper 12-string by doubling your part an octave higher. This is especially effective in arpeggiated rhythm parts. If you play a rhythm part in the key of E using open-position chords, capoing at the 7th fret and playing in the A position will yield the same part exactly one octave higher. That's because E and A have the same voicing, except that A is a 4th higher. When you then jack up A another 5th (7 frets) via a capo, you have the octave part. The same is true for the open chords of G and C.

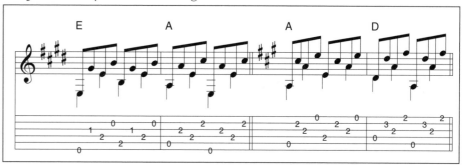

Fig. 9.1

The first two bars show a basic alternating-thumb arpeggio using E and A. Bars 3-4 show the pattern transposed, using A and D chord forms. If you capo up 7 frets and play the passage in A, you'll be doubling the E part exactly in octaves.

Look at the picking pattern in Fig. 9.1. It shows a basic fingerpicking pattern in E, using the first five strings. Play that same right-hand pattern in A one set of strings up, capoed at the 7th fret, and boom—instant octaves.

If you plan your strumming patterns in advance, you can create an exact octave-doubling of your original. Wouldn't it be easier to just grab a 12-string? you ask. Isn't playing two parts an octave apart exactly the same thing? No. The doubling system has three distinct advantages over a single 12-string. When using two guitars—one high, one low—you've introduced these new factors:

- Attack times of notes are slightly separated creating a bigger sound.

- True upper octaves are attained on the top two strings.

- Coloristic and stereo panning options exist, because different instruments can be used and each is recorded onto a separate track.

Let's discuss the above points one at a time.

1) Even if you wanted to, you couldn't double exactly the attacks of your first part with your second pass. You couldn't even get it as close as a double-course attack on a 12-string (strings in pairs, as found on 12-strings and mandolins, are called courses). This randomness is a good thing, musically, as it creates a fuller-sounding part.

2) A 12-string doubles the octaves of only the lower four strings, so you don't get a nice sparkling sound in the upper register. A doubled, capoed guitar "octavates up" the top two strings, which even a Nashville-tuned guitar won't do.

3) This one's obvious for the mere fact that with a 12-string, you have only one guitar giving you octave-separated courses, and these can't be split for individual processing. By using two separate guitars, however, you can make the second guitar actually be another kind of guitar—a small "baby" version, a bright-sounding guitar, a nylon acoustic-electric, etc. Because this second guitar necessarily goes to a separate track, you can give it a different pan position, effects treatment, EQ, etc.

And speaking of effects treatment, here are three tricks to perform on your doubled tracks. Either do these yourself in your own studio, or tell the engineer about them and see if he'll bite. Any one of these create a ghostly, haunting effect that is subtle but effective.

Trick #1: Take just the reverb of the high guitar, not the straight signal, and have it follow the low guitar. Keep the low guitar completely dry. The easiest way to do this is to patch a reverb into a pre-fade aux send, and pull the high guitar's fader down completely. Remember, pre-fade aux sends maintain their level independent of the channel's fader.

Trick #2: Set up different delay times for each track (with at least a 50 ms between the lower guitar and the upper so that discrete repetitions can be heard). Have the lower slap back first, followed by the upper guitar. This will give you a "prepared guitar" sound (as if you had paper clips and other resonating paraphernalia dangling from the strings).

Trick #3: Combine Tricks 1 and 2 by having just the slap-back of the higher guitar against the lower. Put close enough to the original (by lowering the millisecond value of the repeat time) you can get an eerie, ring-modulated sound.

Doubling yourself with complementary parts is an important recording skill. And as with any technique, once you gain facility with it, you can put creative variations on it, altering your timing in certain ways to achieve different effects. The best part, though, is that a doubled part—unlike an effect generated from the original signal—is not merely a clone or a predictable by-product. It's another original, authentic piece of music.

TABLES OF USEFUL NUMBERS

Everyone uses "tables." I don't mean the kind you eat off of, though most people I know use those, too (with the exception of some guitarists I know). No, I mean tables in the sense of reference charts that provide important information—important enough to have ready access to, but too extensive or complicated to be committed to memory. A table could be something as simple as your personal phone book. You can't memorize all your friends' telephone numbers, so you keep this "table" (organized alphabetically on separate leafs of paper) close to you.

Tables can exist for other reasons, too. You may need certain numbers that you can calculate easily enough but would rather keep on a list so that you don't have to do the mathematical legwork each time. Business travelers carry "tip cards" in their wallet for just such a purpose: It's not too tough to multiply the restaurant check's total by .15 (15%), but it's much handier to consult a wallet-sized card (especially after three martinis). Accountants use calculators not because they can't do the math but because it allows them to be more efficient with their time. A calculator is kind of a "virtual table." Many music functions are math-based, so it makes sense to use tables for musical purposes too, such as the circle of fifths, and of course lead sheets.

Over the years I've created various tables to make my life a little easier by not having to tax my dwindling cranial powers calculating things I could look up on a chart. I'd like to share with you some of the more common charts and tables I've devised.

Harmonics

Natural harmonics on the guitar—the ones found on open strings by laying a left-hand finger lightly over a fret—are a great weapon in the arsenal of a recording guitarist. Often a well-placed harmonic is just the thing a sustained note needs at the climax to a solo. But when you're in the studio, the pressure can be on to hit the harmonic the first time, or to hit it repeatedly. For that kind of situation you can't leave it to chance or experimentation. You have to know where the harmonic falls exactly so that you can nail it consistently.

I originally charted all the natural harmonics on all six strings because it used to facilitate transcribing solos. When transcribing, I could hear the note clearly, but since I couldn't see the guitarist's hands, I always had to hunt and peck for the right string and right fret. Calculating harmonics from scratch got very tedious ("reinventing the wheel" was the analogy that often sprang to mind), so one day I just took time out and made myself a chart that had all the natural-harmonic possibilities for all six open strings. So now when I hear a natural harmonic on a recording—or I want to produce one of my own—I look at my chart (see Fig. 9.2).

HARMONICS

Fret	Oct. + Interval	Open String Pitch*					
12	1	E2	A2	D3	G3	B3	E4
7/19	1 + 5	B2	E2	A3	D3	F♯3	B3
5/24	2	E3	A3	D4	G4	B4	E5
4/9/26	2 + 3	G♯3	C♯4	F♯4	B4	D♯5	G♯5
3	2 + 5	B3	E4	A4	D5	F♯5	A5
6/15/22	2 + ♭7	D4	G4	C5	F5	A5	D6
17	3	E4	A5	D5	G5	B5	E6

FRACTIONAL-FRET HARMONICS

Fret	Oct. + Interval	Open-String Pitch*					
1.6	3 + 5	B4	E5	A5	D6	F♯6	B6
1.7	3 + ♯4	A♯4	D♯5	G♯5	C♯6	F♯6	A♯6
1.8	3 + 3	G♯4	C♯5	F♯5	B♯5	D♯6	G♯6
2.0	2 + 3	F♯4	B♯4	E♯5	A5	C♯6	F♯6
2.4	3	E4	A5	D5	G5	B5	E6
2.6	2 + ♭7	D4	G4	C5	F5	A5	D6
3.3	2 + 5	B3	E4	A4	D5	F♯5	B5
5.8	2 + ♭7	D4	G4	C5	F5	A5	D6

*C3 = Middle C. The guitar sounds an octave lower than written. For example the high E string sounds E3, lowest line of the treble clef.

Fig. 9.2

Table showing natural harmonics on the open strings

In addition to making transcribing a whole lot more efficient (especially for Steve Vai solos!), I found it helped my own playing. For example, if I were soloing in A and I knew a high A would be just the thing to nail at bar seven of my eight-bar solo, I could quickly scan my chart and see where all the available As were. Or, if I was playing on a floating-bridge guitar, I could hit a G and bend up a whole step. Figure 9.2 shows the chart that gives all the harmonics for all six open strings.

Note the fractional fret harmonics. These occur not directly over the fret wire but at the indicated distance between two frets. For example, fret 1.6 is a little more than halfway between frets 1 and 2. Very handy for figuring out Steve Vai solos.

THAT DIGITAL DELAY THING

Another situation that can take advantage of a table is the now-common "cascade effect." This is explained in detail in the section called "The Digital Delay Cascade Effect," but this is the crash course for those who just want the numbers. The cascade effect is where you play in eighth notes and set your delay to spit back a single, equal-amplitude repeat three 16th notes later. This doubles the rate at which notes come from your guitar, and you can produce some spectacular results with this trick. (Van Halen's "Cathedral" from *Diver Down* is a well-known example.)

Mathematically, you can calculate how to set your delay, assuming you know the tempo. The formula is 45 divided by tempo equals seconds (e.g., $45 \div 120 = .375$, which is 375 milliseconds). But when I'm fooling around with this technique, I don't think of numbers—I set my drum machine to a certain tempo based on feel and then consult my table to see what the delay's millisecond setting should be. Figure 9.3 shows a table that goes from moderately slow to pretty darned fast, so it should suffice for most of your cascade needs.

DDL Settings: 45 ÷ t = ms

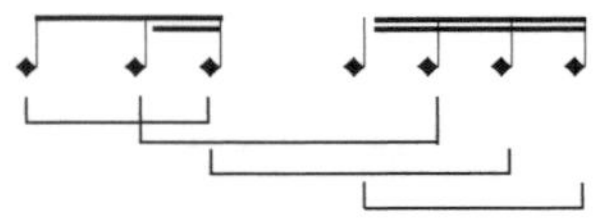

Tempo	Ms	Tempo	Ms
60	750	135	333
65	692	140	321
70	643	145	310
75	600	150	300
80	562	155	290
85	529	160	281
90	500	165	272
95	474	170	265
100	450	175	257
105	429	180	250
110	409	185	243
115	391	190	237
120	375	195	231
125	360	200	225
130	346	205	220

Fig. 9.3

Tempo markings (in beats per minute) and the millisecond setting for deriving the "cascade effect"

WHAT'S THE FREQUENCY, KENNETH?

More obscure but still useful to EQ fanatics is the chart I use for common guitar frequencies (see Fig. 9.4). These include the frequencies of the open strings and middle C, because from these numbers you can adjust your EQ (parametric or graphic) with some intelligence. The open D string on your nylon-string is causing runaway feedback? Look at your chart and dial out (if it's a parametric) or pull down the slider (if it's a graphic) on 146.8 Hz. Remember, an octave, by definition, is half or twice a certain frequency, so the D found on the second string, third fret, is 293.6 and the open, dropped sixth string D is 73.4. This is also useful if you want to create feedback, such as the technique described in "Control Room Feedback."

CASCADING CHANNELS

When you set up two parallel channels that have the same signal flowing through them, you can do a couple of cool tricks. To cascade (or set up a mirror of) a channel, start by plugging your guitar into, say, channel 1 and taking the direct out and putting that into, say, channel 2. Be sure to split channel 1 by pushing the patch cord part-way into the insert jack. This will allow channel 1's signal to continue to go to the main mix as well as providing the doubled signal to feed channel 2. Channels 1 and 2 will now both go to the main mix and channel 2, if all settings are left neutral, delivers the exact signal as channel 1. (Actually, you may have to adjust the trim control, as channel 1's input might be an instrument level, which is lower than the output of channel 1's direct out, which is line level.)

Now you're free to set up a different sound on channel 2. You can then move between channels using the mute switches. This allows you to have two completely different

EQ settings and switch between them, sort of like presets on an effects processor. For example, you might set up a full-sounding EQ for the rhythm guitar on channel 1 that will serve as the main accompaniment for the intro and verses. But in the chorus, where you want the quality to change a little bit, set up a bright-sounding EQ on channel two. Or, perhaps you would set up channel 1's EQ for a boosted mid section with a low and high cut, and channel 2 with the more punchy-sounding boosted highs and lows and a scooped out middle. In either case, keep channel 2 muted during the verses, but then just before the chorus (like, an eighth note before) simultaneously mute channel 1 and unmute channel 2. You can also change the pan position, which might help to distinguish the two parts. Hint: If you know you might want to employ this technique, leave yourself a little "transition room" when tracking the guitar parts.

Guitar Open-String Frequencies	
⑥ =	82.4
⑤ =	110.0
④ =	146.8
③ =	196.0
② =	246.9
① =	329.6
Bass	
④ =	41.2
③ =	55.0
② =	73.0
① =	99.9

Frequencies from 5th Str. A – mid. C	
A —	110.0
A♯ —	116.5
B —	123.5
C —	130.8
C♯ —	138.6
D —	146.8
D♯ —	155.6
E —	164.8
F —	174.6
F♯ —	184.9
G —	195.9
G♯ —	207.7
A —	220.0
A♯ —	233.1
B —	246.9
C —	261.6

Fig. 9.4

Frequencies of the open guitar and bass strings, plus 1⅓ octaves of single-note frequencies

"Comb filtering" is the technique where you set up reciprocal EQ in each channel and then pan each channel hard left and right. The "comb" part is because a graph of the EQ bands, one with its frequencies cut, the other boosted, resembles the teeth of a hair comb. The effect can be spacious and phasey, but still subtle, because you're playing with just the EQ and no time delay or modulation. An effective comb filtering scheme is to use just cuts rather than boosts, which seem more artificial sounding. Try cutting only the even-numbered bands in the left channel and only the odd-numbered bands in the right channel.

Cascading two channels can often act as a work-around for boards that lack an insert point or whose insert point/direct out falls after the fader. For example, if you wanted to put a compressor into a channel insert that is placed after the fader, bringing the level up and down via the fader affects the input to the compressor (not a good thing). In other words, as you bring the fader up, it "fights" the compressor, and the result is an increasing squashed signal, not one with a fixed compression ratio that merely gets louder or softer (which is what you want).

Enter the cascading-channels technique. In this case, you don't want to split channel 1, you want to interrupt it, so push the cord all the way in to remove channel 1's signal from the main mix. Then plug the cable from channel 1's direct out into the input of the compressor. Take the compressor's output and plug that into channel 2's input. Make all your settings on channel 1, including gain settings that will affect how the compressor interacts with the signal. Channel 2 now serves as merely a volume fader because it's dealing only with the compressor output. You can now use channel 2's EQ controls to shape the final sound, if it needs it. Sometimes, especially after heavy compression, you may find it necessary to restore a little top end, and it's best to do this on the channel after the compressor, not the one before it.

You may ask why give up two mixer channels and go through this maneuver rather than plugging into the compressor directly. The answer is that by using a mixer channel's direct out, you're giving the compressor a line-level signal, not a guitar-level one. Unless your compressor is of the stompbox variety, it's happiest seeing a line-level signal.

CONTROL ROOM FEEDBACK

In this trick, you can use an aux send to create a non-recorded, sustain-enhancing feedback signal. The procedure is explained in detail in Chapter 3, but here's the quick-'n-easy version. You can create a dynamic feedback generator (meaning the feedback is based on the music's frequency content) by taking an aux send from the mixer channel of your guitar signal and running it into a nearby combo amp. Make sure that no open mics are near the combo amp because we're not recording this amp. We're merely using it to "excite" or oscillate the strings (which is what feedback does). The best way to do this is leave your main amp (the one that's miked) in another room while you sit in the control room with the amp. That way you can monitor the mix off the studio monitors and you'll be near the mixer to get the mixer's line feed.

Run the aux send from the guitar channel into the amp. Begin playing and face your guitar into the amp when you want feedback to occur. If it doesn't occur naturally, have an assistant boost either the amp's volume or EQ at the appropriate time to drive the sound into overdrive. Again, any changes made on the amp are not reflected in the original signal (the one going to tape), because that's coming from your main amp. All that happens is that there's an increased sustain and feedback quality.

RE-AMPING

Re-amping is a technique that allows you to take an already-recorded, direct guitar signal and run it back through an amp and onto a different tape track. It's an incredibly valuable trick to know in case you have to capture a guitar part in a hurry, but don't have the time to devote to getting a proper amp setup.

There are any number of scenarios where this might occur. Consider just some of the possibilities where you've got to get the performance down and worry about sonic niceties later:

• Your guitarist (or you yourself) has to leave in five minutes and can't wait around while there's a change of amps, re-miking, and EQ tweak at the mixer.

• You stumble across a cool lick you just know you'll forget if you don't get it down immediately. If it doesn't go to tape now, you won't even remember how to play it, let alone improve on it.

• You don't have the right amp or mic available for that session, or the one you do have has broken down.

• You want to perform a guitar trick—like wah-wah in rhythm or rolling off the volume knob on every attack—but your coordination is rusty.

• You want to audition one raw signal through several amps, with no pre-existing amp coloration or processing.

Any of these situations is a case for re-amping. You can capture the performance through a direct-to-tape recording, and at a later time, run that signal back through an amp with the proper gain, mic placement, and board setup. If properly delivered, the amp doesn't know whether it's listening to a live guitarist or a recorded signal. It's just seeing a plug with electrical impulses coming from it. As long as the signal it receives is convincingly guitaristic, the amp doesn't know or care whether it's Jimi Hendrix or an ADAT on the other end.

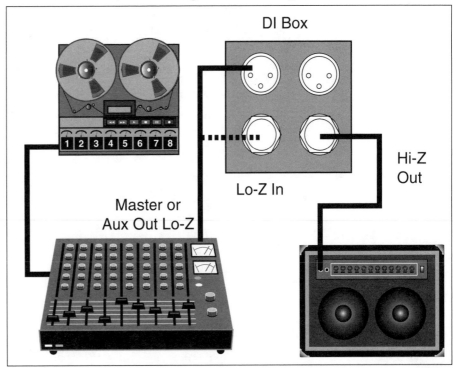

Fig. 9.5

Re-amping is the opposite of "going direct." Here, we take an untreated tape signal and process it through the front end of an amp

Experiment with re-amping in a non-emergency setting, so you can learn which levels work best. If you distort or come in too low while going to tape, you'll never get a good sound later on, even with a vintage '60s Plexi Marshall. Record the signal to tape or disk hot, and don't let it distort. Do not use compression, but you might try employing a limiter set to kick in at the very upper end of your loudest and most percussive point in the passage. When you have a good level onto tape, you can turn your attention to the playback.

The trick is getting the tape signal to masquerade as an instrument signal. If you plug your guitar straight into the board, you encounter an impedance conversion as the signal passes through the mixer channel's preamp. Then when you play the recorded signal back through the mixer's output bus, that signal operates at yet another impedance and level value.

You don't need to know the math here; it's just important to know that the signal is being changed at two stages—upon input into the preamp and upon output through the bus. Giving a guitar amp a tape track, electronically speaking, is not the same as plugging the guitar directly into the amp itself. But you can convert it back to guitar specs, losing almost nothing in the process. It's never going to be the same as if you went to the amp directly, but it's the next best thing, and may not even be noticeable in most situations.

All that's involved in re-amping is an ordinary, run-of-the-mill passive direct box (or "D.I.," for direct injection). A direct box simply converts high-impedance signals to low-impedance ones and vice versa. There's no battery or other power supply involved, and there's no inherent direction in a passive device—meaning you can't screw up by plugging an output into an output instead of an input. It's like a length of pipe: fit the right end on the device with a matching part and you'll be fine. The water—er, signal—can flow in either direction no matter which way the pipe is hooked up.

What we'll be doing is converting a low-impedance line-level signal to a high-impedance "guitar" signal. This is not normally the way a D.I. is used. A D.I. usually takes a high-impedance signal from a guitar, or more commonly a bass, and converts it to a three-pin XLR low-impedance signal for direct injection into the mic input of a mixer channel.

For this application, however, we're doing the opposite. We're taking from the board a low-impedance line level via an XLR or 1/4" balanced jack and going into the low-Z (XLR or balanced 1/4") of a direct box. Then on the other side of the box, we'll connect the hi-Z 1/4" jack with a guitar cord and hook the other end to the amp. Remember, there's no in or out on a direct box, only hi- and low-Z jacks. Low in, high out, is what you want here (see Fig. 9.5).

At first it can be disconcerting to plug a tape recorder into a guitar amp. All your instincts tell you not to do this, that the sound will be dreadful, but with the right levels—both on the amp and from the mixer—you'll get excellent results. If possible, take the same guitar the recorded track was made with and compare your levels and tone along the way. This will ensure you've got everything set correctly.

THE DIGITAL DELAY CASCADE EFFECT

Using your digital delay to create the so-called "cascade effect" is definitely one of the coolest things you can do with a delay. It's also one of the most elusive techniques to nail down at first, but once you get it, it's like riding a bicycle: You never forget how, and it's a no-brainer to jump right up and go for a ride. To pull it off, you have to know how to set the machine (the math), how to play against the chosen setting (the rhythm), and what to play to create the effect (the patterns). Lots of guitarists have used this technique, including Eddie Van Halen ("Cathedral"), Nuno Bettencourt ("Flight of the Wounded Bumble Bee"), Blues Saraceno ("Never Look Back"), and country flashmeisters Albert Lee ("Country Boy") and the Hellecasters' John Jorgenson ("Orange Blossom Special"). Like right-hand tapping or sweep picking, it's a technique you should have a certain mastery over to become a modern, well-rounded player. Besides, this isn't nearly as hard as sweep picking because the technique is actually in the manipulation of an effect.

What It Is

The cascade technique, for all its flashy effect, is surprisingly easy to play (that's why it's in a chapter called "Tricks & Tips"). The tricky part is what you have to do with your ears to not get confused. Musically, what's happening is you play steady eighth notes and set your delay to spit back a single repeat, at equal volume, three sixteenth notes later (a dotted-sixteenth's duration), or on the fourth and second sixteenth note of the beat. This produces a steady stream of sixteenth notes. Figure 9.6 shows the sound rhythmically. You play only the upstem part (eighth notes). The downstem part shows the notes produced by the delay. Practice the part by first playing the upstem part, and then to hear what you should be hearing when you kick in the delay, play both the upstem and downstem part (all notes).

The Math

Memorize this formula or write it on masking tape and stick it to the bottom of your delay pedal: 45 ÷ t = ms. This determines the millisecond delay setting or time setting, of your units (a millisecond is a thousandth of a second; stompbox owners will have to estimate, but you can get there with a little trial and error). The "t" in this case is the tempo, "45" is the number that produces the second and fourth sixteenth notes, and "ms" is the delay's time setting. If you're wondering where the number 45 came from, it's because 60 is used to convert tempo to seconds, and 45 is 3/4 of that—one sixteenth note sooner, or the fourth sixteenth note of the beat. For example, if you play eighth notes at a tempo of 120 bpm (beats per minute), you divide 45 by 120 to get .375 (.375 is actually .375 of a second which equates to 375 milliseconds; I ignore the decimal factor in my original equation). So if you set your metronome or drum machine to 120, then you set your delay like this:

Delay Time = 375; Feedback = 0; Effect Level = 100% (making delayed notes equal in volume to played notes).

Begin playing eighth notes and *voilà*—instant cascade. If your tempo is a slower q=60, set the time for 500 ms.

Subdivide and Conquer

If you have your rhythm chops together (or if you're just a musical masochist), you can derive your delay settings by ear if you already know the tempo (this is how Albert Lee does it on his instructional videos). Let's say you already have the tempo because you're playing along to a pre-recorded rhythm track. You don't know what the tempo is numerically. To find the ms setting for the delay device, tap your foot to the quarter-note pulse of the tape, and move the delay time back and forth until the note spat back by the delay falls exactly three sixteenth-notes, or a dotted

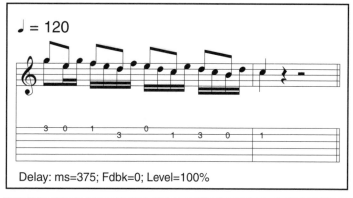

Delay: ms=375; Fdbk=0; Level=100%

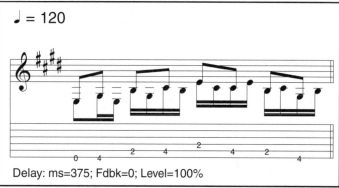

Delay: ms=375; Fdbk=0; Level=100%

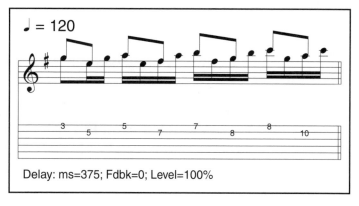

Delay: ms=375; Fdbk=0; Level=100%

Figs. 9.6 – 9.8

Set your metronome for ♩ = 120 and your delay setting for 375 ms. Begin playing the upstem (tabbed) part only. Delay produces downstem notes

eighth note, later (just slightly before the next foot tap).

I find it easier to work by the numbers (setting the drum machine, etc.), but you don't always have the luxury of knowing or influencing the tempo, so you have to be conversant in both methods of setting the appropriate delay time.

What to Drive

For the delay effect to work, you must play certain patterns that will yield musical results. After you master the effect and your ears no longer get confused by a machine playing in the "holes" where you're not playing, you'll begin to know what will work and what won't. Figures 9.7 and 9.8 show two different types of lines that show off the cascade effect nicely. Practice these to a drum machine and have them solid as an eighth-note line before kicking on the delay. Believe me, if it's not down cold, you'll get tripped up the moment the delay spits back that first note.

Many effects processors that feature a "tap delay" function can create the cascade effect automatically, by doing the math and setting the delay time for you. You tell it that you want the cascade effect, set or tap the quarter note tempo, begin playing eighth notes, and it's there. It's definitely a time saver, and for a situation where you don't know what the tempo is numerically and have to tap it in along with, say, a click track, these machines can be a lifesaver. But it's always good to know how to achieve any effect manually. Even if you own a processor with a cascade feature and tap-tempo option, you might someday have to re-create the effect from scratch. Imagine not knowing how to create distortion from an amp if your fuzz pedal broke one day. Same thing here. Know the theory even if you don't have to do the legwork.

TRICKS WITH OPEN-REEL MACHINES

Don't ever throw out those old behemoths of yesteryear, the open-reel two- and four-track machines. And if you ever see one at a garage sale, snatch it up. There's still life in this not-much-used-anymore medium, and you can do tricks with these antiquities that you can't with their more-modern brethren. Read on for some tricks and cool moves that you can perform on open-reel machines.

TWO-TRACKS AND SYNCHING

Here's a scenario where an open-reel machine functions like a multi-track and is useful in a way that a DAT or cassette player is not. Say you have a friend who's written a jingle using a SMPTE-striped tape track to drive a MIDI sequencer and various sound modules. He wants you to play lead guitar overdubs, but he wants you to do it in your studio. But your ADAT is broken and all you have is an old two-track. What do you do? Have your friend record the SMPTE track onto a DAT, which you then bounce over to one track of the two-track. You then get a copy of the sequence he used to drive his modules and you hook up your modules to behave similarly. You don't have to match his sound exactly because these tracks are just for reference. Just make sure his bass sequencer track drives your bass sequencer track, etc. Then hook your sequencer up to the output of the two-track so that the sequencer is slaved to the time code coming from the tape track. As you start the two-track and listen to your MIDI modules play the basic backup, enable the record track of the two-track's right channel and record your fills and solo. Repeat until you're happy with your performance.

When you're finished you will have a two-track tape with time code on one side and your guitar fills on the other. Not very musically useful like that, but once you send it back to your well equipped friend, he can have your time code drive his machines.

From Alvin the Chipmunk to Darth Vader

Two-track machines invariably come with two speeds, and always in a 2:1 relationship. That means that anything I record on the low speed and play back at the high will sound exactly twice as fast and one octave higher than the original. Conversely, anything played on the high speed and played back on the low will sound half as fast and one octave lower. If you play a difficult passage an octave lower and exactly at twice the rhythmic values (i.e., eighth notes become quarters, quarter notes become halves, etc.), you'll get an exact copy of what would have happened had you played accurately and up-to-speed in the original octave.

Sounds like a good way to cheat, right? Well, it almost works. The truth is, certain things don't translate well when sped up, such as effects. So if you plan to record an octave lower at the slow speed and then jack it up on playback, make sure not to add vibrato (the left hand kind or electronic variety) or any other effects that will speed up to unrealistic proportions. But for certain effects, like chipmunk voices or a Darth Vader emulation (and when you're not employing this trick simply because you didn't learn your part well enough!), the double-speed/half-speed option can provide new creative possibilities.

BACKWARD REVERB THE TWO-TRACK WAY

Something that's very hard to do on an MDM is a snap on open-reel machines, and that's adding on a click track or intro in front of a tune. When a tune just starts with no warning, it's very hard to know what the tempo is, when the exact start time is, or certainly what the tempo is going to be, say, four beats before the first note sounds. But with an open-reel machine, you can again, flip the reels and hear the tempo of the kick or rhythm guitar and tap your own tempo on an open track. The trick is to keep going after the song ends—uh, begins (remember you're listening to the song backwards from a few bars into the beginning). If no discernible tempo is there when listening to the tape backwards, play it forwards again and tap your own click track in, using crisp, definable clicks. That way, when heard in reverse, it will be a little more obvious what the pulse is. Record as many clicks as you'll need musical space. Sometimes it's only a bar of clicks, but other times, you might want to put on an extended intro, so calculate in advance how many clicks and bars you'll need to record.

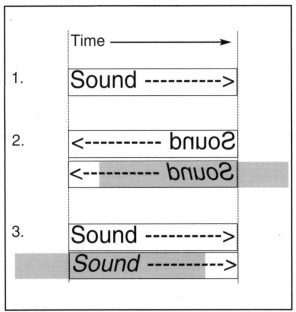

Fig. 9.9

To get a true backward reverb, follow steps 1 – 3. Step 3 shows that the reverb actually precedes the principal sound in time

We talked about backward reverb as an effect, but you can accomplish the real thing with tape flipping. Follow these four steps.

1. Record the sound you want in the normal, forward fashion (is there any other way?).

2. Flip the tape (that is, place the takeup reel on the supply side and vice versa) and play the original track backwards, running it through a reverb unit. Record just the effect sound on an open track, leaving the original untouched.

3. Flip the tape back over again and listen to the two tracks together. You'll not only hear reverb before the actual music, but the effect itself will be backwards. Add reverb again (to both channels) to smooth out the ambience of both tracks. Figure 9.9 shows a graphic representation of what happens to the sound in the procedure outlined above.

OH YEAH, AND PRACTICE YOUR RAZOR BLADE EDITS

You never know when you'll be called on to do this in an analog environment, so practice up while you have the opportunity. When I first saw an engineer execute a seamless splice with a razor blade and editing block (and then heard the results) I couldn't believe my ears. There was no perceptible gap, and I was watching the splice go by under the record heads. A good razor blade edit is just as good as any digital cut, copy, or paste.

PUT YOUR EQ BEFORE YOUR DISTORTION PEDAL

Many amps, including Marshalls and Soldanos, put the EQ section before the preamp, because they feel this makes the interaction of the frequencies more dynamic when the signal hits the preamp. Simulate this effect yourself by putting your equalizer before your distortion pedal. And don't forget to hit your amp hard.

SENDING YOUR SIGNAL INTO A TIME WARP

One of the coolest, most retro, and loopy effects you can apply to your guitar sound is reverse reverb. This is where the normal life of a reverb signal is played backwards, resulting in a diffuse, distant sound that ends in a giant sucking *shoop* and sharp cutoff. It's a common setting on many effects processors, and when used in ambient or atmospheric passages, it can be quite effective. Adrian Belew uses this as one of his hallmark sounds to create interesting textures in his own music as well as in others'.

To have reverb truly in reverse, though, you'd have to have it come before the note itself—something impossible to achieve in a live situation (how do you make the echo of a sound come before the sound itself?). Belew, a master of the technique of simulated reverse echo, works around this problem by masking the attack of his notes with a volume control (either a pedal or the guitar's volume knob), but it's still not the same as having the effect precede the actual note. But there is a way, using a digital delay and a reverb unit, to get the actual reverb sound to come before the dry, uneffected signal.

Do you do that by making time flow in reverse, you ask? No, nothing nearly so diabolical. With a simple digital delay, a separate reverb box that features the reverse effect, and a Y-cable or a mixer, you can easily set up a signal path that outputs the reverb before the main signal is heard. Here are the ways to do it.

You can use a Y-cord (or other splitter) that feeds one line into the reverb unit (set to the reverse setting) and one to the delay. The idea is to combine the sounds at the output and have the delay spit out the signal after the reverb. The best way to do this is to set the delay for a healthy millisecond delay (250 or greater), put the feedback at 0 (to produce one repeat only),

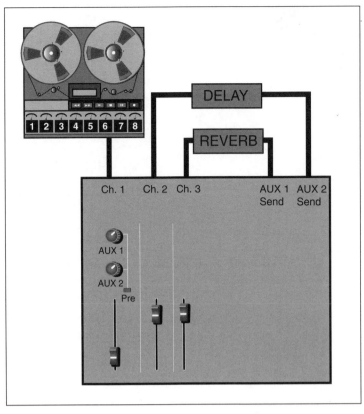

Fig. 9.10

Reverse reverb is achieved here by delaying the dry signal and allowing the reverbed portion to come out first

and have modulation and phase at 0. What you're getting then is the exact input signal outputted 250 milliseconds after the original—with no fancy stuff added on. The signal that goes to the reverb unit sounds almost instantaneously, albeit with a backwards effect on it (be sure to set the effect-dry mix to 100% effect). By tweaking the delay time on the digital delay, you can separate or push together the reverbed sound with the straight signal, creating a smooth, seamless blend of the two. It's still a good idea to employ Belew's trick of masking the attack with a volume device, as this contributes to the psycho-acoustic illusion of sound in reverse.

The difficult part of this system is that it's very confusing to play guitar while listening to your signal arrive a quarter of a second later (a long time in musical terms, especially when you're trying to keep time). A way around this problem is to monitor the straight sound off of the guitar's mixer channel and use the pre-fader aux sends to do your reverb-delay magic. The other benefit to using a mixer (in addition to being able to monitor the straight sound) is that your input doesn't have to be you playing guitar; it could be a tape return. This way, you could play the line as you wanted it to sound (forward, anyway), and then use a tape return as the input to apply the reverse reverb effect—tweaking along the way and not having to worry about performing. If you have multiple tracks that need to be in sync with the guitar, send them to the delay (but not the reverb) as well (see Fig. 9.10).

If you don't delay your other tracks, your guitar will be 250 ms late. This means that the conventional application of this trick works best in passages that aren't highly rhythmic or driving. If you were to play a guitar part along in time to backing tracks and then offset that part by 250 ms or so, you'd be pretty far behind the beat. That can range from disconcerting to disastrous to the listener. If you want the principal (non-effected) note to fall precisely on the beat, there are several ways to achieve this:

1. Assign all the backing tracks to two stereo submaster buses (left and right). Assign one submaster to the left master and the other to the right master. Then patch in a second digital delay line, with the same settings as the one used for the guitar, into the submaster insert points.

2. If you're working with any digital random-access editing format, create a mono, scratch mix of the backing tracks. You'll be using this as a reference, so copy only as many tracks as you need to help you keep a beat and find your place in the music. Copy this onto an open track, and then slide it to the left (forward in time) to 250 ms before the normal tracks start. Use the counter to help you find the start time; you may have to insert a blank measure or partial measure to accommodate your scratch track. You can also perform this trick with an open-reel tape recorder by flipping the reels and giving yourself a pre-click. See the section on "Tricks with Open-Reel Machines," p. 142.

3. If you own an MDM (like an Alesis ADAT or TASCAM DA-88), you can use the track delay feature and delay every track except the guitar tracks. This will have the relative effect of pushing the guitar track forward. (This is like that old Laurel and Hardy sight gag where they're in the army standing in formation and the officer asks for any volunteers to step forward. All the men except the clueless Stan and Ollie step back, leaving them in front and making it seem as if they have stepped forward.)

Keep in mind when dealing with this technique that there are different meanings to "reverse reverb." The eerie vocal ghostings in Led Zeppelin's "Whole Lotta Love" is actually a forward echo placed before the source signal, so that only the "order" of the parts is reversed (you can still hear Robert Plant singing "Way down inside . . ." in a forward orientation). Flipping an open-reel tape or having your hard-disk audio recorder play a sound segment in reverse creates a true backward sound, while playing the backward reverb setting on your effects processor only simulates the behavior (or envelope) of a backward reverb—and it still comes after the main sound. But using this simple trick of a delay and reverse reverb gives your music a retro sound—a truly retrograde sound, in the literal sense of the word.

CHAPTER TEN

Scoring to Video

"Scoring" is the term used to describe the process of writing music to moving images. Moving images can be many things: an abstract montage of shapes and patterns; animation; single, fixed-camera live action (such as a dancer on a stage); or quick-cut edited action sequences (think Terminator movies). These images can exist in either a video or film format. In all cases, the requirements for the composer are the same: Capture the mood through music, and enhance the visual so that it becomes even more dramatic with music. You only have to imagine your most vivid movie moments without music to realize its power. Think of Superman's flight over Metropolis without John Williams' grand orchestrations, or Batman's ride through the outskirts of Gotham City without Danny Elfman's humorously sinister music, or even Jaws' cruise for a human snack without (once again) John Williams' terrifying two-note "shark-theme."

Music can't make a bad movie good, but it can make a good movie great. If you think you have the ability to enhance a movie or video's impact though music—or the process fascinates you enough to try—this chapter shows you what you need to have, both in hardware and brainware, to make it happen in the multimedia world.

Where to Start

Scoring is an art unto itself. You don't need to be a guitar god, you don't even need to be able to write hit songs. What you need is the range of talent and the emotional reservoir that will allow you to create music that is cinematic in nature—be it scary, sad, suspenseful, or jubilant.

Most successful scorers started out pretty much the same way: by watching TV with sound off and noodling on the guitar to the action. That's great practice, and so is renting different types of flicks at the video store: nature films, surfing and hang-gliding films, exercise videos, and especially cheesy horror films—the cheesier the better. If you've already taken care of the creativity aspect, and you've got some cinematic ideas, then you have to consider how to present your talents in a way that enables you to work with others. Assuming you can play well enough to record the thoughts and musical ideas you hear in your head, the next step is committing those ideas to tape or hard disk. But there are certain procedures a scorer must follow if he or she is to interface with the film and video world. These procedures break down along two basic paths: one involves no extra technical equipment; you just need a stopwatch and the ability to "quantify" your music in terms of beats per minute, tempo and feel. The other approach necessitates synching your music to the video itself, so that the audio is "locked" and permanently stamped onto the master tape itself. This requires some extra hardware, but fortunately it's not very expensive.

Non-Synched Music

Some videos do not require precision scoring, such as single-shot videos (one camera) where scene changes are gradual and dramatic action does not depend on musical reinforcement. To be sure, there is a craft in selecting the appropriate mood and general length, but for the most part the synchronization aspect is a non-issue. You don't have to worry about a cymbal crash coming at the exact moment someone slams a door.

If you find yourself in the position of setting music to video, first find out if you'll be looking at the final cut. If not, you can use a stopwatch for timing the various scenes and then "rough out" music to present it to the director. If he or she likes what you've done, you can keep tweaking it until you get the final cut. It's then that you'll re-time the scenes and decide whether you can get away with recording the music conventionally and bringing it on several DATs to the studio when the master is made. If the timing is not critical and there are gaps between the music cues, this is how you should approach it. You'll sit in the studio with the video editing engineer and the director, align the start point of the music and visual and let the two run their course. When your cue is finished, you stop the tapes, roll the video ahead to the next cue and begin again. If you're recording short, isolated spots, you won't run into a sync problem.

But most scoring requires the composer to craft his music around pre-existing audio, and to synch his cues to the visual. To see what's involved in that process, let's take a hypothetical situation that guitarists can related to easily.

The Task

We'll start out by creating a scenario that happens to pretty much every scorer early in their career. Let's say your friend's Uncle Bob owns a motorcycle shop in your home town and is thinking of advertising on the local cable TV channel. He hires a video production company to script and shoot a commercial, and then deliver a broadcast-ready tape. He knows you play guitar, so he's asked the video team to use your music. That's as much as you know. What should you do next?

Seeking Common Ground

You'll first have to ask a lot of questions, so you know what each person in the chain (Uncle Bob and the director) envisions for the music and to set common goals. If the tape is available for viewing, or if you can secure a copy, get rough timings of the various scenes in the commercial. Then run your musical ideas by both the video team and the client (Uncle Bob). Discuss such subjects as emotional content, style, feel, tempos, and instrumentation.

You'll also have to agree on the format your final music is to be submitted on. It will probably be one of these media: 1/4" open-reel tape, DAT with time code, Hi-Fi VHS, or Beta SP. You should try to mix to the final format so you don't suffer a generation loss, but in most cases, it isn't critical. For example, mixing to DAT and then making a transfer to Beta is usually acceptable. Make sure to have the final-format deck well in advance of the delivery deadline, so you can acquaint yourself with its workings.

If the music you plan on composing is just instrumental guitar (provided by you) backed by a rhythm section, you can record in the normal fashion—i.e., onto a multi-track machine first and then mix down to two-track stereo DAT; or if you're fearless, live to two-track DAT. But first you must establish one other key factor before discussing specific creative aspects with the director: Is the music to be pre- or post-production?

Pre Vs. Post

"Pre-production" and "post-production" are processes that determine whether the video people fit the picture to you, or you fit the music to the video. For you the composer, pre-production can be technically easier because you just have to write good music, observing only a few parameters (e.g., it has to be 27 seconds long or three minutes long, etc.). The director either edits the video to your music or fades your music in and out to the images on screen (this process was described previously in "Non-Synched Music," p. 148). Music videos are an example of pre-production music. The musicians record a song first; they don't concern themselves with the visual challenges it may pose, they just try to write a good song. The director rehearses scenes dictated by the music (including getting a convincing lip-synched performance from the on-camera talent), or he edits the picture to fit the music.

Robin Williams' inspired genie scenes in Disney's *Aladdin* were done pre-production. Williams had a script and recorded his dialogue first—including his manic improvisations. The animators then made the genie's actions and facial expressions match the rapid-fire patter and verbal asides that cascaded off of Williams' quick-silver tongue. Similarly, when Gary Hoey scored the music to the surf flick *Endless Summer II*, he may have reviewed the preliminary footage (called "dailies"), but he essentially wrote complete songs that the editors later chopped up, dissolved and otherwise fitted to the picture, so Hoey approached his music as a pre-production process. But chances are, if you're scoring to video, you'll be living in the post-production world, where you have to adapt to the visuals and not the other way around.

"Post-production" means you must write music to match the video (sometimes down to sound effects coming with frame accuracy) and sync that music to a master timing reference. To do this, the video people will give you an edited copy of the video with time code "striped" onto one of the audio channels (channel 2 is the standard). There is also a visual representation of the time code "burned" into the video called a "SMPTE window dub" or "burn." It shows hours, minutes, seconds, and frames, and corresponds to the audio code (the actual sync tone) on channel 2. You're expected to adhere to this code and provide accurate records as to where your cues begin and end with regard to the SMPTE (which is pronounced SIMP-tee, and stands for Society of Motion Picture and Television Engineers, but commonly refers to the actual time code this organization standardized). To deal with SMPTE you'll need specific hardware, discussed a little later on (see "Synching to Video Step by Step," p. 154). But before we get into the nuts and bolts of the hardware, let's first consider some of the unique problems real-life scorers face, regardless of whether the music process is pre- or post-production.

The Setup

In our motorcycle commercial, you might see all the standard images: a guy (most motorcycle owners are guys) tooling down the open road with the camera following him from the side or above. For this you'd break out your best ZZ Top and Steppenwolf music—chunking power chords and pentatonic blues lead. When the close-up camera pans lovingly down the sleek contours of this hog—and the narrator describes its sexy stats—you might write a smoldering 12/8 blues shuffle, with plenty of string bending and swampy slide work, but you would be careful not to detract from the voice-over. Then as the bike glides off into the sunset, some arpeggiated fingerpicked acoustic guitar would be in order. (The narrator intones "All's right with the world when you're ridin' one of Uncle Bobs' bikes." [slow fadeout])

The Trap

Seems straightforward enough, right? But hidden in this simple scenario are the seeds of disaster. Here's an idea of what can happen. After you compose some basic themes and time them out to the pre-agreed-upon lengths, you and your band record all the ensemble stuff the night before your drummer leaves for Mexico. You then meet with the video director and see if you're both on the same wavelength. Typically, if all goes well, the director will like what you've done and offer some suggestions: "Right where the camera stops for a moment on the gas cap? I'd like a little suspension in the musical motion. Can you redo it with that change and have it to me tomorrow morning? Oh, and it needs to be two seconds shorter, because I want to tack on our logo over a black screen in total silence. And the director says to use a little less crash cymbal at the end, because over a TV speaker it will be too prominent."

Welcome to Crisisville. If you had dragooned band members from all over the area to produce this one cue, and now the next day, you have to redo it (and your drummer's on a plane to Cancun), you're out of luck. But last-minute changes are a fact of life in the scoring biz, and facile composing and recording skills are what make or break a successful scorer. It doesn't matter how great your music is if you can't be flexible with it. If you can't shorten a cue by two seconds, or have the drums add a crash cymbal on request, or drop a beat to make the music sync better with the on-screen action, you're not ready to score.

Technology to the Rescue

How, then, do you change music that's already been recorded? Simplest answer: Make it editable in the first place—either through MIDI and/or hard-disk recording. If your tracks were recorded with MIDI instruments on a sequencer instead of live instruments onto tape, it's a simple process to go back and change any aspect of the cue and then re-record the results. You still can play live guitar, because you're the one who's going to be there anyway, making changes to the score. But use MIDI and sequencing, at least in the preliminary stages, so you can re-tool your arrangements at will (yours and the director's), until the arrangements are finalized.

To work with MIDI and be able to tweak timings and such, you need a computer and a software-based sequencer. Even though hardware sequencers exist, no one uses them for scoring in a studio. They're better off for stage and live work. You'll also need some modules to generate different sounds like bass, drums, keyboards, pads (strings and horns), and sound effects (chain saws, engines revving, explosions, etc.). To input all your MIDI-based music, you'll probably need a MIDI-equipped guitar, unless your keyboard skills are up to snuff. You can either keep the MIDI- and sample-based tracks, or swap them out with the real thing after all the timings and edits are finalized.

Frank Serafine, a noted feature film and TV composer, says the first thing a guitarist should do if he wants to score is go MIDI. "You need a MIDI guitar setup, first and foremost," Serafine states. "That's how [former Police guitarist] Andy Summers does it, and I've collaborated with him on countless projects. Then you need a sequencer. I use Opcode's Studio Vision Pro, but any high-quality sequencer will do the same thing. With MIDI you can play your ideas into the computer and then have the synths and samplers play back the music and orchestrations. You can then actually print the score from your guitar and have an orchestra play it. So you could arrange all of your instrumentation and orchestration—via MIDI overdubbing and synth playback—on the guitar. That's how I score. I record everything on synths. If I want real instruments, I print out the parts and give them to the orchestral musicians to play."

Real Musicians Do Math

But what if it's just solo guitar? Should you still have a computer? Absolutely. A sequencer allows you to build a tempo track—sort of a sophisticated metronome—that allows you to play at the same tempo every time, even if there are ritards and accelerandos. Another area where computer sequencers are particularly useful is in timing conversions, which is indispensable for scoring. For example, you time the point where your music begins on the slow pan to the gas cap, and you time it out to about 6.5 seconds. If you're using a pro-quality sequencer, you can see not only beats and bars in the display window, but elapsed time (in minutes, seconds, and frames). You scroll to where 6.5 seconds occurs and the counter tells you that it's bar 2, beat 3½. Remember, this is where the director wants a "suspension." What you've now got to do is rewrite the music so that there is a hold at that point (you put in a half note or something). But how to re-work the music?

Quick quiz: If you're in 4/4 and the counter tells you that at 6.5 seconds you're at bar 2, beat 3½, what is your tempo? The answer is q=60. That means you've set your click track or metronome to 60, which is 60 quarter notes per minute or one per second. 6½ seconds equates to 7½ beats (beat 1 starts at clock 0, beat 2 at 1 second, and so on; this is called an offset). In 4/4, that's one bar plus 3½ beats. You simply re-write the music to look something like this:

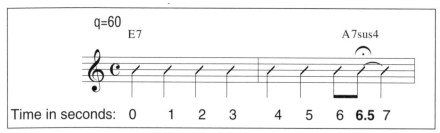

Fig. 10.1

A hold occurs in the music at exactly 6.5 seconds

So the bad news is you must not only own a computer, you must understand the mathematical nature of music. But you're lucky in that a computer will do most of the nettlesome computations for you. A great example of this is the "fit time" function. Remember how our director wanted the cue to be exactly two seconds shorter? Instead of calculating and converting the tempo to shave off exactly two seconds, you can highlight the region and go to the window displaying the "real time" (minutes and seconds instead of bars and beats) and dial in the new time (which is the original minus two). The sequencer re-calculates the tempo to fit the new time. Best of all, if you're dealing with MIDI instruments, the pitch doesn't change. And most hard-disk audio programs have an audio-processing algorithm that will allow you to shorten recorded-music passages by a small percentage without any noticeable effect on the audio quality. This process is called "time companding."

If you don't know what the heck I'm talking about, don't despair. That's all the math involved. But know that you must learn how to convert musical time that musicians deal with—bars, beats, and tempos—into the real time increments of hours, minutes, seconds, and frames of the video world.

In our above problem, say you didn't want to put a half note on an upbeat—you want the hold to fall on either beat 3 or beat 4 of bar 2. What would you have to do? You'd have to make the tempo slightly faster or slower. But by how much? Doing it manually, you'd have to pick a new tempo so that when you divided it by 60 (to get beats per second) and multiplied the result by 6.5 seconds and added 1 (the offset), you'd get exactly 7 or 8 (depending on whether you wanted the hold on beat 3 or 4). The new tempos—one slower than 60 and one faster—would be 55.39 and 64.62, respectively. That's the kind of calculating that goes on every minute of every day in the scoring world. Even if you never use computer-generated music (MIDI), you'd still need a computer for any post-production scoring tasks. The computer converts the video deck's time-code signal into meaningful commands that all the instruments and devices in your studio can read. It not only calculates and plays back tempos at metronome settings to the hundredth place, it interfaces the time code with your recorder.

To the Post

Post-production work requires that you know how to use a computer to read the time code on the video tape. You often need the hardware to stamp the time code into your tape as well. Then when you ship it off to the production company, they can marry your audio tape with frame-accurate resolution to their copy of the visual tape. The industry-standard method of synching machines together is SMPTE. SMPTE is a sync tone carrying information of hours, minutes, seconds, and frames (in most videos, 30 frames per seconds is the standard). Computers (or actually the software that runs on them) convert tempo, bars, and beats to SMPTE times, and vice versa, saving musicians the slow and tedious process of doing the calculations themselves.

Eric Aubrey, a guitarist who scores many network TV shows in his home studio in Chalfont, PA, describes how he works with SMPTE when scoring: "When I get a tape of an episode, it has a SMPTE window dub at the bottom. That tells me where each scene starts and ends and where important 'hit points' are in the scene. I slave my hard-disk recording system to the video, so that when I rewind or fast-forward the video, the computer moves right with it." Eric takes the audio output of his VCR (which has the SMPTE tone) and hooks it into his SMPTE reader/generator. The output of the SMPTE box goes into the computer, and from that moment on, all recorder locations are locked to the video. After he records his music to hard disk, Eric can stop the video at any point to see which frames correspond to which notes in the music. If he finds that his music is a little early or a little late he can tweak it by sliding the entire section forward or back a few frames. His hard-disk system, the Roland DM-80, provides all sorts of tools for manipulating music.

Frank Serafine uses a similar approach: "What I do is sit down and actually log in all the time codes on paper so I know where every section is. And I design everything from scratch. I sit down and I figure out—pretty much on paper—what I've got to do. Then I sequence the parts on my sequencer, Vision. I also do all my sound-effects editing on Vision. It's my production tool. I edit sound effects the same way I do my music; I'm a sound-effects orchestrator. And I'm performing on a synthesizer: an explosion comes up and I go *ka-blooey*! I play it on a keyboard. If it's off a few frames, I go edit it. So it's really like playing music with sound effects. It could be like a major action-adventure sequence, and the stuff that's going on is actually bigger than the score: you've got explosions, you've got a car engine roaring, you've got the sound of gravel on wheels, you've got the squeak of the suspension—everything. I do all of my sound effects the same way."

The basic difference in the two approaches is that Frank makes all his edits in the sequencer window, not in the actual recorded data. Eric moves sound around on the hard disk, after it's recorded. But they both use the SMPTE track as their guide as they tweak their edits.

Take a look at Figure 10.2, which shows how to wire up a studio to synch to video. Note that some lines are audio and some are computer or sync commands. It doesn't take much to hook all your gear together, just the right cables and the SMPTE generator, which acts as the hub for all the networking.

Is it possible, though, to score without all this fancy gear? Theoretically yes, but that would be like scrubbing the deck of an aircraft carrier with a toothbrush. "You have to work very fast in this business," cautions Eric. "You would think that because, say,

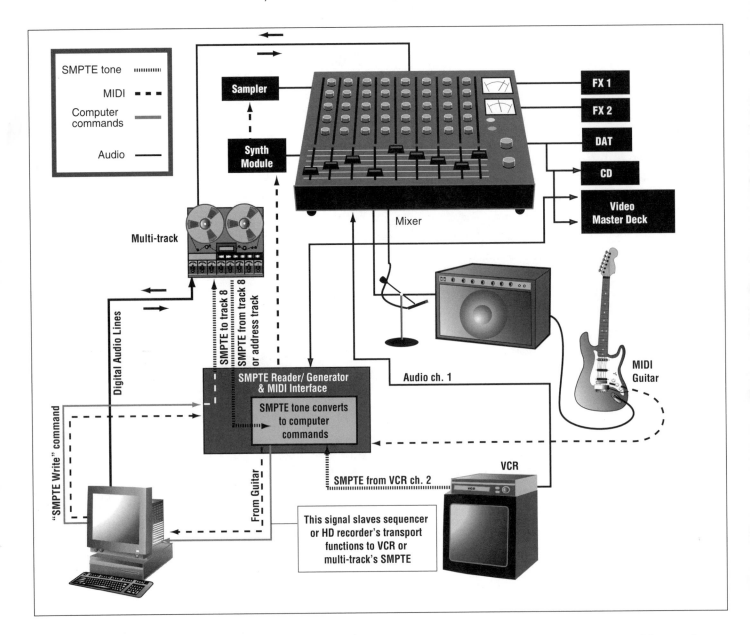

Fig. 10.2

How the essential scoring components in a studio hook together

it's network TV, things would be done way in advance. It's just not so. I learned very quickly where the latest FedEx drop is in my area. Also, the people you're working for know what's humanly possible, even if it is unreasonable. They know you can re-orchestrate something in a night because of MIDI. They realize you might have to stay up all night to do it, but they know it can be done."

Synching to Video Step by Step

The essential gear you need to synch to video includes a Hi-Fi video deck (with stereo outputs) a computer with a pro-level sequencer, some modules to create sound, a multi-track tape deck or hard-disk recorder (which could be included with your sequencer), and a sync box, which can double as the MIDI interface. To actually get the synching part happening, refer to the diagram and the five steps that outline the procedure.

The Magic Box

Sync boxes exist in all flavors, but you'll want to secure a SMPTE reader/generator. You don't have to be using video gear to appreciate the benefits of synching with SMPTE. You can sync together just your four-track cassette and sequencer if you like. Two low-price boxes that work great are the JL Cooper's PPS (which stands for "poor person's SMPTE") and Opcode's Translator Pro Sync (both cost about $150). Once you get one of these boxes (and assuming you have a sequencer that is SMPTE savvy, e.g., Cakewalk, Master Tracks, Vision, Performer, Cubase, E-Magic), you have all the tools necessary to marry your multi-track to your computer. Here's the step-by-step breakdown:

If you stop the video tape, the sequencer will pause too. If you rewind or fast forward the video tape and then press play, the sequencer "chases" the video tape and catches up to it in just a few seconds (this is known as "chase lock"). You can now

Fig. 10.3

Five steps to incorporating SMPTE

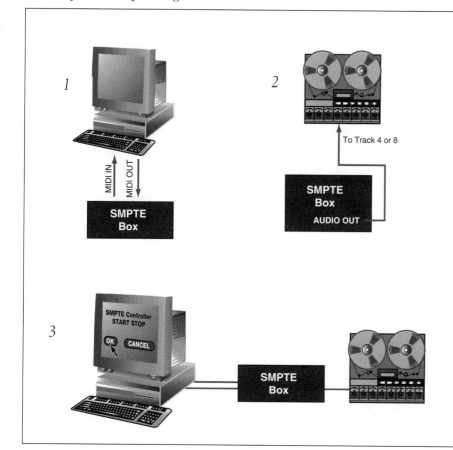

1) Hook up MIDI cables from your computer's MIDI interface to the sync box.

2) Attach a cable from the audio output of the box to the channel input of your multi-track (it's the convention to use the last track—#4, #8, etc.).

3) Launch your sequencer and invoke the SMPTE controller from the menu bar. (The sync box itself is "dumb," meaning it requires an external controller to drive it.) Press the Start command and you should hear the SMPTE squawk from your multi-track (via headphones or monitor speakers). Adjust the record levels so that the signal comes in at about -6 dB. (Zero is too high, and you'll risk cross-talk, especially on analog machines.) Once you get a level, hit "Stop" on the computer window's SMPTE controller. Put the deck into record mode, roll tape (defeat noise reduction if you have it), and again hit "Start" in the SMPTE controller window. You'll now be recording SMPTE onto track 4 (or 8). Hit "Stop SMPTE," then stop the tape and rewind.

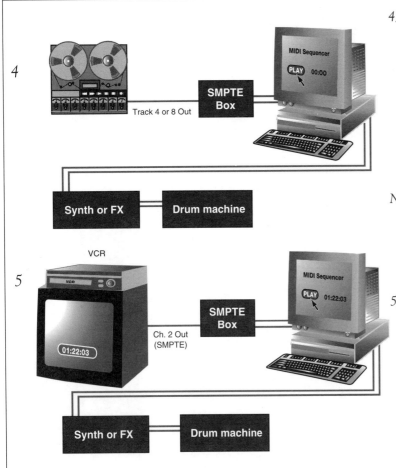

4) *Test that you've successfully recorded the audio SMPTE tone to track 4 (or 8). Then rewind, and take a cable from the multi-track's output and connect it to the input of the SMPTE box. The box will now be able to "listen" to the tone on the tape. The box will then convert the SMPTE tone into MIDI commands (called MTC, or MIDI time code), which it will send back to your computer. Be sure to change your computer's sync source from "Internal" to "External" so that it knows to listen for an outside command. If all goes well, your sequence will start and stop in step with the SMPTE tone.*

Now you're free to record on tracks 1-3 while SMPTE plays your MIDI modules and drum machines from track 4. With this method you don't even have to put MIDI tracks on the multi-track; you can play them live to the mixdown deck in stereo. Record just your live, non-MIDI performances (guitar, vocals, etc.). That's all there is to it.

5) *For post-production scoring to video (putting music to an existing set of images), simply substitute a VCR for the multi-track in Step 4. The video tape must already have the SMPTE code recorded on track 2 (handled by the video production company), and have a window dub showing the hours, minutes, seconds, and frames on your TV monitor. These numbers will match perfectly the counter in your computer sequencer window, because you've "slaved" it to the tape, meaning you've told the sequencer to derive its timing from an external source, in this case the audio track of the video tape.*

note the location of an event in the window dub of the video, record a "hit" at the corresponding point in one of the sequencer tracks, rewind and roll the video again, and the computer will play your hit at precisely the right location. If you've "missed" the exact point, there's no need to re-record. Just go into the sequencer's editing window and move the hit forward or backward in the track (noting the SMPTE time in the counter window as you do) and roll tape again. After you've logged all your hit points in the sequencer, you can substitute a sample, a guitar chord, or whatever cue is called for. The important thing is that you've created a "map" or EDL (edit decision list) indicating where the important cues fall.

Even if you're performing all live music (like solo guitar), you can make critical timing decisions with "scratch tracks" on the sequencer using precision editing techniques (including tempo and meter adjustments), and then match your performance to the sequence. It may take some practice to follow a sequence with a live performance and to make it sound natural and organic, but it can be done with practice, even if there are ritards, accelerandos, pauses and holds. Just make sure that when you make the final recording that it's your performance that goes to tape and not the "glorified click track."

A Hardware Checklist

Here are some essential items that you'll need to familiarize yourself with to become a successful scorer.

Hi-Fi VCR with a jog/shuttle wheel and audio inserts

The jog wheel allows you to move the paused image forward and back by frames (the remote control should do the same thing). Audio inserts allow you to add your own time code to a video tape if there isn't already one, and read the SMPTE code from the hi-fi outputs. Recommended is the pro-quality 3/4", but you can get away with 1/2" VHS format.

SMPTE reader/generator

This reads and writes SMPTE, hooking up in between your computer and video deck. Many DAT players come with a center track for SMPTE. This allows you to put your master timing reference on the stereo mixdown master. There are many varieties of SMPTE generators, the cheapest costing as little as $150.

Computer and pro-level sequencer

You can get either a PC or Mac computer, but choose your computer by which software it will run and the recommendations of the people you'll be working with. As for sequencers, Master Tracks Pro, Studio Vision, Performer, Cakewalk, Cubase, E-magic, to name a few, all have the ability to display SMPTE and convert bars, beats, and tempos to hours, minutes, seconds, and frames. Even if you're playing live acoustic guitar into a hard-disk recorder, the sequencer can provide a click track.

Video monitor

Here is where you can skimp, because a monitor is there for information purposes only (unless you're doing precision hits, and then go easy on your eyes and invest in a high quality unit). You don't necessarily need high resolution to see at which frame the car door slams or the muzzle flashes or the cork pops, you just need to see the image and time code display.

DAT recorder

This is still the industry standard for mixdowns because unlike CDs (which are popular for audio-only applications), many DAT recorders come with a provision to stripe time code on their tapes. You can buy a consumer model without the time code feature for as little as $500, while more expensive pro models include a jog wheel and the ability to record at both 44.1 kHz (the CD standard) as well as the more consumer-oriented rate of 48 kHz. If you record at 48 kHz, you'll eventually have to convert to 44.1 kHz before you master.

A digital multi-track recorder

This is last on the list because if you deal strictly with MIDI sequencer tracks (synths, samplers, and drum machines), you can get away with an analog recorder by editing all your sequenced tracks in the sequencer and then "printing" just your analog material (guitar, vocals) when you mix down to two-track stereo. But if you deal with acoustic or other non-sequenced music, you'll make life a lot easier on yourself with a digital multi-track. You can use either a hard-disk-based system (such as Digidesign's Pro Tools, Opcode's Studio Vision, Cakewalk Pro, Mark of the Unicorn's Digital Performer, Steinberg's Cubase VST, Emagic's Logic Audio, etc.) or tape-based systems (like the Alesis ADAT or TASCAM DA-88), but having your recorded music in the digital domain means precise editing, and that can be a real time-saver. In tape-based systems, you'll need the manufacturer's sophisticated controllers for frame-accurate manipulation.

In addition to the above-mentioned items, you'll need your standard home-studio gear: a mixer, good quality mics, compressors, reverbs, multi-effects processors, monitors, patch bays, dubbing decks, etc. These are individual choices and are not unique to a scoring facility versus a normal recording environment.

The best way to become a good scorer is not to acquire great gear, but to compose and score as much as possible. Successful film and video scorers aren't just good, they're fast, well-oiled, and wear their chops on their sleeves. It's part of the persona. Don't worry about trying to acquire all the gear at once, either. A computer and a sequencer are essential, yes, but nothing else is necessary for improving your skills. Get videos from your film-making friends and have a video production company put a SMPTE window burn on them with the SMPTE code on channel 2. The cost is between $35 and $50 for a 30-minute tape. Then with pencil and paper, make an edit decision list yourself, writing down start and end times for music cues, and then marking the hit points with those times. It might look something like this:

Girl opens door	*1h:23m:20s:14f*	*(creepy slide gtr.)*
Severed arm falls	*1h:23m:25s:03f*	*(power chord w/trem.)*
Girl screams	*1h:23m:28s:29f*	*(wild tapping & fdbk.)*

Then work to connect these hit points together with cohesive musical ideas. It ain't easy, as you'll soon discover. You'll begin to see scoring as an integrated skill, one that involves working your creative themes around hit points, tempo, meter, and how all that relates to real time. When you can be creative within the problem-solving confines of a video, then you're ready to start taking direction from other people, which is another skill altogether. Get as much experience as you can collaborating, as that's one of the key ingredients in scoring. You must be able to work with the director and to take direction.

You might offer your services to the local university's film school. That's a great way to get involved in the collaborating game, and you'll be dealing with people who are more concerned with creativity than the clock (of course, you probably won't make any money either). If you find opportunities, take on as many as you can handle. This way you'll not only get better at scoring, you'll get better at writing music and recording guitar.

A Scoring Glossary

Animation: A format that refers to more than just cartoons. Titles, logos and other rendered images are also considered animation, and they are a staple of industrials and infomercials. These types of animation usually call for a relatively simple musical bed, with sounds highlighting specific text or hit points.

Bed: A piece of background music intended to lay under dialogue without being overtly dramatic or distracting.

Beta, Beta SP: Though Beta long ago dropped off the consumer format map, it's the format of choice for many professional video producers. Beta SP machines are as expensive as top-quality audio multi-tracks.

Bumper: A short musical cue used as a segue between segments, such as music leading into commercial breaks.

Chase: A machine being controlled from an external source via time code is said to be chasing time code.

Cue Lists and Edit Decision Lists (EDL): Text lists used by film makers to keep track of all the edits and segments of a program, referenced to time code. Film makers may supply you with a cue list with specific text about music.

Dissolves, Tears, Cuts and Jump-Cuts: These are examples of different types of video edits.

Dubbing: Adding audio to a video master without affecting the picture.

Educationals: Videos sold directly to schools covering just about any topic and age group you can think of. Since the target audience is young, educationals often call for creative, hip music.

Fly Wheeling: SMPTE can be prone to dropouts, especially on VHS machines. "Fly wheeling" means the unit receiving time code will continue for a specific number of frames in the event of a dropout.

Hit Point: The specific SMPTE location. A graphic appearing on screen, an explosion, or an edit, can all be hit points.

Industrial: Nine Inch Nails it ain't. An industrial video is a non-commercial release used to disseminate information about a product, train employees or communicate about a company. Though most industrials are low-budget affairs using "needle drop," some have high production values and call for original music.

Insert Edit: Editing video with or without changing audio.

Jam Sync: When a unit can receive time code at its input, and spit the code out its output at the same time, it's called "jam synching." Very useful for feeding SMPTE to several devices at once.

A SCORING GLOSSARY—*continued*

Layback: Dubbing the final audio mix to picture.

MTC: MIDI Time Code—MIDI translation of SMPTE.

Needle Drop: A carryover from the days of vinyl, "needle drop" refers to the use of pre-recorded music libraries.

Offset: Sometimes the time code on a video and the time code on your work tape disagree. The offset is the difference (usually in minutes or frames) between the two tapes.

Post Production: Editing, mixing, foley, and layback are all elements of post production. Unless you're working on a desktop production, the final mix to picture is done at a post house. That's where you'll be delivering your mixes.

Rough Cut: A preliminary edit. You may get a rough cut early in a project so that you can create your basic theme and show the direction the music will take.

SMPTE Time Code: An audio signal in the form of linear time code that keeps track of tape position in hours:minutes:seconds:frames:bits. The Frame Rate refers to the number of frames per second (FPS). While 24 FPS is the film standard, most videos come to you striped with the higher resolution 30 (FPS) non-drop frame. If you're striping the tape yourself, be sure and ask the film maker which frame rate to use.

Striping: Recording time code to tape.

Talent: The people appearing on screen.

Window Burn: Time code displayed on screen is called a "window burn." A visual reference helps you find hit points. Always ask for one.

1/2" Video: Another term for VHS.

3/4" Video: A pro format that many people use but few seem to like. 3/4" machines offer pro features (like the ability to chase time code and dub audio) that VHS machines lack, but they're not noted for having good audio quality. Many professional composers get work prints on 3/4", then make their own VHS copies.

CHAPTER ELEVEN

Setups and Small Studio Solutions

With the advent of digital technology, the cost and space required to create a professional-level studio has plummeted. Like the "hardware-downsizing" that computers experienced, the digital-audio horsepower that used to take up a good chunk of a room can now fit inside a unit that sits comfortably on a table-top. Price tags for recording technology have also shrunk just as dramatically. Digital multi-tracks used to cost a hundred thousand dollars; now, for just a couple thousand, you can enjoy the same quality in a machine that at one time only a commercial studio facility could afford to purchase, house, and maintain. And then there's the whole area of affordable digital technology. You can get eight recordable tracks of digital audio for under a thousand dollars, including a mixer, phantom power, effects, and some other handy extras, and the competition is just beginning to heat up.

Better quality, smaller packaging, and downwardly mobile pricing structures all spell good news for the recording guitarist. If you have an unlimited budget and an airplane hangar's worth of space to devote to a studio, this chapter is not for you. But if you're looking to outfit or upgrade a studio in a small space with a meager sum of cash, read on.

STARTING FROM ZERO

The best way to assess what you need in a studio is to take stock of what you already have, even if you think it's insignificant. As a guitarist, you may have been collecting stuff that can be used in your studio without even knowing it. Some gear, like multi-effects processors, can be pressed into studio service, even though you originally acquired it to process your guitar sound. Even if you think you're starting from scratch, you may not be, though your digital delay is the pedal version rather than a nice rackmount unit. Just don't get discouraged when you look at other studios that are better appointed than yours. Remember, Rome wasn't built in a day.

I thought I was forever suffering from the "grass is always greener" syndrome until one day a friend of mine walked into my home studio for the first time and said, "Jeez, look at all this stuff! I just have a little four-track—and a piece of crap, at that. But not you. Oh, no. You have an arsenal! I might as well give up now." Now, my home studio is not that impressive. But I have been cultivating it a long time—longer than my friend has been cultivating his. So when he walks in off the street and compares his to mine, the differences seem drastic.

What my friend doesn't consider is that every piece of gear in my studio was at one time also a "piece of crap." My digital eight-track was once a cassette four-track with a broken rewind button. (I had to flip the tape and fast-forward—talk about a work-around!) My rackmount Lexicon DDL was once a Boss DD-3 stompbox that I used to have to unhook from my studio to bring to gigs and vice versa. This borrowing back and forth can be dangerous, by the way. Sometimes on a gig, I'd open my gig bag, and, as Yogi Berra would say, "There it was—gone!" I had left it in my studio . . . again. Anyway, I had nothing beyond my delay—no compressor, no DAT machine, no monitors, no multi-effects processors, no drum machine, no patch bay, nor microphones at all. Each of these were hard-won prizes: I'd sacrifice taking a vacation, buying a new pair of shoes, and I once drove my car around on the emergency-use-only "donut" for three months instead of buying a proper tire so I could afford a new piece of gear (kids, don't try this at home).

But the beauty of home studio setup is that it's by nature a modular, component-driven enterprise. You can buy one piece of gear at a time and it won't significantly change the way you make music. It might enhance, improve, or streamline the process, but it won't change your basic approach to it. The first thing I did when I brought the Lexicon home was to say, "Okay, now how do I get that sound I got with the Boss stompbox?" Get the stuff when you can and in a year or two, a friend will come over and say, "Look at all this stuff!"

The question of which stuff to get, and in what order, often confuses people. My approach is to get a lot of cheap stuff and upgrade it over time, rather than scrimping and saving to buy one quality piece at a time. As I said, studio-building is modular; replacing each piece will only improve the process, but if you don't have enough of the basic gear, you won't learn any skills. Here's my priority list of must-have gear:

• **Multi-Track Recorder** You don't need a state-of-the-art digital eight-track or a computer-based hard-disk recording system. Four-track cassettes with built-in mixers are ubiquitous these days and for good reason: they sound great. All come with EQ, versatile signal-routing schemes, dbx or Dolby noise reduction, and footswitch operation. Where you have to be careful is with tape speed. Many come with tape transports running at standard cassette speed ($1\frac{7}{8}$ inches per second). These don't sound nearly as good as the ones that run at double speed ($3\frac{3}{4}$ ips). And I'm not just talking EQ or noise floor. I'm talking actual tape-crinkle garble and warble. If you're using your machine for demos only, the occasional dropout may not be enough to outweigh the convenience and economy of standard-speed models. But I personally would never buy one. If you ever get the chance to compare a standard-vs. double-speed machine, you'll discover the double-speed ones are clearly superior.

If you can go one step beyond that, consider the self-contained workstations. The advantage is the all-in-one approach. They're portable and fairly versatile with signal routing, track bouncing, etc. The disadvantage is that they are non-modular, so if you decide to upgrade your mixer, you have no way to ditch the redundant, built-in mixer that's attached to your recording device.

• **Digital Reverb** Nowadays it might seem hard to buy just a reverb; they're usually part of a multi-effects processor. But I've included that as a separate entry, because I feel it's essential to have a separate, stand-alone reverb—a box designed to use all its processing power to produce strictly reverb. Reverb is used on literally every recording you hear, even spoken-word-only pieces. You should use a different reverb for the entire mix than for individual tracks, and having two units will allow this. Also, combining your dedicated reverb with additional reverb from your multi-effects box will produce more complex results.

• **Microphone** Even if you can't carry a tune with a bucket, you'll learn a lot about music by singing and harmonizing your own tunes, and getting acceptable tape takes. To do this you need a microphone. Don't buy one at Radio Shack; go to the music store and buy a Shure SM-57 or SM-58, or comparable mic. They're the industry-standard dynamic (as opposed to condenser) mics and one of these, or a similar model, will serve you for years.

• **Multi-Effects Processor** You might have one of these for your guitar, but you'll need another one dedicated to your studio. I would try to get one with compressor and gate functions, as this will save you from having to buy separate versions later. (The difference between pro and amateur recordings can usually be traced to lack of smooth compression and gain normalization—the principal function of a compressor.) Try to get a processor that contains exciter or signal-enhancement circuitry, since these are especially useful for mixing. Parametric EQ is usually included with multi-effects units, and this is indispensable for recording too. Remember, this is for the studio, not your guitar. Don't get hung up on "guitar" features. Look for quality effects and algorithms designed for versatile applications.

• **Drum Machine/Rhythm Composer** Guitarists are rhythm section players and must know the other instruments in their group. Even if you use just the presets and never program a note, a drum machine will keep you rhythmically honest and will inspire you to make music in grooves you might not intuitively produce or couldn't emulate if the unit weren't there. The Roland Dr. Rhythm units are great, and feature accompaniment instruments as well.

• **Bass** The same sermon about knowing the other instruments in you section applies here. Auto-accompaniment boxes will never replace live bass playing, so learn bass licks in standard grooves (straight-four rock, shuffle, funk, etc.), and write and play your own parts. Remember, you're not just a guitar player, you're in charge of a total sound. I've never known any producer worth his salt who couldn't play at least a couple of different instruments passably.

You can of course record music with just your guitar and a multi-track tape machine, but the above five items will allow for a wide variety of musical possibilities. You'll also never remove them from the creative chain. You may replace one for a better unit, but the purpose for the original box will still be there. I look at my most expensive multi-effects processor and in the display I can see the ghost of my MXR phase shifter.

A No Frills, Self-Contained Recording Rig

Guitarists are unique in that they need more gadgetry than other instrumentalists to get their sound to tape or disk. Unlike, say, a wind player, who just needs a mic, a reverb, and a recording deck, guitarists have to be able to reproduce an entire rig's worth of gear to present to a tape input. That might include not only effects like chorus, delay, and flanging, but also a wall of Marshalls or a close-miked Vox AC30, or a set of matched Fender Vibro-Kings in a layered split, one close-miked and the other ambient-miked. Plus, you have your acoustic setup to drag along as well, which may or may not involve a pickup as well as a miked signal. And unlike our wind-playing friends, guitarists are invariably asked (not that we're complaining, mind you) for a double-tracked part involving not only a complementary part, but sometimes a complementary part using a complementary instrument.

So how do you possibly get this amount of stuff into a reasonable space?

Depending on what you want to do and how truly miniaturized you want to become, you can fit a "recording studio" into a unit the size of a cereal box. Multi-track digital recorders that come with onboard effects now exist for under $1,000 street price. After tracking on one of these all-in-one multi-tracks, you could then do a master mixdown onto a portable DAT recorder, which is the size of a Walkman. Plenty of mega-selling, chart-topping CDs have been made this way. Well, maybe they haven't been recorded entirely from a workstation to DAT, but many tracks of a master recording have been cut on a lower-end machine and "bumped up" to a larger format.

The approach of producing not just demos but "keeper" tracks from small studios or even home studios is finding more and more favor these days. Veteran producer Phil Ramone says, "Home is where the inspiration occurs, which is where you'll find the real music. I've spent too many hours in big studios trying to capture the groove and feel of the demo. I know that sometimes it's just impossible to re-create that original moment. That's why I say as long as the audio quality is there, I'll use a home-recorded track any day. Especially as a kernel of a groove or an overdub. I don't think I'd want to get a drum kit sound that way, or a string section, but for spot stuff—with a nice Neumann mic, a Yamaha 02R, and a DA-88—why not?"

Encouraging news for those of us who can't afford to build The Record Plant in our studio apartment, or whose budget doesn't allow for a 72-input Neve Capricorn with Flying Faders along with rent and macaroni and cheese.

The clues for a well-balanced recording facility lie in Phil Ramone's above quote. You need a mixer, a mic, and a recording device. Guitarists will also need a way to get great sound coming from their equipment, but I can assume that most of you came to recording as guitarists, and not to guitar from recording. In other words, whether you're a solo acoustic player or a mega-rig guitar hero, you probably have your sound together (or we can at least treat that as a separate issue). Now you just need to lay it down for posterity. Let's start by considering the components that will make up our studio, starting with the core of the operation, the multi-tracker.

If you're looking at the best bang for the buck, you can't beat the current trend for producing self-contained units that include a recorder, mixer, and onboard effects. The Akai DPS 12, Roland VS series, Korg D8, Yamaha MD-8, and Fostex FD-8, are the best multi-track buys once you leave the four-track arena. With the exception of the Roland VS-840 (which has circuitry and features to specifically accommodate a guitar input), you'll need to prepare your guitar signal. But because the 840 has not only included their excellent distortion and amp simulating effects, but a properly prepared input jack as well (it boasts an input impedance modeled more after a guitar amp's than traditional mixer channel).

If you have your multi-track and your "input-prepared" guitar signal (either through direct boxes or guitar-effects processor), you have a studio. Well, at least a guitar-based one. But this is fine for guitar-based producers and composers like Waddy Wachtel, who's served as session guitarist for the likes of Linda Ronstadt, James Taylor, Bob Dylan, Melissa Etheridge, Stevie Nicks, the Rolling Stones, and the soundtrack to the Adam Sandler film *The Waterboy*.

"I had asked Joe Walsh to sing this song I'd written for the movie called New Year's Eve, and I recorded his vocal right into the 880. When we finished, I brought the 880 down to Ocean Way Studios and, using a Mark of the Unicorn MIDI TimePiece, transferred it all onto big tape, added real drums, did some minor remixing, and there it was. So when you hear Joe singing in the movie, that came straight off the 880. When you go to 'big tape'," Wachtel advises, "You pick up a little of that analog warmth as well."

Tracking on a portable unit and transferring up has now become Wachtel's favorite approach for creative production. "When you're doing lead solos or vocals," he says, "and you finish the take and want to do another, all you do is switch virtual tracks with one turn of a knob and you're ready to go again, instead of having to take that track out of record, get another track into record-ready, switch mic inputs, and re-match the levels."

Wachtel is a living example of the peripatetic producer. He records his own guitars, as well as, say, the vocals of Joe Walsh onto his VS-880 and then picks it up and carries it with him. In this case that was to a larger studio in New York City, where he simply plugs into a patch bay in the control room.

Well, the theory of what you should buy and how you should set up is all well and good, but nothing illustrates the concept of studio-building like taking a look at some real-world examples.

The following pages take you on a tour of the studios of some working professionals, all guitarists, who have tackled and solved the problem of outfitting a small studio.

Fig. 11.1

The Brewery board

ALLAN HOLDSWORTH
The Brewery

A view of the Trident 24-series mixing board that drives Allan Holdsworth's studio. Allan prefers the EQ of this old British stalwart for its musicality. He's beefed up the power supplies of some of the channels so that he can drive them hot. Note the SynthAxe between the board and the rack of three ADATs.

Fig. 11.2

Guitar corner in The Brewery

Allan's approach to effects sometimes outstrips any single unit's functionality, so he'll often employ two or three of the same effect in one rack (witness the four Deltalab Effectron II's and the four Yamaha 1500's).

Fig. 11.3

The amp room

Allan close mics many of his cabs and doesn't like to play so loud that the cabinets themselves resonate and create standing waves, which is why he's not too concerned about the reflective surfaces (i.e., the hard paneling) lining the room. Allan shapes his signal by running it into a separate preamp and feeding that into a power amp, taking the speaker output of the power amp and running that through his self-designed load box, The Harness. From there, he typically goes into a Carvin power amp.

SLASH
Descend into the Snakepit

Note that in the live room of Snakepit, Slash's home studio, the drums have been walled off by dividers to form an island in the center of the room. This gives the drummer wide visual access to everyone else in the studio and a good sight line to the control booth. Note the rack of Marshall heads off to the right as well as in front of the drums.

Fig. 11.4

Snakepit's live room

Like Holdsworth, Slash likes British boards, and so his studio features a Trident Series 80 B board. That's a Studer 24-track analog machine on the right. Through the control-room window the drum kit vies for center stage with a Marshall stack.

Fig. 11.5

Snakepit's control room

MICHAEL WHALEN
Scoring and Post-Production

The sloped walls hint that this successful film and TV composer has built his studio on the top floor of a house. Whalen keeps three video monitors active for easy reference, and bases his studio around the legendary Synclavier system (whose keyboard is centrally located under the three monitors). Note the Roland-ready Strat (left) and the Roland GR series guitar synth. Whalen recently switched mixers, opting to go with two Yamaha 02R's which give him automation (critical for scoring), flexible signal routing, and great sound.

Fig. 11.6

Whalen's studio is outfitted for state-of-the art post-production scoring

Fig. 11.7

Pete Wasner's control room

Fig. 11.8

Pete Wasner's live room

Fig. 11.9

Kent Wells' control room

Fig. 11.10

Kent Wells' live room

PETE WASNER AND KENT WELLS
Nashville Cats

Unlike the home studios in, say New York City, where space is at a premium, Nashville-based guitarist/producers can capitalize on that city's relatively inexpensive living space. Here are two views of the studios of Kent Wells (whose board is a Mackie SR24 and 24 tracks of ADAT) and Pete Wasner (whose studio runs on a Yamaha 02R and 24 tracks of TASCAM's MDMs—one DA-88 and two DA-38s, one from the live room, one from the control room. Note that in both cases, the control-room facilities are compact, and could easily fit into a space much smaller. The live rooms, by contrast accommodate the different gear amply.

TONY BERG
Squeezing Quality out of Small Quarters

Tony Berg, producer of The Squeeze, Michael Penn, Edie Brickell and Real World, got his board, an API, from the Record Plant in New York, where it had been used for making hit records for 18 years. Tony tells the story that after he paid for the board, "they forgot that the console, which was on the 10th floor, did not fit in the freight elevator. They

Fig. 11.11

The API mixing board, formerly of the Record Plant

had to get a crane to lower it down to the street. And they didn't charge me a dime for that." Berg has recently gone back to analog as a recording medium, employing a Studer A80 Mark IV. Note the Kleenex box atop the right monitor, which Berg had installed to help dampen high-frequencies.

Seen in Fig. 11.12 is one very busy corner of Berg's control room: a remote controller, a couple of racks, and a patch bay sit at the left side of the API board. Above the patch bays sit three monitors—two audio (Audix, Tannoy) and one video (Radius).

Fig. 11.12

Snug but efficient is the left side of the mixer

SIMON TAYLOR
Coad Mountain Studio

Simon Taylor lives in the bucolic rolling hills of County Kerry and has set his control room up in a second-floor gable of his house. The window to the right lets in fresh air and sunshine (not a bad thing to have if you're spending a lot of time in your studio, and the live room is on a different floor, off of the kitchen. At the center of the control room is Taylor's Soundcraft Spirit Auto 24x8x2 inline console.

Fig. 11.13

The control room of Coad Mountain, an ADAT-based studio that specializes in Irish music and recording idiomatic Irish instruments

YNGWIE MALMSTEEN
House of Chops

Yngwie Malmsteen's precision fretboard assault is also evident in his approach to recording. In his South Florida home, he has hardwired many of the rooms with XLR jacks. "I've converted the original maid's quarters on the other side of the

Fig. 11.14

Yngwie in the control room of his studio. The racks include gear by Focusrite, TubeTech, Summit Audio and Urei

house into an isolation room for the Marshall cabinets. The cabs and mics are hardwired into the house with XLR connectors that go straight to the control room upstairs. Up there I have my three Marshall 50-watt heads, my new Studer 24-track tape machine, two TASCAM DA-88's and all the outboard gear. I'm a big advocate of analog recording, even though I have the TASCAM 16-track setup. I'll use the digital setup mostly for playback and for interfacing with other musicians who record digitally, but I like to capture all my guitar stuff on the Studer."

MOBY
Cutting-Edge Art through Traditional Means

Moby leads a varied recording career, creating everything from ethereal voices in an ambient wash to driving groove-based electronica. He uses a Soundcraft 24x8x2 board and four ADATs for tracking, preferring to mix at an outside facility, if possible. His two main effects are a Yamaha SPX-900 and an Eventide DSP4000. He mics amps whenever possible (Mesa/Boogie and SWR being current faves), using SM-57s and lots of compression. When he does go direct, Moby swears by the original SansAmp.

Fig. 11.15

Moby's avant-garde setup

Fig. 11.16

Alex Lifeson performs some finger magic

ALEX LIFESON
Solo Artist and Rush Guitarist

Alex Lifeson's studio is a mix of analog and digital, but he clearly prefers the former technology for his own music. "Although I tend to compose on Logic Audio and use the hard-disk recording feature of the sequencer in the writing stage," he explains, "I'm a little too traditional to go that way for finals. I like faders. I like the board. A lot of people work with a disk-based system, but I like to move the faders with my fingers rather than a mouse. hard-disk systems are terrific for editing, but not as good—at least for my purposes—for recording. For me, if I don't like it, I'll re-record it. But for writing, you can do things very quickly: copy things, move them around, leave space for something else. So for that, I really like the random-access approach."

As one who has produced classic guitar sounds for decades, Alex offers this advice for setting up guitar sounds: "Keep the mixer EQ flat for as long as you can," he urges, "and try different mic combinations. Move the mics around. Fiddle as much as you can before EQ'ing because then you know the sound is there. It's much easier to deal with the sound before it's processed unless EQ is part of the sound, of course.

Fig. 11.17

A Manhattan flat is where it's at for Steve Postell

STEVE POSTELL
Little Blue, Lotta Guitars

With his band, Little Blue, Steve Postell recorded the album *Angels, Horses & Pirates*, which featured guest tracks by Eric Johnson, Robben Ford, Warren Haynes, Jeff Golub and David Grissom. The way he went about it represents a popular paradigm of small studio recording: He started by recording the basics at a big commercial facility (Unique Recording, in New York) and had all his tracks transferred to 24 tracks of ADAT so he could overdub in his studio.

"We prepared tapes for the guitarists by mixing the rhythm section down to two tracks, placing a lead vocal on the third, and a click on the fourth track on an eight-track ADAT tape," explains Postell. "In Eric's case, we made a digital transfer to a TASCAM DA-88 to accommodate the studio where he was to work. It is one thing to listen to Eric's records, it is another to sit at a mixing console with nine tracks of his amazing guitar work your fingertips." Note the mixer faces a bay window in front of the board and that the live room is off to the right. Postell keeps his patch bay in a separate rack, conveniently located just to the right of the mixer. The wooden structure on the far left is the wooden mantle of a fireplace. All the things for a cozy evening: Bay window, fireplace, mixer.

TRAVELING SETUPS

Having survived the era when recording gear was heavy, bulky, and unwieldy, I'm enamored of portable and miniature setups where the goal is to provide the best quality in the smallest possible package. People have been creating miniature live rigs using this philosophy a lot longer than they have for recording, but it's now becoming very popular to build recording rigs that boast the optimum in space-efficiency and pro-level sonic quality. This section is for guitarists who want to take it with them when they go.

In Praise of Portability: A True Story

Most problems you'll solve—in recording as well as life—come out of necessity. You often don't have the option of thinking, "I could do this any way I want because I've got unlimited funds and all the time in the world . . . what's the best way?" It's usually, "Yikes, I've got 50 bucks and 24 hours. How am I going to make this happen with what I've got?"

Case in point. I've thought about creating a portable recording rig for some time, debating portability versus price, and it's never quite gelled. Then the call came. My friend needed an acoustic slide-guitar overdub consisting of fills and a short solo for a jingle he was producing. He was recording it on two synched ADATs, and was just going to send me a copy of one of the tapes, with an open track for the slide overdub. Since I have an ADAT in my studio, compatibility was not a problem. I throw the tape on my machine, listen back to track 1 (which contained a rough mono mixdown of the tune for my reference), record my fills and solo on tracks 7 and 8 (giving him two choices, one busy, one sparse) and then mail it back. He would synch that tape back up to the master, erase the reference track and use whichever track he liked (or a combination thereof).

The problem was, I was going on vacation to a cabin in the woods of Vermont the very next day, and the tape was due back while I was still to be away. Working with the ADAT was going to be impossible. Before I called him back to decline, I looked around my studio to see if I could cobble together a setup I could take with me. I came up with the idea of recording the part onto my stereo MiniDisc recorder, which my friend could then bounce. I didn't have a portable DAT, which would have been ideal, but this was reality (and I wasn't about to lug my full-size DAT deck). The MiniDisc doesn't have the fidelity of DAT, but since this was for unexposed fills tucked in the mix of a TV jingle, it just might do. MiniDiscs still sound pretty darn good, and there's no noise like on cassette. He might go for it.

Then there was the question of miking. Although I have a pickup in the acoustic, it doesn't sound that good, let alone realistic, and it wasn't what my friend was used to hearing. I would have to mic the guitar. I took my trusty AKG 451 (a small-diaphragm condenser mic), powered it with my ART Tube MP (which has phantom power, a 12AX7-powered preamp, and level controls), ran it through my Alesis

Fig. 11.18

The miniature components for recording acoustic guitar: AKG 451 small-diaphragm condenser mic, ART Tube MP mic preamp, Alesis Microlimiter, Sharp MiniDisc recorder, and Fostex T120 headphones

Microlimiter (which allowed my to keep my levels hot, hot, hot without distorting), and then ran into the MiniDisc. After A/B'ing this setup in my studio with my "real" gear (high-end preamp, compressor, and DAT), and placing the track in context with a mix, I couldn't tell the difference. Emboldened, I called my friend and explained my scheme.

After a long silence, he responded: "Yeah, I have no problem with the sound-quality issue," he said with less enthusiasm than I thought was justified, given the brilliance of my scheme, "but how are you going to synch up to the reference track?" "Easy," I replied, trying to sound casual, though I hadn't thought of this and was winging it, "You're going to burn your reference track onto a CD, and I'll play it back through my Discman, monitoring off of that." Long pause. "And how will I sync your track once it comes back to me?" he asked. "I'll give you four taps on my guitar before the first entrance, which you can use to digitally slide the track around until it aligns with your click. Then to prevent inevitable drift, I'll gave you four taps at various places in the song, well away from any playing, which you can use to re-align if necessary." I shut my eyes tight and held my breath. After another long silence, he agreed.

Fig. 11.19

Master quality on the go with Martin J40-M guitar, Audio-Technica 4050 large-diaphragm condenser mic, Sony 57ES DAT recorder, Sony HR MP5 multi-effects processor, Symetrix SX206 Multi-Dynamics Processor (compressor, limiter, gate, expander)

Figure 11.18 shows my "setup." Pictured are the Microlimiter (a 1/3-rack-width unit), the Tube MP (on top of and about the same size as the Microlimiter), the 451 mic in its shock mount, the MiniDisc (about the size of a thin wallet) and the closed-ear headphones which I used to monitor the Discman (not pictured) containing the reference track. I didn't get to monitor my own playing through the preamp, because I didn't have a mixer to combine the guitar and Discman signals, but I could hear fine acoustically, and I was relying on the Microlimiter to do my listening for me. The hardest part about the whole thing was creating a quiet environment in which to record (nature is noisy) and finding a Fed-Ex depot in rural Vermont when I'd finished.

My friend reported back that this system worked perfectly for him. He didn't even have to re-synch during the tune. "I certainly wouldn't use this method with bass and drums," he remarked, "but with slide guitar it really worked out. It's not a critical, dead-on-the-beat, lockstep thing." "Yeah, especially the way I play," was my witty riposte, although he didn't laugh, which kinda spooked me.

I have since created a "real" portable setup, pictured in Fig. 11.19. The whole shebang fits into a three-rack-space carrying bag. Notice that the same types of items are there, just upgraded. The mic is now the versatile, large-diaphragm, switchable-pickup-pattern AKG 4050, the recorder is a Sony DAT deck, and the Microlimiter has been replaced by a Symetrix compressor/limiter. I added a Sony MP5 multi-effects processor (it fits conveniently with the other half-rack unit, the Symetrix), which I use primarily for parametric EQ, and, if I decide to print with effects, reverb. There is one constant between the two setups: my trusty ART Tube MP mic preamp. Can't beat that thing with a stick.

Fig. 11.20

Verheyen's "emergency" direct rig

Here are some other approaches to portability in recording.

A DIRECT SOUND IN A RACK

As a sideman, you can travel with your self-contained sound in a space of only a couple of rack units. Carl Verheyen may have a cartage company bring his full rig to a studio, but in case of emergencies, he's got an instant direct rig, in the form of a 2RU setup shown in Fig. 11.20.

Carl keeps an "emergency" rig always in his car, so that no matter where he is or under what circumstances, he's ready to track. Pictured here is a Mesa/Boogie Studio preamp, Sony HR GP5 multi-effects processor, Lexicon LXP-1 reverb unit.

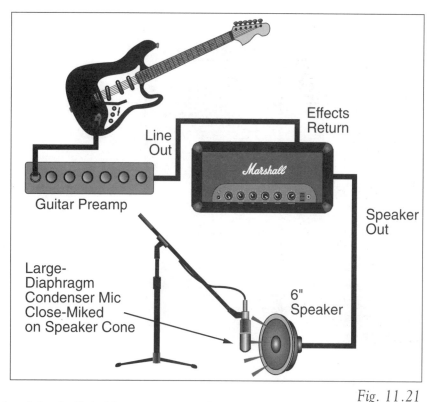

Add a Speaker for Unbeatable Realism

Of course, there is no substitute for a speaker, and even if you don't travel with a Marshall 4x12, you can get that certain *je ne sais quoi* that only a magnetic cone and vibrating paper can deliver. Here's the schematic of a basic setup that requires components you'd probably take on a live gig: a distortion box, an amp head, and a mic. The only addition is a small

Fig. 11.21

A "direct recording" setup that utilizes a small speaker

Fig. 11.22

The photo of a "studio in a suitcase." Note that this setup allows for a variety of amps or speaker combinations

speaker, say around 6", that you'll use to get that sound. Run the preamp hot and hook the output (line level, if there are more than one to choose from) into the effects return of your amp. You don't need to plug into the front, because you've already "preamped" your signal. It now has the right tonal shadings and is electronically compatible with the line-level input of your amp's effects return jack. Keep the master volume of the amp low, so as not to severely distort or damage the speaker. Connect the speaker out of the amp to your small speaker (you may have to solder together a jack and some lead wires to do this) and you have a recording setup. The absolute volume will be low, so it's perfect for situations where you can't necessarily make a lot of noise. The distortion comes from your preamp, but you'll still get that power-amp tube response, and the realistic ambience, and frequency and phase response that only comes from using a speaker.

Suiting up for Speakers

Like other travel setups, this "studio in a suitcase," designed by Douglas B. Lucek, is comprised of many miniature effects, but with an added advantage: speakers. Even though they're small, they provide a realism that processors and simulators have a tough time matching. Especially at low volumes, even a low-quality, underpowered, and thin-papered speaker can sound awesome, if it's miked and processed well.

Figures 11.22 and 11.23 show how to mount small amps or speakers and signal processing gear into a suitcase. It's best if you run the amps themselves as clean as possible so as not to compound the distortion situation by over-distorting the speaker. Get your sound from the stompboxes and EQ, and run the amps at a low volume, especially since they're solid-state and offer little or no dynamic advantage in their response characteristics. The choice of effects here

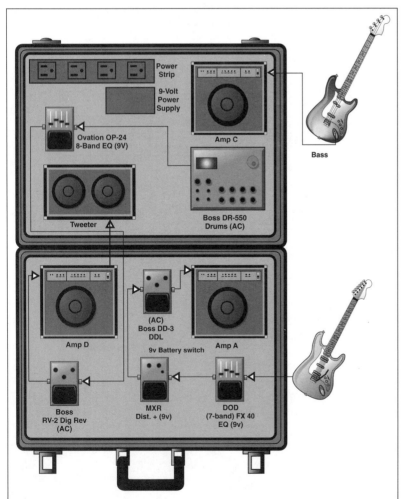

Fig. 11.23

The schematic of a "studio in a suitcase" including the AC power strip and the 9-Volt power supply

represents only one of many possible solutions, but obviously you can use anything you want.

Hard-disk Recording and the Whole Nine Yards

Perhaps of all the miniaturized setups possible, this one wins the award for quality contained in as small a space as possible (see Fig. 11.24). This scheme shows a Fernandes travel guitar, a Texas Instruments PC laptop computer running Cakewalk hard-disk audio/MIDI sequencing software, an effects processor (the Korg Pandora, currently the smallest full-featured processor available), the Roland PMA-5 rhythm composer, which can be used as a MIDI trigger, sequencer or as audio-only output source. The silver pen-like object on the right is a stylus used for programming the PMA-5 from the front panel, though you could use the software sequencer to create your MIDI tracks and use the PMA-5 as just a "slave" or playback-only module.

Fig. 11.24

Cakewalk, Fernandes travel guitar, Roland PMA-5 rhythm composer, Korg/ToneWorks Pandora multi-effects processor, Sony Walkman-style headphones, stylus for programming PMA-5. What's more, it's all battery powered

Figure 11.25 shows another approach to the traveling recording studio. This one features a Chiquita Travel guitar, a Rockman x100 Guitar processor (which accommodates an external input), a Sony Walkman for play-along or mixdown purposes, a Macintosh laptop running Opcode's Vision, MIDI interface, Walkman-style headphones, and a Yamaha MU-5 rhythm composer.

Fig. 11.25

A complete traveling setup including MIDI interface and connective cabling

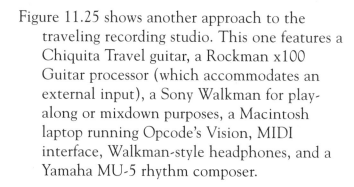

CHAPTER TWELVE

Recording the Perfect Demo Tape

THE ALL-IMPORTANT DEMO TAPE

A demo tape is an essential part of any recording guitarist's arsenal. Just as every 9-to-5 businessman can produce a spiffy business card and résumé on demand, so too should a guitarist be able to proffer a cassette, DAT or CD that demonstrates his abilities to anybody willing to pop the thing into a boom box or car stereo. It won't take the place of a live performance, but it is one more way to circulate your name and get your music heard. And demo tapes seem to have a way of creating their own need; after you have one, opportunities to distribute it will materialize out of thin air. Just having one in your pocket will probably inspire people to blurt out, "Say, you wouldn't happen to have a demo on you, would you?" You'll pass them out liberally—to the curious and the polite—so when you're not around, your music can still be heard . . . something that can't be said of a live performance. Also as recording guitarists, and not just guitarists, you have a double-edged showcase. People can respond to your production chops as much as your fretboard ones.

If you've never made a demo, the task can seem daunting. But like any other new endeavor, like changing your brakes or house painting, once you do it a few times, you'll be an expert—ready to give authoritative advice on the subject, and ready to recognize faults in others' efforts (as well as your own). The one thing about making demos (regardless of the level of playing) is that you get better at making demos the more you make demos. And consequently, you get better at recognizing the good demos from the bad. As someone who's made a lot of demos, and more important, listened to a lot of bad demos (which are different from bad music), I can offer some insights about the common pitfalls guitarists stumble into when putting together a demo. I'll present some classic dos and don'ts that I've gathered over the years as both a submitter and receiver of guitar demos. We'll start with Side A, which I call What to Know Before You Push the Red Button.

• **Don't Get Hung Up on Technology.** It's a demo, remember? People will appreciate production values like high signal-to-noise level, full-spectrum frequency response, and dbx or Dolby C, but not at the expense of your playing. Most people spend too much money on external qualities when making a demo. If you're selling the song, don't hire a seven-piece band and five backup singers. If you're showcasing your lead skills, consider a MIDI-sequenced rhythm section rather than a live one. The idea is not to fool people, but to get them to focus on the issue of primary importance. Only if you're certain you have the above issues covered should you then worry about the overall production values like reverb, compression, noise reduction and sequencing (how the tunes or segments flow into one another).

• **Don't Overplay.** I've heard demos where the guitarist is either playing all the solos, filling every hole, or playing as if he were paid by the note. People hear stuff like that and think, "My God, what a hog! He doesn't let anybody else be heard. He doesn't let the song breathe!" Don't think that just because it's your demo you can skip over the principles of good musical taste.

• **Watch Your Intonation.** Most guitarists, especially when they're shouldering recording duties, lose themselves in technique, and often miss the fact that they've drifted out of tune. This happens a lot when you work marathon sessions, woodshedding to get a certain passage just right. In the real world, non-guitar-playing musicians and astute listeners are on their guard for out-of-tune guitarists. Don't let them add you to their list. Listen to your tapes for tuning as well as execution. See the whole forest, not just the trees.

• **Don't Make the Tape Too Long.** I've seen people submit 14 full-length songs on a demo. Ridiculous. True story: A friend of mine caught the ear of a record company executive and asked if he could submit a demo with his best tunes on it. "Sure," the exec said, "let me hear three of them." "Actually," responded my friend, "there are six on the tape, and each one is unique, strong, and represents a different facet of my talent." Continuing his impassioned argument, he said they were like his six children, each one special in its own right, but tended to with equal love and attention from the same creator. The exec gave this whole plea a moment of thought and said, "Yeah, great. Pick the best three and send only those." Three or four tunes are plenty for most situations.

• **A Demo Is Its Own Format—Arrange/Produce the Music As Such.** I've seen people just throw three or four songs on a tape and call it their demo. Wrong. A demo is a musical slide show, a teaser, a movie trailer showing your range of talents. If you're limited to three minutes, it's better to have six 30-second passages than two minute-and-a-half ones. If your sixth example is 45 seconds (15 seconds too long) rewrite/edit the example to fit. When submitting small snippets like this, I will often put the full-length versions on side B. That way, if someone really likes a particular cut, they can find the whole song on the other side. But consider the demo as a mini "concept album." Treat transitions, cross-fades, and overall levels (peaks as well as averaged perceived loudness) as you would any other musical aspect of the production.

Is Your Demo Up to Snuff?

If you already have an existing demo tape, and have dealt with many or all of the issues in the previous section, I'll ask you to take a hard look at your own work, and answer questions that may make you think twice before dropping that 9x6" envelope in the mail. We'll also examine the toughest aspect of submitting demos: taking criticism.

Like résumés, demos have improved over the years, and, more important, people's expectations of demo quality have increased. Prospective recipients are more savvy about what they should be listening for. Cottage industries have sprung up that will produce your demo for cheap. The result of this "demo market inflation" is that demo submitters have to play the game or risk looking unprofessional. For example, when someone at the magazine I edit receives a story or résumé generated on a typewriter or written in longhand (in other words, not produced on a computer), it raises a red flag. They're playing the professional publishing game, but aren't participating in the technology that is recognized as the professional standard. It doesn't necessarily mean the quality is any less; it just puts the sender at a psychological disadvantage.

The above scenario holds true for demos: Don't be a typewriter throwback in a word-processor world, presentationally speaking. Play the game, be a pro, and exercise some smarts. Here are more Words To Live By, for people who may already have a tape and are considering a mass mailing. Don't send it out if you can't deal with each of these issues honestly and objectively. Better to wait and go back and do it right. You never get a second chance to make a first impression.

- **Know Your Listener and Tailor the Tape Accordingly.** Demos, like résumés, should be tailor-made to suit the intended recipient. Don't submit a shred-soloing piece to a bandleader who's looking for a rhythm guitarist. Know when a tape showing your versatility will serve you better than one showing your specialties, and send only the appropriate version.

- **Accompany Your Tapes with Professional-Looking Print.** J-cards (the folded card inside a cassette box), cassette labels, and cover letters (if included) should be typed (computer or typewriter generated), and should be free of typos and have some design flair. People won't care how good your playing is if your handwriting pegs you as a kindergartner or a serial killer. Don't use crayon to scrawl on your cassettes. Spend the extra money and have a friend or local print shop professionally typeset the labels (more on this below). Listeners will often make notes on the J-cards to aid their memory. Don't clutter the card with extraneous information.

- **Your Best Playing Doesn't Always Make for Your Best Demo.** Many's the time I've avoided putting a tune on a tape simply because I've been playing it for years and I'm bored with it, or all my friends are sick of hearing me play it. A demo tape is not for your friends, it's not even for you. It's for people who don't know you. If the song's appropriate, put it on.

- **Don't Be Married to Your Tape.** Just because you've sweated and toiled for days in the studio doesn't mean you necessarily got it right. Solicit opinions and live with the tape for a while. Leave it and come back. After you've taken a break from it for a day or so, you may come back and say, "I'm out of tune!" or "The bass is way too loud!" Give yourself the flexibility to change something if you discover you don't like it.

CDs: THE NEW STANDARD FOR DEMO?

The recording media of choice was, until recently, DAT (digital audio tape). Recordists would mix down to a master, first-generation DAT and then make copies from that. Those copies could be additional DATs—recorded by digitally cloning the original or running the signal through the analog ports and a mixer for more control—CD, open reel tape (rarely seen these days), a wave (or other computer-generated audio format) file for Internet transfer, or, most commonly, cassette tape.

Now, more and more demos are appearing as CDs. Even if you only use four minutes of the possible 74 on your demo CD, the economics make it worth it. Recordable CDs (which hold 660 megabytes of data or 74 minutes of high-resolution audio) cost only about a dollar apiece, and you can easily find them at Staples, Office Depot, Radio Shack, and other office supply and electronics stores (though for better prices, you have to buy in bulk).

CD-writing drives (as opposed to the read-only kind, called "CD-ROM" for "read-only memory") cost only a couple hundred dollars and are getting cheaper (partly because they're being pushed out by re-writeable CD media). New computer systems are even including them as an option. Burning your own CD is as easy, if not easier, than duping a cassette. The only catch is that you have to own a computer to take advantage of these low-priced drives. CD burners that accept analog ins (and which function like a tape deck, receiving a stereo mix from your mixer's main outputs) cost many more hundreds of dollars.

The reason for the disparity between "SCSI" (small computer systems interface, pronounced "scuzzy") drives and "stand-alone" or audio CD burners is that the SCSI-based models hook up to your computer—just like an additional disk drive. You then copy "data" (in the form of audio files, like .wav, .aiff, etc.) and manipulate the audio via software. Before you start to glaze over because computers and software have been brought into the picture, let me repeat myself and say that CD burning with a computer is stupid-simple. It's simpler in fact than using the stand-alone kind, even though these function like just another tape deck. The reason the SCSI burners are so easy to use is because you have the benefit of the computer's graphical interface (read screen and mouse) to construct your CD. You can assemble all your tunes (or

- **Get a Variety of Opinions Before You Send.** You'd be surprised what people close to you—musicians and non-musicians—will say. Some will listen intently to your technique and rhythm; some will listen only to the melody; some will begin talking as soon as the music plays—chattering amiably over weeks of your sweat and blood. Take it in stride. Each is reacting in his or her own way to a piece of music. Be a psychologist and examine each response objectively.

- **Don't Get Defensive When People Respond.** You'll learn a lot more if you stay quiet and let people talk. They can't help what they feel, and launching defensive salvos only discourages people from talking. I once recorded Gershwin's *Rhapsody in Blue* for solo acoustic guitar, played the 20-minute tape at a big Thanksgiving get-together, only to have someone from my own family say "Ee-yoo, what's that *skritching* noise?" "That's just finger noise," I say. "It's part of the acoustic guitar's inherent sound." "Too bad; it's so distracting," was the only response. So if somebody says, "That last song is kind of stupid-sounding," jump in right away in agreement—as if they picked up on something really subtle—and say, with a straight face: "It really is, isn't it? I didn't know if anyone would get that. Very astute of you." You may not like what they say, but you may manage to acquire an ally.

- **Don't Show People Your Work Until It's Finished.** Unless it's to my closest friends, I don't show people works in progress. It destroys the illusion and exposes some of the guide wires of a magic musical flight. As tempting as it is to give interested people glimpses of your greatness, avoid the unveiling until the work is complete. Show your work in its best light or not at all. Make them wait. I'll repeat myself: You never get a second chance to make a first impression—and music is a highly subjective matter. The very fact that it's recorded makes it a fairly unforgiving situation. The means, materials, and sonics of a demo tape can be cut-cornered, but the illusion has to be perfect and flawless.

ALL IN THE PACKAGING

This next section covers how to cheaply and easily put printed color covers and professional type on your tapes. Don't overlook this important step in presenting your work. As MTV has taught us, packaging your product is sometimes as important as—if not more important than—the substance within.

Your demo has to be as professionally packaged as possible to exploit every psychological advantage it can while it sits there in the record-company bin with all the others that scream, "Pick me! Pick me!" What that means production-wise is having a well-designed J-card (the folded card inside a cassette box) with printed type and possibly a logo, along with an adhesive cassette-shell label, also bearing typewritten or computer-printed text.

As a musician you really are an independent businessperson selling one product: you. You may not get a gig because you have a snazzy-looking demo package, but you certainly won't lose one for it, and if I had time to listen to only one more, I might pick the one with a nifty design rather than the one in crayon from the guy with serial-killer handwriting.

fragments thereof) in a list and play them down to see if you like the sequencing. Tightening up transitions, closing inter-song gaps, assigning pre-rolls (where the CD counter counts down from -3 to allow for more time between cuts), changing levels or bridging two tracks with a cross fade (very handy for demos) are all simple intuitive operations. You can then review the changes, make additional tweaks, and audition your CD in preview mode. When you're finally satisfied, hit "write" and go get a cup of coffee. When you return your finished CD is ready for you—and the world.

It should be noted that all of the above operations are not unique to SCSI-based burners. Stand-alones can do them, and just as well, but you'll be dealing with a front-panel interface with tiny screens and numerical data, instead of big, friendly graphics with icons and lists of titles to help you see your CD's contents at a glance. Stand-alone CD burners are more expensive, because they convert audio to digital data and burn the CD within the same box. This means that essentially there's an onboard computer. The SCSI burners require you to get audio converted by your computer first (through the soundcard and software) and saved onto hard disk as a file before it can perform its magic. If you're thinking of buying a CD burner and don't already have a computer, consider taking that extra few hundred bucks' difference between a SCSI-based drive versus a stand-alone, and apply that money towards a computer. Then buy a SCSI-based burner and enjoy all the benefits that a computer provides to the recording guitarist.

CD Advantages:

• Media is cheap—about $1 apiece.

• Media is readily available at most office supply stores.

• CDs can hold data (for computer backups) as well as audio, and can mix data and audio on the same disk.

• Indexing and locating tracks is much easier on a CD. This is especially good if you have numerous cues or tracks.

• CD index numbers are absolute, meaning 2:32 is the same exact spot in the program material on every copy of that CD.

• CDs are found in more places than DAT, and provide better fidelity than cassettes—and are cheaper than both.

If you own and are facile on a home computer—or know someone who is—you can create the demo cover in an illustration program. If you don't have a computer yourself, or don't have an illustration program, find a friend who does. You can design your J-card on a whole host of programs: PageMaker, QuarkXPress, CorelDraw, MacPaint, PhotoShop, Illustrator, Ventura, FreeHand, MultiMate, as well as many others. Virtually all of these programs support color, and since it's so cheap now to print in color (more on that below), you might as well spend the extra time and get something really splashy. You can make it easier on yourself by getting an artist friend to design and produce the art beforehand and just scan the images in, or the two of you can design it right on the screen with the program's drawing and text tools. This takes a little longer, but it's lots of fun, and you learn something about computer design in the process.

If you take the deluxe route, you can first design a background in PhotoShop (a program that allows the digital importation and manipulation of photographs), import that file into an illustration program (such as Adobe Illustrator) for more tweaking and then import that into a page-layout program (such as PageMaker or QuarkXPress) to add the type elements and set up the specs (the J-card's dimensions, like where the folds, or "scores," fall), and make "clones" on the same page. After the file is finished, take it to your local print shop. Most print shops have computers now, so just make a few phone calls, tell them you have a disk with a file that you want to print, and see if they can help you. Tell them you want to generate a "fiery proof," which is a high-quality color proof printed from your disk. You'll have to bring all the original images and fonts (typefaces) with you on disk, but beyond that it's a simple matter of slipping your disk into their machine and having them output a fiery proof. Cost for this? About nine bucks.

Your fiery proof is a color sheet with multiple color copies (as many as you can squeeze into the 8.5x11" dimensions) of your J-card artwork. Now you tell them you want to make color photo-copies from this proof on their color copier. These typically run about a buck apiece, but you might have eight J-card covers per sheet, so it comes out to 12.5 cents per color label. Ask for "card stock," which is heavier than flimsy paper and will keep its shape in the cassette box better. Your fiery is your master. Keep it where it won't get creased or exposed to light, and bring it into the print shop every time you need more copies. Cut the color copies out at home using a metal straightedge and an X-acto knife.

Cassette-shell labels can be ordered from any office-supply store. If they don't have them in stock, the brand and catalog number is Avery #5198. These come in packages of 50 sheets, with 12 labels per sheet (600 labels for $25). You have to design a document in the aforementioned page-layout program that puts 12 clones of your shell info onto one sheet. Then, instead of using regular printer paper, manually feed in the label sheet so the image prints on the 12 individual labels. This takes some trial and error to get all the labels to print on center. You have to go back to the computer screen and bump some clones up, some down, some rows right, some left, but eventually you'll get it to where you'll be able to print 12 labels on one sheet. Then just peel 'em off and stick them on the tapes themselves, and you're ready to pop them in the mail. If you've got a modem, however, you can retrieve a file from America Online and CompuServe that already has the labels placed on a page for you. You simply type in the text appropriate to you (e.g., keyword: "Avery" Desktop Publishing Forum). This is typical of helpful items people upload to these online services, and is one more reason to join the Internet age.

A demo tape with color graphics and a typeset shell label is truly an impressive thing to behold, and it "primes" the listener for good times ahead. Get your art friends to look at this article if you don't understand every aspect yourself, and get busy.

An ironic footnote. One friend I know who went through all these steps *did* get more work because of his demo tape. All his musician friends have commissioned him to design their demo tape covers. It's not quite what he expected, but hey, at least he's making some money in the music business.

Conclusion

Hopefully, you've picked up a few tricks and techniques from this book that will help you in recording your guitar. I've tried to present the various procedures and guidelines in a practical, applied approach, so that you can actually try the tricks out when you sit down to record. And hopefully, too, the gear and technology discussed here has been somewhat de-mystified and seems a bit less daunting, even alluring.

Remember though that while the tools and techniques of guitar recording may present a fascinating world of cool gear and sexy technology, they exist merely to serve a greater purpose: making music. The pitfall for many guitarists who get bitten by the recording bug (I'm way guilty of it myself) is they sometimes get so enamored with the technology that they forget that all this gear exists only to make your music-making more efficient. I love my toys, but when I spend too long with an owner's manual or perfecting some obscure synch-tempoed auto-panning move, I know I'm just dodging the more difficult task of addressing and dealing with the music. Recording is meaningless where there is no music to record, but certainly music can exist where there is no recording. It has for centuries and continues to do so everywhere music is made and there's no oppressive red light and some guy croaking "Take one."

Never forget that the best recording techniques are the ones that are transparent to the listener. The listener should be aware of only the music and not how many channels the mixer has or how powerful the multi-effects processor is. Recording is, after all, a subtle skill. The better you get, the less intrusive your technique will be on the music itself, and the more the music will dictate the production rather than the producer dictating the production. I listen to mixes I've done years ago and am horrified. Did I really think the listener wouldn't hear that phrase without me shining a searchlight (in the audio sense) on it? Was I that in love with my new reverb? Couldn't I trust the background vocals to be panned a little wider for depth instead of using the center-panned frontal assault to show off my vocal blending skills? I have a much softer touch now.

You will find that like playing the guitar, recording is a skill that develops over time, requires practice to keep it well-oiled and under your fingers, and is tempered by your ever-evolving sense of taste and judgment. But like guitar playing, recording becomes second nature and you don't always have to "think" every time you set up a mic, dial in a distorted sound, or solve an EQ problem. Your ears take you right to it. A good recordist isn't thinking technique or rules or acoustic principles, he merely uses his ears to solve problems and get things happening. Recording and guitar playing then fuse to become one overall creative, musical process.

Glossary of Audio and Recording Terms

A/D Converter: Analog to digital converter. The circuitry that converts an analog audio input signal into digital data for processing or recording.

Amplitude: The measure of a signal's intensity, whether it's acoustic (air pressure) or electric (current). The higher the amplitude of an acoustic audio wave, the louder it is perceived by a listener.

Analog: In audio, a signal that produces varying and continuous levels of electrical energy, reproducing (is analogous to) the stimulus from its input source, such as a microphone's diaphragm movement or the current from a guitar pickup's changing magnetic field.

Attenuation: The diminution or reduction of a signal's intensity, level or amplitude.

Audio Signal: Any electrical signal that's eventually converted into acoustic energy and occupying the spectrum of human hearing, which is roughly between 20 Hz (cycles per second) and 20,000 Hz (also written as 20 kHz).

Baffles: Movable absorptive panels used to acoustically isolate instruments from one another in close proximity.

Balanced-line input: A three-way signal. One signal is the sound coming from the source. The second signal is exactly the same but flipped out of phase 180 degrees. The third signal is the ground. The reason for having two identical signals but out of phase is an ingenious electronic invention. As the two signals travel down the line they pick up identical versions of noise, be it radio frequency interference (RFI), spurious electrical surges from nearby electrical devices, or normal high frequency hiss from random electrons in the circuit. The trick comes at the end where the second signal is again flipped 180 degrees and paired with the first. The signals are now exactly in phase and reinforce each other. The noise, however, is now 180 degrees out of phase with itself and cancels out. Simple and very effective.

Band-Pass Filter: An EQ device that allows passage of all frequencies between a user-definable high and low frequency band.

Bandwidth: The frequency response range or measure of the band of frequencies that a signal, device or circuit passes. Can also refer to the number of different frequencies or signals a device can pass.

Bouncing Tracks: In multi-track recording, this is the process of playing back one or more tracks and recording them onto an empty track. This combines the two playback tracks onto one track, allowing you to use the original tracks for recording new material.

Bus or Buss: On a mixer a common circuit or path that signals share to reach a common destination point, whether that's an output jack (as in the case of an aux send) or a master left/right channel (as in the case of a submaster bus). An aux send, for example, is a bus shared by every input channel on a mixer. Plugging in a device, such as a reverb, at the aux send's output jack allows every channel to access the reverb by sending a portion (determined by a volume knob on each channel) of its signal to the aux send bus. The output of the reverb unit (which carries all the channels' processed signals) is returned to the board at another input, such as an aux return or even another input channel.

Calibration Controls: Controls on a tape recorder that adjust level, frequency response, bias, and the physical position of the heads.

Cardioid: A word meaning "heart-shaped," and used to describe the pickup pattern or directivity pattern of a unidirectional microphone. A cardioid mic has the widest part of the pattern (the top of the heart) facing in front of the mic, on axis, with the sides sloping towards the back of the mic. A cardioid mic picks up sound primarily in front of the diaphragm and rejects sound from the sides and rear, making it a good stage mic. A Shure SM-57 is an example of a cardioid mic.

Channel: A single, electrically isolated path for a signal to flow through. On a mixer, channel is used to describe the input channels; on a stereo system channel refers to either the left or right output.

Clipping: A type of distortion, usually undesirable, where the signal's electrical current exceeds the circuit's capacity, resulting in the upper region of the waveforms getting cut off or "clipped."

Compressor: A signal-level-altering device that reduces the dynamic range of a signal, or the distance in amplitude from its loudest to softest level. Usually compressors do this by applying a gain-reduction ratio to the signal. For example, a compressor set for a 3:1 ratio and a threshold of -10 dB, would apply 1 dB of gain reduction for every 3 dB rise in level above the threshold. Compressors are used in studio work to deliver a smoother, more consistent mix. In guitar playing, a compressor is often used to enhance sustain by applying a high compression ratio and playing well above the threshold setting at all times.

Condenser Microphone: A type of microphone that uses an electrically charged variable capacitor to produce sound. Condenser mics require external power to operate, in the form of phantom power (supplied by the mixer or outboard preamp and delivered through one of the wires in the mic cable) or battery power (where the battery, usually a AA fits inside the shaft of the mic).

The Recording Guitarist

Console: Another name for a mixing board or (as the British refer to them) mixing desk.

Control Room: The space where the mixer, outboard gear, patch bay, monitors and usually recording devices sit. In studios with an isolated control room, the musicians can either play in the control room (if they're recording direct) or in the live room (the room on the other side of the glass of the control room).

Cue: In mixing terms, the monitor or headphone output. A cue mix is the headphone mix distributed to the musicians in the studio. Cue controls are the monitor levels used by the engineer or listener for tape playback. In scoring terminology, a point in the visuals where an audio event (such as a sound effect or melodic fragment or chord) occurs.

Cue Mix: Headphone or monitor mix used by recording musicians.

D/A Converter: The counterpart to an A/D converter, a D/A, or digital to analog, converter takes digital data and converts it back to analog wave forms to be processed or output as audio signals.

dB or decibel: A unit of relative power or loudness, expressed as a ratio. Used commonly to refer to loudness as when someone asks that the "EQ's 1 k be turned up a few dB."

DDL: Digital delay line; a device that samples (records digitally) an input signal and plays it back at a user-specified delay, expressed in milliseconds. DDL's also include controls like effect level, feedback, and modulation.

Diaphragm: The sensitive, movable membrane in a microphone or speaker.

Digital Recording: A recording process where analog signals are recorded digitally, using sampling. The recorder takes discrete samples, or snapshots, of a continuous sound according to its sampling rate (44,100 times a second is the current CD standard) and storage capacity or bit depth (16-bit or 65,536 separate storage locations is CD standard).

Direct Box: A device, either active or passive (with or without external electrical enhancement), that converts 1/4" unbalanced instrument-level signal into an XLR balanced line-level signal, and vice versa. Direct boxes allow guitarists to plug straight into a mixer channel input, something that is not recommended without electronic conversion.

Direct Out: An output on a mixer channel that taps the signal and takes it to another device, such as a multi-track recorder. Direct outs are usually used to remove the signal from the master bus of a mixer, but sometimes they are used in split mode, where the tapped signal is also allowed to proceed to the main outputs.

Distortion: What happens when a signal is too high in level for the circuitry to handle. Distortion in recording is usually undesirable, with the only exception being "slamming" analog tape. Otherwise, distortion is desirable only as a guitar effect, unless a specific non-musical effect is desired.

Dynamic Microphone: A type of microphone that converts acoustic energy to electrical energy by means of a diaphragm that moves in accordance to the sound pressure it receives. See Condenser Microphone.

EQ: An abbreviation for Equalization or Equalizer.

Equalization: The shaping of a signal's audio frequency content. EQ devices achieve different tonal results by boosting or cutting the levels (increasing or decreasing the amplitude) of specific frequencies or frequency bands. Equalizers can be either passive (involving resistor-based filters) or active (where an enhancing electronic signal is introduced). Graphic EQs adjust by bands, presenting the controls as a series of sliders arranged from low to high (forming a visual graph of the EQ's shape). Parametric equalizers use rotary controls that allow you to dial in any frequency and adjust the bandwidth based off of that center point (called Q).

Equalizer: A series of variable filters to shape a signal's tone by altering its frequency response.

Expander: The opposite of compressor, where if signal levels don't reach a user-defined threshold point, they are reduced (usually) in gain according to a specific ratio.

Fader: On a mixer, a linear, vertically oriented level control (sometimes called a slider), but can also refer to a rotary knob that controls a signal's level.

Fade-out: The smooth, gradual reduction in level of a signal or mix. Used at the ends of many radio-based pop songs instead of a hard cut-off.

Feedback: A situation where an output is connected back into its input resulting in a loop where the signal is amplified with each successive pass. Sometimes desirable and musically useful in guitar playing (where distortion helps generate and enhance the feedback), it is almost never acceptable in microphones.

Filter: An electronic device designed to cut or boost certain frequencies, either through active or passive electronic means. Filters can be dynamic, meaning they react according to the level received at the input (such as an envelope follower or electronic wah). Filters can also pass or restrict bands of frequencies. A low-pass filter allows all signals below a given frequency to pass; a highpass filter allows all signals above a given frequency through.

Flanging: A time-based effect where two signals are combined, one original and one delayed slightly, to produce a whooshy, underwater sound. The term originated from the technique where engineers used to press down on the flange of one reel of a tape recorder running in sync with another, slowing it down slightly and creating this exotic effect. Modern flangers then sweep this delayed signal with modulation to enhance the effect. Flanging is similar to Phasing.

Frequency: The rate at which a waveform, acoustic or electronic, vibrates.

Frequency Response: The amplitude variation of a certain frequency or frequency range. How a device can faithfully reproduce the frequency character of the input signal.

Gain: The amplitude or level of a signal. Not all gain equates to loudness. Sometimes a gain control is in a stage where it's modified by another gain control after it, and it is this second, or later, gain control that determines the absolute output gain or loudness. Separate gain controls is how guitarists achieve distortion; they boost the first gain control to overdrive the circuitry and then use the second, or final, gain control to determine loudness.

Gobos: Another word for baffle, or movable divider used to isolate the sound of instruments in close proximity to each other. The term is a corruption of the phrase "go between."

Graphic Equalizer: An equalizer that uses sliders or linear level controls, arranged by frequency from low to high, to form a graph of the signal's frequency alteration. The filters are in increments of one-octave to one-third octave widths.

Harmonics: Frequencies above the fundamental, or lowest and principal pitch, that occur naturally as mathematically related multiples of the original frequency. Commonly heard and reproducible harmonics are the octave, 5th, and second octave.

High-Fidelity: A term used to describe quality audio or accurate sound reproduction.

Hypercardioid: A microphone pickup pattern narrower in focus than a cardioid mic.

Input: The initial or entry point in a device or circuit to introduce an electronic signal.

Insert Point: A jack on a mixer that allows the signal to be taken out of the normal path and routed to an outboard device and then returned back to the path at the same location.

LED or Light Emitting Diode: Tiny, sensitive lights that require very little current and last indefinitely. LEDs are used to indicate status or behavior of a signal or device. LEDs draw so little current that they have no effect on the signal itself, yet can mirror the signal's behavior with extreme accuracy (such as in the LED meters showing a mixer's output).

LED Meter: A series of LEDs arranged vertically or horizontally and designed to light up in succession, based on a signal's strength. Used in place of VU meters or other analog-style meters that passed current to a wire coil which then drove a needle to various distances to the right of its resting point.

Level: The amplitude or intensity of an electronic signal.

Microprocessor: A miniature computer or controller that consists of one IC (integrated circuit) chip used for controlling other functions, analog and digital, on an electronic device such as a multi-effects processor.

Monitor: In audio, the practice of listening to a signal as a reference, either through headphones or through reference monitor speakers.

Multi-track Recorder: A recording device (tape or disk-based) that allows for more than one track to be recorded simultaneously and in synchronization with other tracks. Some two-track recorders (like reel-to-reels) can be used like multi-tracks, but not DATs, stereo cassettes, and stereo MiniDiscs.

Near-field Monitors: Speakers designed to be listened to at a close enough proximity so that no reflected sound reaches the listeners' ears before the direct signal. Near-field monitors are the most popular types of small studio monitors, because the engineer/producer is usually in close proximity to the speakers, which are typically positioned over the board. Yamaha NS-10M, Tannoy PB, Genelec 1029A, Mackie HR824 are all popular near-field monitor models.

Noise Gate: A device that shuts down the signal path when that signal falls below a certain, user-defined threshold. Noise gates include a rate control that determines how fast the path is shut down, to allow for a more natural-sounding signal decay.

Noise Reduction: A system of circuitry designed to reduce noise (specifically high-frequency tape hiss) using an encoding and decoding scheme, usually involving the compression and expansion of the signal's high-frequency content of a signal.

Off Axis: Any position that is not on a perpendicular line, or axis, to a speaker or microphone diaphragm. Engineers place close-miked dynamic mics off axis to a speaker to help reduce rumble and standing waves from the speaker to the diaphragm. Singers who go off axis of a mic cause a drastic level reduction in their signal.

Omnidirectional: A type of mic pickup pattern that picks up sound in all directions with equal sensitivity. Unlike a directional microphone (such as a cardioid mic), an omni experiences no proximity effect when the source is at close range.

Open-reel or Reel-to-Reel: An older, seldom-used tape format that uses a system of spools, or reels, and capstans and tension arms to hold and pass tape, as opposed to cassettes.

Outboard: Refers to external processing equipment, as opposed to onboard, which means the processor is built in.

Out of phase: A term used to describe a signal or waveform that is not at the same cycle or period relative to itself or an identical signal from the same source. A speaker that's out of phase will pull in while others push out. Two mics picking up the same source that are out of phase with each other will create a hollow sound, reduced in level and frequency content, because one mic's waveform dips will combine with the other mic's waveform peaks, resulting in a cancellation.

Output: The final stage of a device's signal path before it leaves to go to another device.

Overdub: Recording new musical material in synch with pre-recorded tracks that are monitored during recording. Through overdubbing, one person (if he's versatile enough) can create the music of an entire band and make it sound like all the different instruments recorded simultaneously.

Pad: A resistor-based circuit designed to attenuate an input signal, usually by a fixed amount, like -10 dB or -20 dB.

Pan: On a mixer the control that determines where in the stereo field a signal is placed, or which submaster bus it gets assigned to.

Parametric Equalizer: An equalization device that features rotary knobs instead of progressively arranged vertical sliders (see Graphic Equalizer). A parametric has more precise control over specific frequencies because it features a frequency select control, a width or Q control, and a level control to boost or cut that specific frequency. Parametrics are often used to remove problem frequencies (such as wolf tones and feedback tones) by dialing in the trouble frequency, setting very narrow Q and cutting the level drastically. This is called "notching out" a frequency.

Patch Bay: A centrally grouped collection of jacks used to connect the various input and outputs of different devices to each other. If all the inputs and outputs of a mixer and outboard effects unit are run to a patchbay, then any two connections can be made at the patch bay using short cords called "jumpers."

Patch Cord: An electrical cable used to connect devices together. On a mixer a patch cord connects inputs and outputs together on the same device.

Phantom Power: The external DC voltage supplied by the mixer or mic preamp to condenser mics. The power runs on pins 2 and 3 of the existing XLR cable; no external wires are necessary to run a condenser mic versus a dynamic mic, and no damage results if a dynamic mic (which does not need external power) is hooked up to a phantom-powered cable. The dynamic simply "ignores" the voltage.

Phaser or Phase Shifter: A time and EQ-based signal processing device, similar to a flanger, that creates a swirly, out-of-phase sound.

Pickup Patterns: The directivity or directional characteristics of a mic. Patterns include cardioid, hypercardioid, supercardioid, bi-directional and omni-directional.

Pitch-Changer: Electronic device that alters the pitch of a signal without changing the time relationships. Using smaller increments produces chorus-like effects, while larger intervals can create harmonies based on intervals of the chromatic or diatonic scale.

Pot or Potentiometer: A variable resistor used to control level.

Preamp or Preamplifier: A signal-conditioning device that takes a low level signal (from a mic or guitar) and amplifies it to where a higher-gain amplifier can then drive speakers. Preamps usually feature other controls besides level, such as EQ, phase and phantom power.

Pre/Post Selector: In mixers the switch that determines whether an aux send is tapped pre-fader or post-fader. A pre-fader aux send signal ignores the fader movements at the board and is good for setting up a monitor mix, but generally bad for effects processing because the wet-to-dry ratio in the main mix changes as the fader moves. A post-fade aux send's wet-to-dry ratio remains constant.

Presence: In equalization, the high midrange frequencies from about 2 kHz to 4 kHz. In microphone technique, the distance of the source (such as a singer) to the diaphragm.

Proximity Effect: The phenomenon in cardioid mics where bass response increases dramatically as the source approaches the mic. Can be problematic or advantageous depending on the desired effect.

Punch In: In recording, the process of recording onto an already existing track by pushing the record button at precisely the time you want to replace or add material, and pushing the button again ("punching out") when you've finished so as not to erase material after the desired section. Most tape recorders put punch-in and punch-out functions on a footswitch, allowing a solo-guitar-playing recordist to perform "hands-free" punching.

Q: The width or resonance of a frequency. In parametric equalizers, the control that determines the width around the selected center frequency.

Radio Frequency or Radio Frequency Interference (RFI): Frequencies used for radio and wireless communications (including AM, FM, short-wave and CB) that sometimes creep into amplifiers and other electronic equipment and become audible or wreak other havoc.

Re-Amping: Taking the tape output of a recorded guitar and passing it back through an amp to create a realistic amped sound. This involves stepping down the tape output's line level to an instrument level.

Resonance: The frequency at which a filter, instrument, or room shows an increased level response.

Reverb: The natural echo or ambience of a sound that occurs when placed in an environment with a variety of absorptive and reflective material. Not to be confused with "delay," which is a discrete repetition of the original signal, reverb is a complex acoustical phenomenon, and processors designed to re-create or simulate that ambience require much more sophisticated design and much more powerful microprocessors to reproduce the different environments convincingly.

RF, RFI: See Radio Frequency.

Ribbon Microphone: A type of microphone where the vibrating medium is a metal ribbon suspended in a magnetic field.

Roll-Off: A control used in microphones and mixers to attenuate certain parts of the audio spectrum, usually the low end. Many mics feature a bass roll-off which helps reduce stage rumble and feedback from sub-audio sources.

Rough Mix: A hastily constructed mix that's meant to be used only as a reference, such as in monitoring for an overdub, or to teach another musician the song's form. Rough mixes are often made in mono to preserve tracks.

Scratch Vocal: A reference vocal to be used in the building of a mix that gives other performers a reference. A scratch vocal is "wiped" (erased) when the final vocal is "laid down" (recorded).

Slate: The vocal announcement used to label a take. Derived from the movie industry when a slate chalkboard showing the scene's title and take # was held up to the camera.

Sound pressure level or SPL: The relative energy of an acoustic signal, expressed in decibels. A Shure SM-57 is a good mic for close-miking a Marshall stack because it can handle high SPLs.

Splice: Originally the term to describe joining together of two pieces of tape in an edit, but now used to describe any edit where two audio segments must be joined together.

Stereo: Processing two discrete channels or paths of audio information. Stereo recording means that two mics were used to record the same source and that those two paths were preserved through the output stage. In the looser sense, stereo refers to the stereo spectrum or stereo processing, where one input signal can be split into two output signals with stereo-simulated ambient effects.

Supercardioid: A pickup pattern wider than the normal heart-shaped cardioid pattern. A good mic for picking up a widely diffuse source where some back-and-sides rejection is still desirable.

Synch-lock: The synchronization of two devices, such as tape recorders, so that they are locked together. This allows, say, two eight-track recorders to function as a 16-track.

Tape Hiss: A broad-band high-frequency hiss sound resulting from the random distribution magnetic particles of the tape medium being dragged across the tape heads.

Time Code: A signal that is printed on tape that carries time-based information and is used to synchronize multiple machines or to locate various points on an existing audio or video tape.

Transient: A short, non-pitched signal that usually precedes the sustained, pitched portion of a musical instrument's tone. Transients are often louder than the sustained portion of the signal and sometimes create problems in the areas of compression and clipping. A guitar's transient sounds like a click, flutes produce a chiff, bowed instruments a scrape, and brass instruments a blatt.

Trim Pots: Variable gain controls on a mixer or other device that raise or lower the level of an incoming signal to optimize it for the rest of the circuitry. The trim pots on the channels of a mic and guitar might be set to drastically different positions so that each sounds at an equal volume level when their faders are both at 0 dB.

TRS or Tip/Ring/Sleeve: The configuration of a quarter-inch plug to provide for a three-way circuit. TRS plugs and jacks can be used for stereo (left, right, ground), balanced (hot, cold, ground) or insert jacks.

VU or Volume Unit Meter: A level-driven meter consisting of a wire coil and a needle used to indicate the average level of a signal at any given time. Now it's more common to see LED meters, which are faster, more sensitive and can be switched to different modes, like average or peak.

Waveform: A visual representation of a sound wave, tracing its frequency and amplitude.

XLR: A three-pin connector used in audio applications that carries balanced signals, such as mic signals and other pro-level connections.

INDEX

Numbers in boldface indicate headings; numbers in italics indicate figures